LIVING THE DREAM

LIVING THE DREAM

Membership and Marketing
in the
Co-operative Retailing System

BRETT FAIRBAIRN

Centre for the Study of Co-operatives
University of Saskatchewan

Cover design by Brian Smith, Articulate Eye
Editing, layout, and interior design by Nora Russell

NATIONAL LIBRARY OF CANADA CATALOGUING IN PUBLICATION
Fairbairn, Brett, 1959–

Living the dream : membership and marketing in the co-operative
   retailing system / Brett Fairbairn.

Includes bibliographical references and index.

ISBN 0–88880–479–2

1. Consumer cooperatives—Canada, Western—History.
2. Federated Co-operatives Limited—History. I. University of Saskatchewan.
Centre for the Study of Co-operatives. II. Title.

HD3290.A3P63 2004   334′.5′09712   C2003–907457–9

Printed and bound in Canada by Houghton Boston, Saskatoon
04 05 06 07 08 / 5 4 3 2 1

Centre for the Study of Co-operatives
101 Diefenbaker Place
University of Saskatchewan
Saskatoon SK Canada S7N 5B8
Phone: (306) 966–8509 / Fax: (306) 966–8517
E-mail: coop.studies@usask.ca
Website: http://coop-studies.usask.ca or http://www.usaskstudies.coop

CONTENTS

CREDITS AND PERMISSIONS

Front cover credits: (upper left) Calgary
Co-op exterior, Airdrie, AB, Wes Raymond;
(upper right) Marketplace at Attridge Drive,
Saskatoon, SK, Sean Martin, Dark Horse
Studio; (centre right) The Grocery People
truck and warehouse, Edmonton, AB, staff
member; (lower right) convenience store/gas
bar, Saskatoon, staff member; (lower left)
FCL Home Office, Saskatoon, Sean Martin,
Dark Horse Studio; (lower centre) Quality
Fresh semi, Sean Martin, Dark Horse Studio;
(centre) mother and daughter, Sean Martin,
Dark Horse Studio; (spine) convenience store
interior, Wadena, SK, staff member.

Back cover credits: (upper left) feed plant,
Saskatoon, staff member; (upper right)
Canoe aerial, BC, staff member; (lower right)
bulk plant and delivery unit, High Level, AB,
staff member; (lower left) semi unit and
Calgary warehouse, unknown; (centre left)
agro centre, Regina, SK, staff member;
(centre) Consumers' Co-operative Refineries
Limited, Regina, Kevin Carlson Photography.

Unless otherwise noted, credit for the interior
photographs in this book belongs to employees of the co-operative retailing system that
comprises FCL.

"Just a Little Dream" (p. 249) and extract
from "Harsh and Unforgiving" (p. ix)
reprinted with permission of Connie Kaldor.
© Coyote Entertainment Group Inc.
Box 51541, 699 Taschereau Blvd.
Greenfield Park, PQ J4V 2H8
www.conniekaldor.com

CO-OP EQUITY and CASH BACK	QUALITY CO-OP® LABEL PRODUCTS
PERSONALIZED SERVICE	YOUR COMMUNITY BUILDER

I come from a land that is harsh and unforgiving
Winter snows can kill you
And the summer burn you dry
When a change in the weather
Makes a difference to your living
You keep one eye on the banker
And another on the sky

by Connie Kaldor, from the compact disk
WOOD RIVER: Home is where the heart is…
© 1992 Coyote Entertainment Group Inc.
Canada—Festival Distribution, CD—CEGCD 1010
Reprinted with permission.

This book is dedicated to my mother
Eva Fairbairn (Hurlbert)
1924–2002
a long-time co-op member.

PREFACE

I WAS CHATTING WITH LORNE ROBSON AT THE KITCHEN table of his farmhouse outside Deleau, Manitoba, when he fixed me with a look from underneath his bushy white eyebrows, and said, "We're living the dream."[1] The dream he refers to is the dream of his grandparents, who came here in 1889, and in 1910 established the historic Hereford farm where Robson still lives. His grandfather was there on the pool elevator committee when the elevator was built; he helped develop the local retail co-op; he was the president of the Manitoba Dairy and Poultry Co-op; and he served on the board of the old Manitoba Co-op Wholesale. Lorne Robson has followed in his footsteps by serving on the board of Federated Co-operatives Limited (FCL). The dream that binds together these generations is one of economic and personal development. It is a dream of businesses controlled by people, controlled locally, serving members and their needs.

Robson has seen generations of co-op leaders, and has seen some rough times in co-ops. Small-town co-ops like his local one have not always fared well in recent years; they struggle. When he says, we're living the dream, we're *trying* to live the dream, he means trying to live up to the visions of the pioneers. But he also means the co-op system as a whole is booming in a way they could scarcely ever have imagined; there is new activity and a sense of growth; there is professionalism and a new standard of service and performance. All of this is fulfilling hopes for survival and growth, keeping a dream alive, and sharing it with new and different generations of people.

Sharing the dream—conveying the experience of it, the difficulties involved, the ways in which these have been overcome or not—is also the purpose of this book. Federated Co-operatives Limited Senior Vice-President, Corporate Affairs, Lynn Hayes arranged a meeting late in 2001 where the possibility of my writing a book for FCL's seventy-fifth

1

anniversary was first raised. Subsequently, FCL made a contribution to the Centre for the Study of Co-operatives, University of Saskatchewan, where I work (and of which they are also a regular sponsor), to cover part of the cost of doing the research. Writing this book was a unique opportunity. I do research and teach about the history of co-operatives, and the Co-operative Retailing System (CRS) is an intriguing example of success in a field where others have failed. I had previously written a history of FCL and the CRS up to the 1980s, so there was a certain logic to a follow-on book.[2] This is a much different book—much more contemporary, more immediate, and more personal in its style—but it is still a work of history, concerned with a context, a progression, a continuity, and evolution over time. Federated's leaders did not tell me anything about what kind of book they wanted, but I knew enough about the system to know that the last twenty or so years are a story all their own. To write a history book now, when the system is breaking records and exceeding any past financial performance, is to relate today's success back to the serious difficulties in which the co-ops had found themselves in the 1980s. The current generation of co-op leaders has gone through a harrowing and lesson-filled experience, and it is this experience, above all, that needs to be shared. Their concern that today's success not be taken for granted does them credit, and in any case, recording the historical experience and the culture of a large organization is always worthwhile.

When you ask an academic to write a book, you get more than you bargained for; at least, that *should* be the case. Whether this is always a good thing is another matter. In the case of *Living the Dream,* there are three things, in particular, that my academic training brings to the book. My hope is that these are not too evident: I want this book to be entertaining, personal, lively, and readable, but the academic apparatus is there in the background. First, my eighteen years working at the Centre for the Study of Co-operatives have led me to a number of, I hope, well-considered theoretical perspectives about co-operatives: the ideas in this book reflect the influences of many colleagues. Theory is deeply embedded in what I say, even though I usually do not point it out. Second, the methodology I chose depended heavily on in-depth personal interviews, which these days, in universities, are governed by a rigorous set of ethical guidelines. I know that some of my interviewees found the procedures cumbersome, but they do ensure (as much as any procedure can ensure) that the comments quoted in this book are more than accurate: they represent as much as possible what the individuals *want to say*, on their considered reflection, not words that slipped out or that I put in their mouths. Finally, all the interviews were anonymous and confidential—where I quote people by name, they have given specific permission for the quotation in question, usually because it involves speaking in their official organizational role or capacity.

The interviews were relaxed, open-ended, and conversational, but I took advantage of the confidentiality to probe some difficult topics. I did so gently, not aggressively, but enough to give people an opportunity to say anything that was on their minds. Most of my questions were general ones about roles, relationships, careers, and responsibilities, but to see what people would say, I raised topics such as disagreements and controversies, best and worst moments, confrontations and styles of behaviour they had observed. I asked employees about their bosses, past and present, and I asked bosses about their philosophy towards their employees. I asked about working conditions and career plans. In the context of asking about roles and responsibilities, I inquired whether people knew of any misconduct. I asked them to compare their experiences in the co-op system to other experiences they might have had. I asked people questions about how their experiences had been affected by their cultural background, their age, their gender, or other factors that came up in the course of the conversation. While most of those I interviewed were people in positions of responsibility identified by FCL, I also interviewed people who were not recommended. I talked to ordinary members, disgruntled members, and enthusiastic members. I interviewed some people who had been with the co-op for as little as one month, and others who had been involved for more than forty years. I interviewed staff who had left co-op employment under various circumstances. People told me all kinds of things, many of which are impossible to mention for reasons of confidentiality. But everything I heard informs how I have chosen to present major themes and issues. This book is not a public-relations gloss. It is a serious attempt to investigate, to understand, and to document.

I conducted interviews with eighty individuals, seventy-six of whom ultimately signed transcripts giving me permission to use their words in this book. Nineteen were interviewed in their capacity as senior managers at FCL, twenty-three about their role as retail co-op general managers, sixteen others as employees (middle management or nonmanagement), and I talked to twenty-eight about their role as members, most of these holding elected office in either a retail co-operative or at FCL. (The numbers add up to more than eighty because of individuals whom I interviewed about more than one role.) Of the total, eighteen were retired, while the rest were currently still involved; seventeen were women. Most were interviewed singly, but in a couple of cases participants arranged joint interviews. While I generally asked for about an hour of people's time (or less from employees in the midst of busy work days), participants were generous, often blocking off an entire morning or afternoon to accommodate me, giving a tour if the interview was in the workplace, or chatting over coffee or a meal. Interviews actually ranged from about fifteen minutes to nearly three hours. Obtaining the interviews meant travelling to locations across nearly the full east-west breadth of the system. I formally visited more than two dozen retail co-ops, not counting different branches or facilities of the same co-op, and lost count of how many others I just dropped into for a quick look around and informal conversations with anyone I happened to meet. Perhaps some of them remember the inquisitive stranger who walked around their store taking notes, seemed fascinated by what was posted on the bulletin boards, and stopped to take photographs of signs and bulk petroleum tanks.

The travel, visits, interviews, and on-site note taking probably took about three hundred hours of my time between late January and early July 2003. Reading, editing, and digesting the transcripts took another month, even with the invaluable help of a research assistant, four different confidential typists, and the office staff of the Centre for the Study of Co-operatives, who helped with co-ordination and mailings. I had well over one thousand pages of handwritten notes taken during the interviews, and around fifteen hundred closely typed pages of interview transcripts. My initial file of quotations from the transcripts—the excerpts I thought usable for the book—was five hundred and forty-one pages long, single-spaced. To my interviewees, I have to say that there was good material in every single transcript. I have tried to use something from all of them, but if you don't see your words somewhere in this book, it is only because of lack of space.

The interviews were a remarkable experience. Co-op people tend not to be loud and abrasive; they know they are part of a system, and they think about how others will perceive them, and about what effect their words could have on their unit or their company. But they are *people,* and as different from one another as people generally are. I talked to people who were virtually in tears as they described the tremendous personal support they had received from superiors and colleagues during difficult periods in their lives. I talked to people who spoke with obvious pain and regret about decisions they had had to make twenty years ago, decisions about the closure of co-ops that affected them almost as deeply as the loss of a loved one. I talked to people who were emotionally scarred by what they had been through, and also to people I knew had been through the most unpleasant experiences the system offers, and showed no sign of it when they spoke. Most people in the system simply say something was "tough," or "there was some debate," to indicate controversies that involved shouting and confrontation and anger. I talked to junior managers who are openly ambitious, never wanting the same job for more than a couple of years; and I talked to staff who know the opportunities are there for them in the system, but are deciding, at this point in their lives, not to pursue career advancement. Some praised their superiors and colleagues in language that is almost embarrassing to quote; a few alleged things I can't put in print. I talked to retail staff who were suspicious of FCL, and FCL staff who were suspicious of retails, but there are not as many of these as there used to be. Most of all, I talked to people who were proud, and loyal: those are the qualities of the ones who have served the longest in the system. The most common way they characterized their experience—the single, most frequently-quoted phrase they used—usually after the tape recorder was turned off: "It's been fun."

The interview material comes into this book (other than as background) in one of three ways. First, as already mentioned, some senior officials speaking in their official capacities have been quoted, and with their permission, identified by name. Second, other material is quoted anonymously. I have tried to refer to the speakers and choose the quotations in such a way that no one could figure out exactly who said what. Finally, in cases where confidentiality may be especially difficult to preserve, remarks are attributed to "composite personalities"—essentially fictitious speakers, whose comments may in fact have come from more than one individual. For literary convenience I have given these composite personalities names and descriptions, but to avoid confusion they are introduced with their "name" in quotation marks. This is explained further in a short appendix at the end of the book.

In addition to the interviews, my research assistant, Jill McKenzie, put in long hours at FCL Home Office and in front of her computer to help me with documentary research. There are not many living individuals who have read more FCL reports and minutes than she. She and I received unfailing assistance from Donna Tetrault and from the receptionists and other staff at FCL. My colleagues and co-workers at the Centre for the Study of Co-operatives contributed in innumerable ways, helping me with ideas, with administrative matters, with specific tasks and sections of the manuscript, and as readers of drafts. Students helped as well, both graduate and undergraduate: as always, I learned from their assignments and questions, and developed my own interpretations as I practised explaining the CRS to people who had little prior knowledge. Much of the eventual book was written well away from ringing telephones (with apologies to those who were trying to reach me at the time) in cabins near Wakaw, Saskatchewan. The drafts of the book were improved by three helpful and knowledgeable readers, as well as an editorial committee of five assembled by FCL.

The finished book, particularly the cleanness of its prose, the elegance of the layout and design, the co-ordination of photographs (with help from the FCL advertising department), the management of editorial and production schedules, and the supervision of contractors, was wholly the work of Nora Russell, publications officer at the Centre for the Study of Co-operatives, one of the best book people there is.

Beyond the mechanics of the research, preparing this book was a surprisingly enjoyable experience. It is a privilege to be able to drop in on people scattered across western Canada and be introduced to their lives, their careers, and their co-ops. If only more people could have this experience—to see different co-operatives, to hear from different people in their own words—they would better appreciate the strength and diversity of the co-op system. Perhaps this book can convey some small part of it. Given the elaborate transcription procedures for their interviews, each and every interviewee is really a kind of co-author of this book, although I hasten to add that they are not responsible for any of its failings.

The following pages tell the recent story of FCL and the co-op system as fully as is possible between two covers. For those newly involved in the system, perhaps this can serve as something of a primer. For those who have never encountered the co-op system, the book offers a fascinating glimpse into a successful community-based business model that has adapted in surprising ways to the challenges of globalization. In telling the story, I made great efforts to be as personal as possible. I talk about individual people and particular co-ops wherever I can, within the boundaries imposed by the confidentiality of the research. This approach has its limitations. In striving to be personal, to write about the distinctive, and to pay attention to the unusual, I cannot possibly be representative. The co-ops I describe are not necessarily the "best" or most important co-ops. The managers and directors I name are not the only ones worthy of mention. The price of a personal approach is that the reader's experience will be limited by where I visited, whom I talked to, what I happened to see. In truth, it is impossible to do justice to the people of the Co-operative Retailing System: hundreds of senior managers, thousands of directors, hundreds of thousands of members. Nevertheless, I want readers to think of the co-op system as a place full of interesting people, people you could meet and talk to, real people. I also want readers, as much as possible, to be able to visualize different towns and different co-ops. For this reason I will describe them just as I saw them; I will write personally, about my own experiences and impressions. I do this not because my experience is more important than anyone else's, but because it is a device to enable readers to put themselves in my shoes, travelling across western Canada, dropping in on dozens and dozens of co-ops, if only for a few sentences each.

My special thanks to Norma and to our children, Catherine, Elena, and David, who during long weeks of research, editing, and writing either had to put up with me being absent, or wish I was.

Travelling the Co-operative Retailing System

M Y CHILDREN HAVE STARTED TO GET USED TO ME turning off the highway, pulling into some town or urban neighbourhood, and pointing out to them: look, there's another co-op. *This* one has a brand-new cardlock. Look at how *this* one has adopted the new system signage. *That* one has its own petroleum-delivery truck; see it filling up there at the bulk plant? See that new store? It's owned by the wholesale company, and the local co-op can lease it and earn money without carrying debt on its balance sheet... They have, of course, tuned me out long before I get this far. I don't really expect them to be excited, because retail co-ops are a perfectly normal sight if you live in western Canada. I suppose they are not interesting when you are a teenager—unless, of course, you need a part-time job or are looking for a career in your own community.

Many people today express concern about corporate globalization, about the power of big transnational companies, about the concentration of wealth and responsibility outside the control of people in a region or a country. Small businesses complain about the encroachment of WAL-MART, or whomever it may be. Loyal customers bemoan the loss of familiar Canadian retail outlets like Eaton's. Young activists travel huge distances to protest trade policy. But there are these co-ops, which aren't going away. Locally owned, they have found ways to compete in one of the harshest businesses there is—the retail business. And they are *growing*. If people are more than just superficially concerned about corporate globalization, then it seems to me they have an answer close at hand. What they choose to do about it will testify to whether they really care about where or how a business is owned. Meanwhile, co-op managers would like to make it easy for them by offering *better* value and service than any other establishment on-site.

In an age of globalization, the co-ops run counter to the trend, or perhaps ahead of it. They represent local ownership, autonomous local entrepreneurship, and community participation in business, in an era when (it is assumed) multinational corporations dominate the economy and local people are powerless and dependent. This is the mostly invisible but pervasive difference of the co-operative model: where one sees the CO-OP® sign, it means hundreds or thousands of local people are co-owners. It means there is an autonomous local business, with its own manager and board of directors, making decisions about retail services in the community. It means that the surpluses generated by retail business are reinvested in the local economy or paid out in cash to local people, either way recirculating wealth in the community. Although these co-ops are businesslike and aim to create economic surpluses, they are in another sense entirely nonprofit: the wealth that is created belongs to the consumers and the community, not to outside investors or individual business people. Though they are the heirs of a populist and social-reform movement that swept western Canada in the first half of the twentieth century, they have adapted in the last generation to the circumstances of mass consumer society. As a matter of fact, within their market area the co-ops compete with three of the four biggest business corporations in the world.* So far, they are more than holding their own.

So when I drive across the West, I point out co-ops to my kids. Until recently, you had to look for them, because the co-ops were not always the flashiest or most obvious businesses. For one thing, in small towns they typically stuck to locations near their local members, in the centre of town (often near the Wheat Pool elevator), while their com-

* *The Economist* lists the world's largest corporations by revenue as WAL-MART Stores (approx. US$250 billion), followed by General Motors, Exxon Mobil, and Royal Dutch/Shell (all over US$150 billion). The co-ops do not compete with General Motors. Vol. 368, nr. 8341 (13–19 September 2003).

petitors were out along the highway in plain view. ("I think that we've come front and centre from where we were. I used to say behind every elevator there was a co-op, and I think there pretty much was at one time," a general manager told me.[1]) You had to turn into town and look for it if you wanted to find the co-op. In the cities, they sometimes used to content themselves with out-of-the-way locations known mainly to their members; few co-ops had the kind of foresight and neighbourhood siting strategy exemplified by Calgary Co-op (Alberta), which has made it a universal presence across the city. But now, almost everywhere, the visibility of co-ops is growing, mainly as a result of the system's ongoing expansion in petroleum distribution. Co-ops such as Heritage (Brandon and Minnedosa, Manitoba), Pioneer (Swift Current, Saskatchewan), and Medicine Hat (Alberta) now have gas stations on the Trans-Canada and other main routes. And everywhere, along the highways, the new bulk plants and cardlocks stand out, each one with a CO-OP® logo.

One of Medicine Hat Co-op's gas bar/convenience store facilities.

Today you can drive across western Canada and find nearly three hundred independent retail co-operatives (294 of them in 2002)[2] that are members of the Co-operative Retailing System (CRS). They are spread from the Pacific coast across to northern Ontario, and from close against the US border up to the north of the Prairie Provinces. This doesn't count several dozen more in Yukon and Nunavut: Arctic Co-ops, an affiliate member of FCL, represents the far-northern co-ops, which also use many CRS products and programs.

Many of the CRS member co-ops have multiple branches, facilities, or locations, so the co-op system has a presence in over five hundred communities. As of early 2003, this includes 376 gas bars, 336 propane filling plants, 325 food centres, 215 agricultural supply outlets, 185 convenience stores, 183 cardlock petroleum facilities, 136 bulk-petroleum outlets, 97 home centres, 89 general-merchandise department stores, 54 touchless car washes, 46 pharmacies, 11 family-fashion departments... not to mention a few unique facilities we'll hear more about in chapter three.[3] Sometimes it can seem like the red-and-white CO-OP® sign is everywhere (well, except in Calgary, where it's red and blue and white, with a distinctive emblem).*

The sign is the same, but the co-ops themselves are different. Each is a legally independent business, and they vary in the services they provide. In some towns, people think of the co-op as the place to buy paint and wood-burning stoves. In other places, such as Red River Co-op (Winnipeg, Manitoba), co-op is gas bars offering full-service at self-serve prices. The co-op may be primarily a convenience store, or—in other communities—it may be the fanciest full-scale supermarket for miles around. Some are pure farmers' co-ops, the places to buy feed, fertilizer, chemicals, lumber, hardware, and bulk petroleum. Nor is it only farmers who use a lot of petroleum. In some communities, the backbone of the co-op is its cardlock facility, and the big users are truckers and other businesses. Everyone in each community calls their store the co-op, but they all have different ideas of who and what it's for: co-ops are for businesses, for homeowners doing renovations, for trades people and contractors, for family food shoppers, for people who drive vehicles. Co-ops are not all the same, but they—the ones who call themselves the Co-operative Retailing System—are integrated into a single system, a system that represents the combined purchasing power of a million western Canadians.

For the most part, the items on co-op shelves don't look much different from what is in other stores, though many of the products have CO-OP® labels on them. But a bag of frozen peas or a can of motor oil

---

* This refers only to facilities with CO-OP® logos. There are also 257 TEMPO® gas stations supplied by the co-op system, as well as the independent SUPER A FOODS™, BIGWAY FOODS™, and TAGS™ stores supplied by FCL's The Grocery People (see chapter three).

in a co-op display unit looks much like similar articles on other stores' shelves, and it is precisely in such prosaic articles that most co-ops deal. Here and there, it is true, a visitor may see something about the facilities that hints at a certain difference: in one community, a cafeteria teems on Saturday mornings with throngs of people who busily visit and renew acquaintances. In another community, there is supervised in-store childcare for shoppers' children, or aisles of organic foods and natural remedies, reflecting local members' interest in alternative food and health. On rare occasions, one finds the CO-OP® logo on a housing complex, a cable-television-distribution system, a funeral home, or a prairie grain elevator—a matter-of-fact sight to the local residents, but a surprise to visitors from other towns where co-ops don't do such things. Such exceptional sights are a reminder that co-ops exist to serve their local members in economical ways that those members want and need.

Not everyone will have or take the opportunity to drive around western Canada looking at co-ops, but for those who do not, I hope this book will serve as something of a substitute: a travelogue of the Co-operative Retailing System, showing some of the sights, the places, the people of the co-op network, and above all, illuminating the ways they are connected and tied together. The most important institution connecting the people of the retail co-op world is their federation and wholesale company, Federated Co-operatives Limited.

One person who travels the system a lot is FCL's President Dennis Banda. Banda is a farmer from Marcelin, Saskatchewan, and a person with uncommon skills at dealing with people and getting things done. Political skills mean concentrating on the basics, paying attention to people without losing sight of the one or two key things that matter. Dennis Banda has those kinds of skills. His face is open and he speaks freely, right off the cuff. He clips his consonants and speaks in short sentences that often have upturned intonations that invite you to agree with him. It is clear that he is experienced at getting to know people and dealing with their issues quickly. He never seems to rush, and yet it's amazing how much you talk about with him in a short time.

Banda speaks of his previous experience in the Saskatchewan Wheat Pool governance system as well as in the Saskatchewan Legislature. "I don't think I would be in this position if I didn't have the background that I had with the Wheat Pool and in provincial politics," he says. He joined the FCL board only in 1993, and became president in 1997. Without his experience, he says, "I don't think I would have been … able to win the leadership of all the board people at the point in time that I did."[4]

In putting his own stamp on the position of FCL president, Banda's philosophy has been to concentrate on communication. "It's also been my focus ever since I've been here to travel through the system a lot, and I did that on purpose…. I could see that there was kind of a separation between the retail system and head office…. It was almost like [the] eighth floor [executive level] … was almost prohibited. That's nonsense. So I guess it's been my focus … to make sure and keep that communication between the retail system and our regions and head office always accessible."

FCL's board of directors, CEO, and senior vice-president, Corporate Affairs, in front of Meadow Lake Co-op's new food store during their July 2003 tour of retail co-operatives in districts S9 and S12.

"When I made a decision that I wanted to travel the system, Wayne [CEO Wayne Thompson] said, 'By all means do it. Don't ever question it, because when you're out there we know that you're doing things that should be done.' We found when we had issues developing, I'd say, well,

I'm going to go out there and do some travelling; and I got nothing but support from the management team." The managers, in fact, also spend considerable time travelling the CRS. Directors and managers both go on summer tours of the co-ops, attend numerous regional meetings, and rack up a lot of kilometres.

The eighth floor that Banda refers to—the home base for the co-op system's senior managers and leaders—is in a somewhat modest nine-storey office building on the corner of Twenty-Second Street and Fourth Avenue in Saskatoon, Saskatchewan. Thousands of people who pass it daily likely don't know that it is the home office of the largest business corporation headquartered in Saskatchewan, with $3.55 billion in sales in 2003—the central agency for the far-flung network of local co-ops. Federated Co-op is, so to speak, the corporate arm of western Canada's retail co-op system. Like the local stores, Federated (or FCL— I will use both interchangeably in this book) superficially resembles its competitors, except possibly for a more unassuming appearance, and the fact that its head office is in Saskatoon. When you walk in the front doors, you find yourself in a wood-panelled lobby, adorned with a mix-ture of award plaques, historical memorials, and merchandise displays. The lobby is spacious enough and sufficiently decorated to state that this is a corporate office building, but it is by no means large or showy. It is, like many other things in the system, understated. Only metres away, one finds oneself in tall, functional, neutrally panelled hallways, running straight and narrow down the middle of the building. These halls efficiently connect open-office areas filled with desks and cubicles, with private executive offices lining the outside walls. The halls and ele-vators are filled with accountants and analysts, commodity managers and retail advisors, who are friendly but efficient. There is a clear hier-archy reaching up to vice-presidents and the CEO, who have their offices alongside the boardroom near the top of the building.

Just like the local stores, Federated both resembles the competing, corporate model, and turns that model inside out. The office building in Saskatoon is *owned* by the local co-op stores in the towns and cities, not vice versa. Each local co-op, and its membership, has a stake in those nine storeys of steel and concrete in Saskatoon, and in the people and expertise and information systems contained within. Each local co-op also owns a stake, through FCL, in an oil refinery in Regina worth many hundreds of millions of dollars, and in other production, warehouse, and administrative facilities spread across the region. This is a corporate model turned upside down, where local businesses own the central one. Just as local consumers own the stores, the local co-ops own FCL—it's a three-tier ownership structure with consumer-members at the top.

The inverted pyramid of ownership does not make FCL less important. The tremendous financial success of the retail co-operatives in the last twenty years—success in local towns and cities across the West—has a great deal to do with decisions and policies framed in that nine-storey building, as well as four blocks down the street at the Centennial Auditorium, where the retail co-op delegates hold their annual meeting every March.

I have used the word unassuming to describe the Co-operative Retailing System, FCL, and its member retail co-ops, and that word probably captures the first layer of what people see when they look at the co-op system. It is not pretentious. It is not loud. It is simply there, and most people likely have little sense of what lies behind the stores they see. Perhaps co-ops seem monolithic to those who don't know them well; they certainly present a unified face to the outside world, and cultivate a distinctive internal culture of their own. Scratch beneath the surface, and those familiar with co-ops see a little more. Among co-ops (of which there are many kinds, FCL and its members being only one type) the Co-operative Retailing System stands out, first of all, as exceptional in its financial success in recent decades. Some people are a little puzzled by this success, and because of what looks to them like a cautious and conservative approach to business. Some people's preconceptions don't allow co-ops to be either so successful in business or so fiscally cautious. In FCL's case, the important thing is to see how its approach to business has created its success—how it has succeeded not in spite of, but because of, the system's culture and priorities. This needs to be understood historically, as a process and as the result of the co-op system's experience, learning, and adaptation. This is another layer of understanding, and it might require some readers of this book to discard or modify their understandings of what co-ops are and how they work. Beneath that layer, there is still more ...

But that is the subject of this book.

For now, let me say that no co-operative is ever simple. Co-operatives are not collectives, and they are not Utopias. Co-operatives have different people within them, different groups, different ideas, different interests. There are always, in any human institution, implicit and explicit tensions among people, groups, ideas, and interests. Unity such as the Co-operative Retailing System has displayed in recent decades is never given; it is always achieved. Decisions have to be made, understandings have to be created and lived with, different groups have to buy into policies—not in automatic submission to collective decisions but in processes of discussion, dialogue, education, training, and networks of communication. The ability of the Co-operative Retailing System to work together is the result of the triumph of vision, experience, and communications over competing and divergent interests. The co-op system works *not* because there are no tensions within it, but because, for the most part, those tensions are creatively, productively, dynamically *balanced* and harnessed.

This is what other organizations can learn from the co-operation practised by the Co-operative Retailing System. Co-operation is not like a clockwork mechanism, running perfectly and in the same way forever. A co-op is more like a spinning top, which maintains some kind of equilibrium even though it is constantly moving and changing, dipping and righting itself. A well-functioning co-operative system is a near-miraculous piece of organizational interaction; at its best, the system—the members and their co-ops together—can be more efficient than any other form of enterprise. But the functioning and the interaction can never be taken for granted, never arbitrarily changed or arbitrarily left to stagnate; co-operation is like a living thing. FCL learned this the hard way, through a near-collapse of the CRS in the early 1980s. That FCL even exists today is not a given. Other co-ops, other kinds of organizations, and the Co-operative Retailing System's future leaders and members, can learn from what happened between 1982 and 2003.

This book is an examination of how the Co-operative Retailing System—the consumer co-ops across western Canada—rediscovered membership and marketing during the last twenty years. They almost didn't. In the 1980s, many consumer co-ops were on the verge of bankruptcy; some of them closed, and the crisis was severe enough that it even threatened the system's central wholesaler, Federated Co-operatives Limited. If the Co-operative Retailing System had collapsed at that time, it would have seemed regrettable but normal. During the same period, consumer co-operatives collapsed or went bankrupt in Québec, in France, in Germany, in Austria, and elsewhere. Experts wagged their jaws and said see, co-operatives can't compete; they are inefficient; they can't raise capital; they can't handle globalization and corporate competition; retailing is too tough a business. On that latter point they are right; retailing is a *very* tough business. But the CRS did survive, and today is one of the most successful co-operative systems in Canada, and among retail co-operatives, one of the most successful in the world. In 2003, the wholesaler to the system, Federated Co-operatives, had $3.55 billion in sales and, with $282 million in surplus, twelve years in a row of record profits.[5] The return on members' invested capital was 30.1 percent in 2002.* Some inefficiency.

The story of the retail co-operatives demonstrates that history is not simply deterministic, but can be trying. The CRS's lessons were hard learned. In the 1980s, officials closed facilities, eliminated product lines and services, rolled back wages, laid off staff—there were even strikes at some co-ops. Long-time co-op staff and members must have wondered where it would all end. Most of this, in retrospect, was necessary, but cost cutting did not create the co-ops' present-day success.

A significant part of the system's earnings can be ascribed to two specific factors, which relate to the co-ops' two main lines of business, petroleum products and food. The co-operatives own an oil refinery in Regina, Saskatchewan—Consumers' Co-operative Refineries Limited (CCRL)—and there is no doubt that the profits from petroleum production and distribution have driven the system's growth. On the food side, a single spectacularly successful retail co-op in Calgary, Alberta, has been a leader in urban food merchandising and handles a significant percentage of the system's total food volume. All the co-ops benefit from the volume and marketing practices that Calgary Co-op contributes to the system. It would be a mistake, however, to think that either of these provides a simple explanation for the total system's success.

Other companies have failed even when they did have lucrative components: indeed, they have sometimes been forced to sell off their

---

* 2003 figure not available at time of writing.

best assets. Having their own oil refinery did not prevent giant US agri-cultural co-op Agway from running losses and selling their refinery interest in 1988; or Farmland Enterprises from having to enter bank-ruptcy protection in 2002 and divest itself of petroleum ventures.[6] Contrary to some people's perceptions, a refinery is not a licence to print money. Western Canada's co-ops have fiercely protected their refinery, nurtured it when other things were being cut back, invested their hard-earned dollars in it while foregoing investments in many other areas. And, of course, it takes the retail co-ops to sell the gasoline and diesel fuel, and it takes members to buy it: the refinery does not generate money unless the till rings in the gas station. As for Calgary Co-op, it is fortunate for the system that Calgary was so strong in the 1980s, when many other urban co-ops were in trouble. In 1998–99, how-ever, it was Calgary Co-op's turn to enter the downward spiral towards bankruptcy, and it was saved by inviting in management expertise from Federated to do many of the things there that other co-ops had done in the 1980s. The truth is that no component of the system is strong enough to stand on its own.

A key to the co-ops' success is that in the darkest days of the 1980s they began to rededicate themselves to marketing. They examined the state of their facilities and the image they projected. They looked at their merchandising, store layouts, and shelf displays. They revisited customer service and employee training. They didn't take the easy way out and let debt and investments swallow up their earnings, but instead insisted on the practice of paying patronage refunds to members. This took determination and discipline, but FCL and most member co-ops accomplished it. They renewed the economic benefit of co-operative membership, while also giving members better service and improved facilities. This part of the story is the subject of chapter one.

A successful organization requires good governance, good manage-ment, and the support of its stakeholders. The reorientation of the Co-op Retailing System in the 1980s was no accident, but occurred through definite processes and structures that developed trust, fostered consen-sus, and achieved results. There are three important aspects to these processes. First—the usual stuff of corporate and co-operative gover-nance—is that people have to play their roles, particularly the member-elected boards of directors and the senior managers, but also ordinary members and employees. Routine administration and oversight, planning and policy setting, meetings and information, would be boring if they didn't mean life or death to businesses. But a second aspect of governance and management is to identify and correct problems. The CRS is not free of the same kinds of problems that can surface in any business, but its mechanisms for dealing with those problems seem effective. Finally, relationships in the CRS are structured to promote good practice, excellence, and the development of human resources. The CRS is a business with a difference—a different kind of organizational culture and unique relationships—conditioned by the fact of local ownership and accountability to members. Chapter two is about the roles and relationships that make the system work.

Marketing, membership, and management are three fundamental factors in the system's success, but they would not get very far without innovation. The CRS has adapted to a changing retail environment, and even though change can be controversial, it has done so while increasing its unity and its cohesion. At the local level, co-ops innovate because of their relationship with their members and their communities. At the system level, co-ops innovate through working together. Only people who are unfamiliar with co-operatives would think co-operation comes easily. The CRS co-ops had to learn to set aside historic tensions and suspicions to co-operate more effectively as a system. In this environment, autonomy, mutual respect, and trust are the basis of innovation. The CRS is a decentralized, locally owned, bottom-up federation, and it works, it innovates, and becomes excellent at marketing *because* of its democratic federation structure—a result that is startling and full of lessons. The ways in which the co-ops have adapted to communities and opportunities, planned, set priorities, and introduced innovations is the subject of chapter three.

The chapters outlined above present three different slices from the experience of the Co-operative Retailing System over the last twenty-some years. The first is primarily about products, pricing strategies, dividends, and functional economic linkages between co-ops and members. This is the face of the CRS as members see it when they purchase a product, enter a store, or receive their patronage refund cheque. The second is about internal structures of the system, institutions and patterns that maintain it over time, promote its success, and encourage trust and accountability—the inner workings, as managers and elected leaders know them. The third chapter is about processes and adaptation. It puts together the products, strategies, leaders, and agents to show how the co-op system "thinks" and how it undertakes change.

CHAPTER ONE

Linkage

Rediscovering Marketing

WALKING INTO A STRANGE CO-OP STORE BRINGS an odd feeling. If you have the sense that your local co-op is your own store—that it belongs to your community, or even to you personally as a part owner—then to step into someone else's co-op feels like walking into a club where you aren't a member. They will gladly sell to you. But you don't know that co-op's story.

Every co-op is special—it has dramas, triumphs, losses, quirks—if you know the stories and the people behind it. Take, for example, the co-op gas bars and convenience stores (c-stores) that have spread in recent years around Winnipeg. In and of itself, a gas bar/c-store is a mundane operation. But to those who recall what happened to the co-op in that city, the new facilities are full of significance. The Co-op Marketplace on Richmond Street in Brandon, Manitoba, is one of the newest stores in the system, but it, too, has a history. In other places, you can go into prosperous-looking stores and service centres, and never know the sweat and anguish it took to save those co-ops two decades ago. The staff, members, and managers who lived through those times, however, will likely never forget what one Federated Co-op senior manager described to me as their "trial by fire."[1] Some of them will tell you, *I managed a priority retail; this co-op was on the "A" list.* You would never know what it means unless you know the stories. This chapter tells a few of them, which have to stand for many others.

The other thing to keep in mind is that the visible parts of the Co-op Retailing System, like those gas bars, do not stand on their own. They function because they are linked into a multilevel, multiproduct network nearly three thousand kilometres across and encompassing over a million people—the estimated number of active individual members of all CRS co-operatives.[2] Each gas pump connects back, directly or indirectly, to the system's purchasing and refining power in petroleum; to fleets of tanker trucks; and to the Co-op Refinery in Regina, Saskatchewan, a unique and highly important undertaking. Each product on a store shelf connects back to the voluntary teamwork of staff and co-ops across western Canada, who had to co-operate to put it there; to warehouses that handled it and more trucks that delivered it. But while the visible stores and centres are only one part of the system, they are the most important part of it: that's a lesson the system learned. The refinery is there because of the pumps at the gas bar, not the other way around. The co-op lumber mill at Canoe, BC, is there because of the local retail co-ops' profitable lumberyards. FCL is there— you might say *still* there—because enough retail co-ops changed course in time.

Which brings us to 1982.

Gerry Onyskevitch, now general manager of Moose Jaw Co-op in Saskatchewan, was then a young manager newly installed in a rural retail in Boissevain, Manitoba. The co-op was doing fine. Though interest rates were high and the economy was in recession, the business was stable; it had little debt to carry and its members were solid. Onyskevitch and his family went on holidays. His first intimation of what was going on in the wider co-op system came when he stopped at Fairmont, BC, for the annual conference of co-op managers. It was his first time; he had never before managed a co-op big enough to meet the $5-million sales cutoff to qualify for the meeting. He walked, unsuspecting, into a crisis. "I was a very young manager at the time," Onyskevitch says, "and I didn't understand or I hadn't been made aware that there were a lot of problems." He quickly found out. "At that conference there were all kinds of things happening. There was a lot of, basically, static" coming from his fellow retail managers. "They had received letters [from FCL] saying that you should be taking [wage] rollbacks and all this other stuff to try to survive ... and I remember that all the discussion at that Fairmont Conference pretty well centred around that; there was a lot of bickering back and forth.... There were some retails that really got upset over the whole thing.... I walked in on the middle of this—like, what's going on, I don't understand!" Today he says, "I can't imagine what some of those guys went through in those retails where they had to go to the employees and say, sorry, this is the situation. We're rolling back wages to survive. Or the things that they had to do, the task force reports that went on. I never experienced that because my retail wasn't in that situation."[3]

It seems fair to call it the most difficult moment in the history of western Canada's consumer co-ops. Likely even the Great Depression of the 1930s had not caused such anguish and dissension, possibly because co-ops at that time had less to lose. As in the 1930s, co-ops came together around sound management, eventually emerged financially stronger and refocussed, but also deeply marked by the experience.[4]

This chapter examines how the co-op system learned from its 1980s crisis, and how it achieved today's success. We'll begin by analyzing the problems of the early eighties—how they became apparent and where they came from. From there, we'll look at the short-term impact on the co-ops, the cutbacks and retrenchment, the loss of some co-ops, and the turnaround of many others. In telling this story, I will go back and forth between the wholesale level (FCL) and the retails, to show how the two are interdependent. From looking at FCL's strategy for dealing with "priority" or problem retails, I will move on to look at the gradual ramping-up of the system's marketing efforts, through the sequence of initiatives and programs building over the last two decades. Near the end of this chapter, we'll have a look at how some particular aspects fit into this retailing/marketing story—behind-the-scenes functions such as wholesaling and distribution, exceptional successes like Calgary Co-op, and one of the system's cornerstones, the Co-op Refinery. The chapter will conclude with a few reflections about the meaning of this story in terms of what it shows about western Canadian communities and about success in co-operatives. This chapter is the broad-brushstrokes picture of the system's overall history, leaving other important subjects to be filled in by chapters two and three.

O MINOUS TRENDS WERE BECOMING MORE AND more visible as the recession deepened. By 1982, the combined debt of the individual retail co-ops had grown to $260 million. They had a consolidated equity ratio of 32 percent—that is, the members' stake in the retails (their share capital combined with the accumulated reserves) was less than one-third of the assets; the rest was covered by accounts owed to the co-op, by loans taken on by the co-op, and the like. FCL was better off, but still had $105 million in long-term debt and only 44 percent member equity. Though the wholesale made record savings of almost $51 million in 1981, when it made patronage refunds it was able to pay out only 35 percent in cash and had to retain the rest in shares to preserve its own finances.[5] At the spring 1982 annual meeting in Calgary, CEO Pat Bell had told delegates that the amount of financial assistance required by retails had doubled between 1980 and 1981, and was expected to double again to almost $4 million in 1982. More and more retails were relying on FCL to prop them up financially. Then-Treasurer Wayne Thompson warned that FCL had more than $21 million of outstanding guarantees to retails. At that time, FCL provided direct assistance of $1.9 million in light of the serious financial position of retails. His report mentioned great potential loss for Federated if any of the retails didn't make it.[6]

It was probably hard for the retail co-ops to be too concerned about the warnings from FCL, since its 1981 results had been so good. FCL was still making money; it should just pay more of it back to the co-ops to help them through their troubles—or so it seemed to some retail managers. Resolutions continued to be passed up to 1982 calling for higher cash repayments to members, more development funds from FCL for retail expansions, more free services from FCL, and more financial assistance to retails; not to mention the investment of Federated funds in a variety of ventures, such as Co-op Implements, about which FCL management was more than dubious. Managers who had opposed such spending and who had been concerned about retail viability were overruled by FCL delegates and directors.[7]

Then came the fiscal year 1982. The recession hit FCL now, too, and

though sales increased, earnings plummeted almost 80 percent to barely more than $10 million. The wholesale had to absorb $27 million in
bad debts that year. CEO Pat Bell's presentation to the 1982 Fairmont
Conference—the meeting Onyskevitch remembered as marked by
bickering from the retail managers—was statistical in approach and
hard-hitting in its implications. Bell noted that retail long-term debt
had increased 272 percent over the period from 1974–81; that by 1981
almost all profits were eaten up by interest costs; that the entire economy was in recession; that ten retail co-ops were in "extremely difficult
circumstances" and might not survive, while about one hundred—one-
quarter of the total system—were facing "serious operating problems."
Overall, the retail co-ops were in red ink, losing money on their combined operations; and with FCL's plummeting earnings, there was no
way the wholesale could help them all. "It is now very obvious that we
are not going to survive intact," he told the retail managers. "Our challenge now is to make the turnaround and survive."[8]

Today, if you ask people in the system why co-ops were in such
trouble, they mostly agree: hindsight is 20-20, and the anger and frustration have been tempered by wisdom and experience. One FCL
region manager says simply, "We overexpanded"—his "we" means the
whole system, including the retails. "We overexpanded into areas that
were not profitable. We carried a huge debt load. The interest rates
were in the low 20 percent range, and as a system we just didn't recognize the fact that we had to be profitable," he says.[9] Another manager,
who worked at that time in a co-op finance department, put it this
way: "In the late seventies, everybody was on a roll. They were all
building—it was the thing to do.... Not only the co-ops; there were
many other businesses.... They were building almost beyond their
needs," he says. "If you don't have it, borrow the money and go for it,"
is how he describes the attitude. "And what happened?... Their debt
was virtually killing them and they weren't efficient in their operations," he says. "When the high interest rates started creeping in, in the
early eighties, the retails couldn't service it. And then ... other companies started to move in," new competitors with new and attention-getting retail formats. On the food side, this included the new warehouse-
style retailers and superstores. "They were introducing a whole new
marketing era" based on low pricing. "We didn't have the ability from

the retail and the wholesale side to offer efficiency" to match them, is how he sums it up.[10]

If some explanations make it sound as if the co-ops were caught by factors beyond their control, others are more self-critical. The crisis was due to "a number of things, and I'm not sure if I would want to put them in order of which was the worst," says a long-time FCL employee. "Complacency: I think the managers in Federated and the managers of our retail co-operatives got real complacent. Inflation was rampant, sales were increasing, and the bottom line was being inflated by inflationary factors," he says. Others told me you could be careless in those days ordering inventory: always order a bit extra, keep it lying around somewhere; you'd be able to sell it next year at a smart profit, just because the prices kept rising. Inflationary earnings covered up all kinds of inefficiency. "There was a lot of expansion going on. I think that would have been another cause," he continues. "Some of the expansion was not well planned. There was less concern for the accuracy of the feasibility studies that were being prepared" than there is today. "So a lot of the expansions ... turned out to be very serious problems. Some of the retails were really suffering. They had high-interest-rate loans and just weren't getting the sales volume to cover them." In 1979, 1980, 1981, "there were few of us in the system who were trying to ring bells and suggest that we were going about this the wrong way and that the balloon was going to burst," he says.[11]

It didn't help that co-ops, flushed with ambition and confidence in the 1960s and 1970s, had gone in for some difficult retail formats. Characteristic of the early part of that era were the downtown co-op department stores in urban centres—multistorey, full-range stores where loyal urban members could buy almost any product they wanted, with large selections of clothing, appliances, and so on. But the department-store era was peaking by the time the co-ops were getting into it. Few of these stores remain today, and none with the original marketing concept. Then in the 1970s, the new concept was malls, preferably big malls filled from one end to the other with purely co-op departments. Customers could browse from the co-op food store at one end to the co-op home centre at the other, passing co-op gift shops, clothing stores, appliance and furniture stores, and of course the cafeteria along the way. It was the department store idea in a new form. These were the expensive concepts into which the system was investing money, just as warehouse-style discount retailers hit the urban markets, and began pulling customers in from smaller centres as well. In retrospect it's all very understandable. Co-op people, proud of what they had accomplished, wanted to build stores just like the best ones they knew. Their mental models came from the recent past, not the near future. Today, a number of co-ops make money on those old malls, but usually it's not by the co-op trying to run every service in it.

One of those who joined FCL's senior management in the years leading up to the crisis was Elmer Wiebe, hired into FCL Home Office out of the Manitoba region office by then-CEO Bill Bergen. Wiebe brought with him a familiarity with marketing and experience at the retail level, which he put to good use in the 1980s when he became Federated's VP, Marketing. Marketing came naturally, he says, "with my background, with my dad always being involved in retail … whether it was selling tires or selling oil or selling groceries or selling anything, it wasn't really something that was very strange to me." He recalls how he got his start in the system in southern Manitoba at Plum Coulee. "It was a little general store, so we sold everything from gasoline to groceries to family fashions to a little bit of, you know, their homemade remedies," he says. "So it was just about everything you could think of." From there he went through a variety of other co-ops, through FCL departments and regions, became an FCL retail division manager and eventually a senior vice-president at a critical time in the system's history. Wiebe was in charge of teaching the system how to market.

He recalls the financial pressures on all the co-ops, and on FCL. The retails' own loans from various financial institutions were already backed by verbal guarantees from Federated, which was bad enough; now the retails wanted more loans, and the banks and credit unions were demanding written promises from FCL. "That's exactly the era," Wiebe recalls, "where Wayne and I sat together night after night trying to figure out how in the world—before he was CEO—we were going to cope with this situation." Others from that era say managers' stomachs clenched when they thought about what was going on in the system. "You've got managers trying to manage a mall, and they don't know too much about family fashion units, these huge departments and inventories, they don't know very much about an agro centre.… Some years you have all the equipment and all the inventory in place ... but no volume, because ... you've got a bit of a drought or you've got this or you've got that.... Wheat was ninety-five cents a bushel," in those days, and the rural co-ops were suffering. "All these huge inventories and accounts receivable and ownership of [as little as] 10 percent," Wiebe remembers. "That [caused] years of suffering that should have never happened."[12]

Wayne Thompson—today CEO—joins those who are critical of the standard of management in those days, and adds that the relationships between retails and Federated were not great, either. "Retail general managers, many of them, weren't focussed on standards and weren't good operators in many respects," Thompson says now. "Costs got away on us. Facilities at that time were ones that we couldn't really be proud of, and the way they were managed was no better. I think over-all the system was caught up in a little bit of bureaucracy. There was more overhead than there should have been. It's always hard to know where you get the problem from, but when the focus gets off making money and you start relying on subsidization and the like from Federated, and you start arguing about how you're going to share the money between Federated and retail, I think you've got real problems," he explains. "A big part of the focus with the retails was how to get either financial assistance from Federated or get more money one way or the other from Federated. So we spent all of our time arguing amongst ourselves instead of looking at how the system in total can generate the most money. It can be generated through retails; it can be generated through Federated—wherever the most money in total can be generated by using the system's strength. That's the difference today ... how the different relationships work."[13]

In pointing to *relationships,* Thompson puts his finger on the key to the co-op system. In 1982, the relationships weren't working. There was no money in Federated to bail so many retails out of their problems. There was no effective partnership—retails were not profitable, and FCL was not helping enough to make them profitable. What the crisis did, ultimately, was to draw attention to their interdependence. The retails had the debts, but FCL had the overview of the problems and had to be a source of the initiative to address them. At the same time, FCL couldn't exist in isolation; it would get pulled under unless retails had earnings. They needed each other.

It wasn't apparent to everyone at the time just how serious and how intertwined the system's finances were. It wasn't just that retails expected loan guarantees and subsidies from FCL; there was more. One FCL board member of the day recalls, "The biggest problem was that ... the retails were expanding and they were using their shares in Federated as collateral for their loans. As high interest rates hit at that time, a lot of those loans became very dicey as to whether they could be repaid, and that was the problem. Federated had so many liens—liens against the shares—had they all been called, or gone bad, the entire Co-op Retailing System would have collapsed." He adds, "Today that isn't allowed. You can't use Federated Co-op shares to borrow money."[14] His account of the situation is confirmed by a finance manager of the same period. "If our bankers—the Bank of Montreal, primarily—ever really took a look through our financial structure and recognized just how much of ... Federated's equity was assigned to retail loans, and the total reality of the guarantees that we had out there on behalf of retails, I think we might have been doing some pretty tall explaining.... We had a lot of it out there. Well up into the 60 percent range of our equity being assigned and, like a house of cards, if the thing started to topple, it was going to be a messy situation."[15]

The objective had to be to save the system. It was clear some individual co-ops were not going to make it. In the end, probably fewer failed than some leaders had feared; but some of the failures that did happen were extremely painful, and there are system leaders who still regret choices they made. Before describing how the turnaround happened, it's important to register that the possibilities of failure were real. At the same time, looking at *how* and *why* particular co-ops were closed sheds light on the challenges the co-op system faced.

~

SPEAKING OF JUST MYSELF," ONE FCL MANAGER OF the day told me, "I saw some things that were just so unpleasant—retails like Salmon Arm," he said. "That was a fairly well-run retail; it was well located and well stocked; it was well supported; it was just a very good store." At the time it opened, it was probably one of the most ambitious and most modern in the system, and a key geographically to the development of the BC region. But it had borrowed to build that beautiful store. "Interest rates went to 20-some percent. It was an impossibility for them to make money"—and that's it, they were dead. Not instantly, mind you, since it took a few years, but the death sentence had been passed the moment the interest rates climbed. "You get a situation where a tremendously successful, healthy retail co-operative is simply going to die, and if that one can die, so can lots of others," he points out. "I think the fear factor was probably as big as anything" in motivating people in the system to change what they were doing. "And I think the closer the people were to the financial situation, the better they understood the financial situation, the more fear" they felt.[16]

It all depends how you look at a co-op. If a beautiful facility, large stock, technically proficient management, and imposing presence in the community are the standard, then Salmon Arm was a great co-op. But sometimes, at least, you have to see it differently. A great co-op is what is adapted to its setting, to the needs of the community, so that it can sustain itself through adversity. Then you want to know not about the buildings, but about the balance sheet; not the capacity, but the market; not the volume, but the earnings.

I asked another manager, why did Salmon Arm go down, while Otter Co-op (Aldergrove, BC) and Vanderhoof and Districts Co-op, BC, made it? All three co-ops in the same FCL region were on the priority list as retails that were expected possibly not to survive; but the last two not only survived, they are thriving today. "I think that Salmon Arm was so overdeveloped, size-wise, cost-wise ... even if we had the whole 100 percent of the market it probably wouldn't have survived," he says bluntly—with the bluntness you sometimes see of people who went through those years.[17]

Yet another manager brought out a different dimension by comparing Salmon Arm to Drumheller, Alberta, where the co-op was also in trouble. "Drumheller made it because of the success of the CRS and more so, Federated.... Numerous individuals spent a lot of time in Drumheller chipping away at the operations and making decisions to weed out the bad and the departments that lost a lot of money ... and once the debt was paid off, then they were able to turn [it] around.... But it was as a result of the system being strong, and Federated [being] able to put a little bit of money each year into Drumheller and keep it going … until it could stand on its own two feet. Salmon Arm didn't have the luxury of getting money from Federated during the rough periods, so the decision was, ok, we can't feed everybody, so who are we going to save? So a decision had to be made … some dropped off, some were able to be salvaged." And in Salmon Arm, "you know, a $20-million retail—we had to … give notices, shut down the facility" in 1986. "It was a big part of Salmon Arm.… To shut it down and walk away, it hurt, because a lot of blood, sweat, and tears went into that organization to try to salvage it and try to make a go, and of course, it couldn't. It was sad to see."[18]

If such decisions seem brutal, it has to be added that FCL developed a rationale for making them—after all, the company had to explain to the other retails why it was helping some, pulling the plug on others. In the end, the money that was lost in each case (whether in a closure or keeping a money-losing co-op alive) was money that came from and belonged to all the other co-ops in the system. The basic principle was simple: it was the survival of the total system that mattered most. In each case, they followed the solution that cost the system least. This might mean keeping a money-losing co-op alive, perhaps because of strategic importance (for example, its volume might bring viability to a warehouse on which other co-operatives also depended), or perhaps simply because of timing. The system couldn't afford to have too many co-ops fail at the same time. If the hemorrhage was big enough, closure was cheaper, as proved to be the case in Salmon Arm. For a formerly fractious group of retail managers, directors, and FCL managers and directors to learn to think this way was quite a feat. It was a practical example of recognizing how the good of the whole and the good of the one were interdependent.

Perhaps even more troubling, to more people, was what happened to Red River Co-op in Winnipeg. The ambitious co-op in Manitoba's capital had undertaken a concerted expansion in the sixties and seventies. Despite the expansion, it was not prepared for the competition provided by Superstore—Winnipeg being one of the first cities the new retailer entered. Red River's food stores were burdened by debt or by expensive leases, and just didn't earn enough. "Very, very painful," one manager recalls. Words fail him: "I remember in Red River, October 28,

1982, we delivered 350 layoff notices. That was not a very good day to have, and I experienced, you know ... We personally hand-delivered a letter to each employee and ... Very, very painful," is all he can say.[19]

Red River Co-op's new gas bar/convenience store located at Brookside.

Mel Adams, who since 2001 has been vice-president, Agro Products, for FCL, also remembers being on the front lines in the early 1980s. "I was the finance manager in Winnipeg in 1981," he says (in FCL's Winnipeg region office), "a time when, financially, retails were struggling, and that certainly put pressure on Federated as well." One aspect of this was dealing with FCL's own internal reorganization. FCL shed jobs in Winnipeg as accounting functions were centralized in Saskatoon. As finance manager of the region, Adams also acted as controller of Red River Co-op; later, when he was FCL region manager, he doubled as general manager of Red River. "Red River was in a very dire financial situation in the mid-eighties," he recalls. "Because of its operations and its financial position, it was virtually bankrupt.... Red River at that time was operating home centres, food stores, and petroleum facilities, and through a tremendous amount of analysis it was determined that there was potential for the retail to survive, but it would have to rid itself of all operations other than petroleum, and even then the risk was still fairly high at that time.... So, the closure process at the food stores and the home centres and so on certainly became quite a task." By the time he became general manager in 1994, the co-op had turned the corner, and—specializing in petroleum alone—was progressing again.[20]

The store closures in Winnipeg were controversial and attracted criticism—and not only on the street and in the press. FCL board member and at that time Manitoba Vice-President Ed Klassen remembers that he and another director were called into the office of Manitoba's minister responsible for co-operatives and lambasted for what they were doing.[21] It's interesting that anything a private corporation does within the law normally passes without comment: for-profit businesses can open stores, close them, undercut established businesses or take them over, with little criticism. But co-ops are supposed to do what outsiders, who aren't reading the balance sheet, consider good, no matter what the cost.

Winnipeg was bad, but it was not the worst. While a number of co-ops were lost, and many were scaled back, former Vice-President Wiebe says, "To me the most upsetting thing was to lose the Edmonton market ... and I wasn't the only one ... but we had just too much on our plate ..." he sighs. "I would have fought harder—and I sometimes blame myself for not fighting even harder than I did in terms of saying, come hell or high water, let's right Edmonton ... let's take the hit.... But we had too many hits," he says regretfully. "We just barely had an earning after all the writedowns we took at the retail level." But you can tell he is thinking of Calgary Co-op's tremendous success, and Edmonton not too different in population, its co-op developing nicely... "Lord only knows where we'd be at today."[22]

Edmonton was doubly disappointing because the system did make an effort to save the co-op, and it took nearly a decade before it was finally shut down. Edmonton had similar problems to Winnipeg—expansion; debt; expensive stores; tough competition from the likes of Superstore, Food For Less, and Save On Foods—but at first there seemed to be more hope. FCL sent one of its senior managers to try to rebuild, and a group of younger managers came along. "Edmonton was a very interesting experience," says one of them. "It was a frustrating experience because, while we were newcomers to Edmonton Co-op, there were a lot of long-term employees ... And so there was sort of an us-against-them atmosphere." The managers personally got "our first taste of the pain that we had to start going through in terms of survival in the co-op system. Things like mandatory six-day work weeks, 20 percent salary cuts, giving up a week's holiday, those kinds of things were ... talked about and in some cases enforced" on the managers. The young managers resented the cutbacks; they hadn't caused the problem, so why should they be paying the price? "However, that was the pain that was required, I guess, at the time, to try and get it back on track." It was the staff, though, who bore the brunt of what happened. "A review of the company was done in terms of the positions, the structure, and as a result of that they ... went about trying to eliminate some of the losing departments." He recalls that "it was very frustrating from the standpoint of the people who had been there for a long, long time." They "viewed the action as just a terrible blow to the work that they had done and resented the kind of decisions that had been made in terms of winding down portions of the operation. We learned a lot of new language from folks.... As a young manager, it was a stressful time," he says, but also a learning experience.[23]

"You see a lot of mistakes that were made by management," he reflects. He became determined not to make the same mistakes himself. "I realized that [you can't] ever take any success or any part of the business for granted. Every day is a new day and you have to continue to improve the operations. And Edmonton I guess was my first experience with that. People had assumed that this co-op was going to go on forever. It was expanding. They looked to the south at Calgary Co-op and felt that if Calgary was expanding, therefore Edmonton should be expanding; and I think that they didn't do a good job of managing the fundamentals of that organization. They didn't have a strong base to build on, and a lot of the people's ideas were rigid, in the past. They didn't like change and the company had to change."

As it turned out, 1983 was the last year Edmonton Co-op made any surplus, and that was achieved by selling one of it stores. FCL began managing the co-op in 1986. In 1990, with all five remaining co-op stores still running losses, Federated presented the Edmonton Co-op board with a restructuring plan that involved spinning off its least unsuccessful store as a new co-op. The directors were split and the plan was rejected; some accused FCL of running the co-op into the ground and seizing its assets. Directors who supported FCL said the Edmonton operation had run up nearly $11 million in losses in ten years; that FCL had provided it with $2–3 million per year in financial assistance for four to five years running; had forgiven it $15 million in debt; yet even after this, Edmonton Co-op was still in debt and not making ends meet. Federated put the organization into receivership in 1991, spun off the new Delton Co-op as planned, and liquidated the last Edmonton Co-op assets in 1993—a long, lingering, and acrimonious end to a promising co-op.[24]

Other co-ops were wracked by strikes. Unions tried to resist the closure of FCL's BC warehouse. Co-op employees in Moose Jaw, Saskatchewan, went on a thirteen-month strike. Employees in Saskatoon went on strike in 1983; at one point a mass public meeting of more than a thousand people met to consider impeachment of the board of directors (the petition was voted down). In the mid- to late 1980s, a strike at Pineland Co-op in northeastern Saskatchewan became one of the longest-running labour disputes in the province's history, leading the Saskatchewan Federation of Labour to declare a boycott of co-op stores and products. There was so much labour unrest that an academic study conducted at the time concluded that the co-op sector had a far higher frequency and intensity of labour disputes than other branches of the economy.[25] All of this was painful and frustrating; but it was nothing compared to the experiences of the co-ops that ceased to exist altogether. The spectre that haunts managers who went through those years is not labour unrest. It's Winnipeg. It's Salmon Arm. It's Edmonton.

~

FEDERATED LEARNED, THE RETAILS LEARNED, AND the system learned together; but in many ways the process began at FCL, and it began even before 1982. "There was a realization within our organization," one person told me, "and it grew out of Federated, I think, although it spread easily enough to the retails,... starting in the late seventies, that things were not only not as good as they looked, in fact they were an awful lot worse."[26]

The wholesale company was in the midst of a leadership transition among managers. One sign of a certain instability was the short tenure of two successive CEOs, Bill Bergen followed by Pat Bell. Similarly, the board presidents turned over: Gordon Sinclair to Leo Hayes to Vern Leland. But beneath the top level, new managers were coming into key positions. In 1977, Distribution Division Manager Wayne Thompson moved to treasurer, and Al Roden moved into Distribution, a position he held for twenty-one years. (The terminology changed: Distribution Division manager became vice-president, Distribution—today, Logistics.) They joined Peter Zakreski, who was already vice-president of Human Resources. Elmer Wiebe joined the senior management group as manager of Retail Operations, and became vice-president, Marketing, in 1983. Harold Empey moved from Agro Division manager to senior vice-president, Corporate Affairs, a position he held until his retirement in 1991. Al Robinson moved into the VP, Agro Division, manager role. Norman Krivoshen, food department manager since 1976, became vice-president, Consumer Products, in 1980, a position he still holds today. Ken Hart became vice-president, Retail Operations, in 1983, and he, too, holds that same position today. And finally, in 1983, Wayne Thompson became CEO. Within a span of six or seven years, almost the whole senior management group changed; and much of the core of that group remains in place today, over two decades later.

The changeover in FCL management was underway before the system became aware of any crisis. One reason for FCL's ultimately successful response to its challenges may have been that regular management turnover was ensuring that new managers with different ideas were waiting in the wings, and moving into key positions. Wayne Thompson's appointment as CEO in 1983 was not the beginning but in some ways the culmination of the changes. The process was what Elmer Wiebe refers to as "the changing of the guard." The new managers brought with them what developed into a fairly coherent point of view. He recalls that under CEO Pat Bell "the trend was already established that we had to move away from being perceived as a wholesale organization, and that we were moving into being a retail system," he explains, with a greater emphasis on marketing success, and closer co-operation between the wholesale and the retails. "Really, who are we, you know, other than the retails? So if they've got a problem, we've got a problem; it isn't an us-against-them kind of thing."[27]

There was a variety of thinking in the system. One promising concept of the early 1980s was "Growth from Within." As championed by a group of adult educators and member-relations specialists within FCL, the idea was to deepen co-operative membership and enhance loyalty by making co-operatives more thoroughly democratic organizations. The authors of the concept papers argued that running democratic meetings was a different thing from operating democratic organizations, and that democracy might require many more mechanisms than just a single annual meeting to determine what members want. They advocated that co-ops use a continuous cycle of surveys, interviews, and other forms of information gathering and communication in order to keep in touch with their members. They pointed to low purchases per member and apparent alienation of members from co-ops as problems that could be solved in this way. While Growth from Within continued to be mentioned throughout the 1980s, and helped inspire a continuing focus on loyalty of co-op members, the promoters' ideas were likely never more than partially implemented.[28]

In 1982 the crisis was dire and immediate, allowing no time for long-term strategies. FCL began to respond early in 1982, with proposed remedies increasing in severity as the scope of the crisis became clearer. The January 1982 FCL board-management planning session prioritized "improvement of the viability of retail co-operatives"—helping them be competitive, and finding efficiencies in FCL operations "in order to enhance the savings available for allocation to the retail co-operatives." FCL also promoted "the Area Development concept" among retails— i.e., amalgamations or shared services among neighbouring co-ops—"as offering the greatest opportunity for improving retail viability." The marketing strategy of the system was to focus primarily on "those commodity lines in which it is most successful.... These lines will receive priority in terms of operations and the allocation of resources." Plans for succeeding years were largely similar in overall strategy, with improved retail operations always being the number-one item.[29] Early in 1982, FCL introduced an internal hiring freeze that saw management salaries frozen, work weeks extended, and employees laid off in the spring. This was only the beginning.[30]

Long-time Vice-President, Human Resources, Peter Zakreski recalls a turning point at a summer 1982 planning session. His own message was that there was no point, at that moment, in doing long-term planning. If the company didn't focus on the short term, it wouldn't be there. This called for desperate measures. "We did things that consultants have subsequently developed all kinds of fancy words for," Zakreski says. "I guess we didn't know what the hell we were doing, but there was the reorientating, the reinventing, there was the downsizing, there was a rightsizing, there was the re-engineering—But I think we did it all and we did it from common sense because we couldn't go on the way we were going." He remembers that Wayne Thompson, still treasurer at the time, made the conclusive presentation. "After Wayne was finished, we obviously switched our whole direction in terms of talking about what had to be done. There was no tomorrow. It had to be done today, and there was no time for any more task forces or any more committees."[31]

FCL had already closed its Vancouver distribution centre, and sold the properties, in 1979–80. Other closures and shutdowns soon followed: its Designex prefabricated homes plant; its Downie Street sawmill in Revelstoke, BC; its Retail Development department; its forty-four-year-old *Co-operative Consumer* newspaper; and a number of warehouse and other operations were centralized in particular locations. FCL officials rolled back salaries for senior managers by 10 percent, which would be reinstated only if the company met its earnings targets. They informed lower-level managers that their salaries might be rolled back 10 percent if their departments failed to meet targets. They reviewed all staff positions in FCL Home Office and regions, and eliminated "large numbers ... not absolutely required to handle our existing sales volumes." They sold nonproductive assets and began the process of withdrawing investments from outside companies. "Every expense possible was questioned." In short order, FCL shed more than two hundred jobs, and those who remained were subject to freezes, wage rollbacks, or threats of wage rollbacks.[32]

Zakreski's own area, personnel, was critical. "We had too much bureaucracy in our organization, we were overstaffed; we'd lost our focus, to some extent, in terms of what our purpose was and why we were there," he says. "Then we used an approach on the people side," Zakreski remembers, "in which we identified the people we wanted to keep for the future and then found a job for them from among the jobs that we would keep. So I remember spending one weekend in June, I think it was the last weekend in June, typing up layoff notices."

Unpleasant as the job was, Zakreski remembers doing the best they could for the employees, putting together complete information packages anticipating their questions about unemployment insurance, pension and benefits, transfers, and so on. "As a result," he figures, "all of that happened without one lawsuit from the employees, and we weren't overly generous in terms of our severance pay. In fact, by today's terms, we were rather conservative. But the unions, the same thing, there were a lot of union positions that were eliminated and we did all that without one grievance. We had a lot of communication." And, Zakreski says, "We led by example in senior management" by taking the salary cuts. "The situation was very serious and we took it that way."[33]

The harsh medicine at FCL carried with it the message that retails had better undertake similar survival measures. One of the managers quoted earlier told me that before 1983, "there was a mindset in the system, and it was in general in the system, that as long as there was any money available anywhere … there never would be a time when a retail co-op would be allowed to disintegrate, go under.… That was never a very healthy outlook and it's one that at that stage … we had to dispel, and it was not popular. Sometimes it was at the cost of what people traditionally called the co-operative spirit, whatever that is, but for those of us who … could really see the terrible results of not altering our approaches, it still didn't taste good, but we certainly knew that's what had to be." Thompson was "a leader in that thinking," maybe more direct in financial matters than others had been, "but he definitely was not alone in it."[34]

In this environment, it was around Thompson's way of thinking that the FCL managers and board of directors coalesced. An FCL director recalls how "Wayne came on board and he was chafing at the bit to get things back on track. Certainly he has to take … most of the credit for what happened. He was able to analyse the problems very clearly and he was fearless in suggesting the painful surgery and the bitter medicine that had to be taken," the director told me. "I accompanied Wayne quite often to the retail meetings and he certainly had a clear focus about what had to be done. He had to come out with a very unpopular message and at first some managers reacted quite violently," the director recalls. "But after awhile he became a real hero because they saw the tangible improvement that was taking place year by year.… For me it was very gratifying to see this turnaround because it could have gone the other way. It was the leadership" that made the difference, both Thompson's sense of direction and new board President Vern Leland's communication and persuasion skills.[35]

Because of his determination, even in the face of initial disbelief or opposition from retail managers, Thompson established an impressive credibility among the system's managers. One of the retail managers, new in the early 1980s, says today, "Well, to me, Wayne Thompson is—as a manager, he'd be my idol." Nor was this the most positive comment I heard. Others I can't quote because they would be embarrassing, or possibly sacrilegious. "To me, he is basically the savior of the co-op system."[36] Another put it with a bit more nuance: "He's provided the vision and the leadership for our organization and for many of us as general managers to do the things that needed to be done at our own retail.... It took great leadership to steer us through all of the problems that we encountered in the 1980s," he says, "and without the vision and leadership and the strength of character, in particular of Wayne Thompson, I don't think we would have come as far as we have. And that's not to minimize all of the work that his people—senior management and the entire Federated Co-op staff, or the retail general managers and their staff, and the boards of directors of all the retails—have done. We all have a role to play. But without a strong helmsman to lead us through it, I'm sure that we wouldn't have been successful today."

"I've learned a great deal from the individual," this manager says. "I don't always agree with his opinion or his tactic, but he wins more than he loses. He's more visionary and ... sees [some things] coming long before the rest of us do. I marvel at that."[37]

Thompson himself characteristically draws attention to the direction and the teamwork, not the role of any individual. "I think one of the things that's really worked well for us is that we've had a very, very solid and consistent team of management, and we've had a very, very good relationship with our board," he says when I ask him why the co-ops have succeeded. "They know that everybody has to be together because the one who's offside doesn't get a lot of support from the other guys," he points out. "That's one of the keys to our success; how we achieved our success was in having everything together instead of all this fighting all the time.... The differences in these meetings are like night and day."

"You know," he adds, "one person who deserves a lot of credit, but who has never been mentioned a lot, was the CEO at the time," Thompson's predecessor, Pat Bell. "People like myself and Elmer Wiebe really put a lot into it," and so did the entire executive management group, but "we had tremendous support from Pat Bell.... He was the one who took most of the heat," Thompson says. "If he hadn't supported us as the CEO at the time, and had been willing to let things slide, it wouldn't have changed.... Sure, at the Fairmont Conference I was doing a presentation," he says, "but the tough questions, they weren't asking me.... They were asking Pat."[38]

By mid-1982, FCL was changing course. The issue was to get the retails to follow suit. FCL managers believed that retails, too, had to go into "survival mode," which entailed dissolving some retails, closing departments, selling assets, "reducing costs in every area possible—including layoffs, salary freezes, and rollbacks," strictly controlling inventories and accounts receivable, avoiding all but emergency capital expenditures, and requesting relief from lenders.[39]

The senior management group employed various mechanisms to transmit their ideas to the system as a whole. There were the reports, the studies, and the presentations at the managers' meetings and planning sessions, at Fairmont and then at FCL's annual meeting. These were accompanied by the sharp cuts at FCL, which were designed both to improve the wholesale's finances and to send a message to the retails. But the most important step came after FCL's August 1982 board meeting, which received and approved the proposals from FCL management.

As a result of policies approved by the board, the problem (or "priority") retails were generally divided into two groups. Those with net overall losses in 1981 even after FCL patronage refunds—i.e., the worst off—would be required to adopt a standard "resolution A." These were the "A" list. The "B" list consisted of those with local losses prior to the FCL refund, but still a positive result overall. The retails were asked to call special board meetings to discuss the resolutions, and teams of FCL region and home-office staff (task forces) were sent out to conduct analyses at the retails and make further or more specific recommendations. FCL would not provide the retails with direct financial assistance or any other help unless they adopted the "required recommendations" in the task-force reports.[40]

The B group consisted of sixty-six retails with local losses, but not receiving FCL assistance. They were asked to pass board resolutions accepting FCL's report and recommendations, adopting them for implementation by retail management in "close co-operation" with FCL, setting a minimum target of "local breakeven operation before FCL patronage refunds," and declaring "voluntary" support for this plan in full awareness that financial assistance from FCL would only be forthcoming if necessary improvements in operations were achieved. The retails were to consider salary rollbacks, review operations and management, close departments wherever shutdown losses would be less than operating losses, reduce inventories by 10 percent in departments kept open, and make efforts to increase member support and member equity (Growth from Within). Boards and managers were called upon to keep closer track of operations and support system programs, including promoting Area Development "at every opportunity."[41]

The thirty-six A-group retails, the ones receiving FCL subsidies, had to go further. FCL's recommendations were to be "approved and adopted for implementation by our management staff *under the direction of Federated Co-operatives Limited, as soon as possible*" [emphasis added]. They were required to implement immediately (for nonunionized staff) or negotiate (for unionized employees) a 10 percent reduction in wages, a longer work week, and a maximum four weeks of annual vacation.[42]

Debate at the Fairmont Conference introduced some flexibility and discretion into the application of the restraint plan, but in broad outline it remained as FCL managers had devised it.[43] Within a month of the FCL board's August 1982 meeting, most of the thirty-six priority retails had been visited by FCL teams led by home-office managers, leaving the rest to be dealt with by officials from the region offices. Six retails were recommended for dissolution; the others were given hard-hitting presentations about the need to close departments, dispose of assets, reduce costs "in every way possible," control inventories and accounts receivable, and limit capital expenditures to emergency items. "Unless the retail and FCL came to some tough decisions, even the system might not survive." One of those who led the teams commented,

"At first I believe the attitude was basically one of shock and resistance to the presentation." The idea of a 10 percent salary rollback drew particular opposition. But within a month, twenty-six of the retails had passed the required resolutions.[44]

Ken Hart was among the teams that went out to the retails to give them FCL's message. As vice-president, Retail Operations, for FCL since 1983, Hart's job today is to oversee the services provided to retail co-ops through FCL's region offices. FCL supports the retails in improving their operations, finances, and human resources. "Because of the opportunities, I got to move back and forth between the wholesale organization and the retail sector," Hart reflects. "I got a really good understanding of why the decisions are made the way they are from both perspectives." In 1983, he needed that perspective. "We went from retail to retail with a package to try and say, these are the things you're going to have to do at your retail in order to get the results that are going to let you survive," Hart recalls. "And there's no question we were in a survival mode. There was not time for a lot of questions about why we're doing this or why we're doing that. If we were going to survive we had to act, and we had to act now."[45]

While the crisis and the process of responding to it eventually bonded the system closer together, this wasn't the immediate reaction. Many retails did not accept that there was anything wrong with what they were doing. Managers resisted FCL's message, which might be taken as a criticism of how they were doing their jobs. Boards of directors, who had to take responsibility for unpleasant decisions, resisted it. Members criticized cutbacks and closures. Meanwhile, retails that were not in trouble criticized the aid being given to those that were. This is where the system's least-cost approach became important: it held out a relatively objective yardstick for explaining why some co-ops were to be helped, for the good of the system.

One retail co-op complained in August 1982, "While we are certainly concerned about our sister co-operatives, we do not see where FCL has the financial ability or right to pour millions out in assistance to bail co-operatives out of trouble that have been ill-advised or perhaps not advised at all as to the problems they are getting into."[46] CEO Bell was blunt in explaining the policy. "The amount provided for direct assistance to those retails which are most seriously affected … will hopefully provide us with the time required to rationalize these operations and in so doing, minimize our ultimate loss."[47] In other words, the assistance was *not* being provided on the basis of keeping the retails afloat. It was being provided in order to minimize the damage to FCL, the remaining retails, and the whole system. Bell also said to more than one retail manager: "From where I sit … it appears to me the financial support provided to retails [in the past] … has had the effect of sheltering the recipients from the problems of the real world."[48] That wasn't going to happen any more.

Task-force reports (another region manager recalls) showed that "there was a lot of excess staff. There wasn't a lot of efficiency; staff productivity wasn't being measured; there was lots of waste in [utility] and supply costs. There were a lot of co-ops that, over the years, had banked a lot of land that was unproductive and was costing a lot of money, and that had to be unloaded. There was a lot of rolling stock that wasn't making big money. They were buying lots of big trucks and having them sitting around," he recalls. The reports in many cases pinpointed "service departments that were big money-losers, and those were the toughest ones to get boards of directors … to close down" because they had become "pet" projects of the board and services that the members had "grown to expect." He sums up: "We had to improve merchandising, improve marketing, improve the image of the co-op."[49] This region manager recalls some boards objecting, "We'll have to go to the membership to close this department!" He also recalls countering, "Did you go to the membership to open it?" Of course they hadn't. "You have the same authority to close it. You have to practise good, due diligence in protecting the members' equity and the members' assets," he stressed to boards. According to other accounts, noncompliant directors received letters informing them they could be sued, as individuals, if they made irresponsible decisions—likely an effective way of getting their attention.

There are some examples of co-ops that were able to consult their members and get them to agree, in a majority in public meetings, to close money-losing services. For the most part, however, it was the boards of directors who took action, and had to defend it afterwards in members' meetings. "That was … a difficult thing for our boards," an FCL director agrees. Because of the importance of the message, and the resistance to it, FCL directors also went out to talk to the retails in support of the instructions from FCL management. "Some small retails were into everything—into fertilizer, into lumber—and they were money-losers," this director recalls. "Some of the major retails in our area,… we talked to them about closing [departments], and they were all very much against it," in part because they knew what their members were going to say.[50]

A second director also remembers that the "retails didn't want to accept the fact that there was a financial crunch, and they leaned pretty heavily on me then to say, you know, we're not going to go along with that." They hoped their FCL director might help protect them from the pressure FCL managers were exerting. "We think that we're doing okay," they told him. "It took some pretty shrewd financial messages" to convince them otherwise: "You're not doing okay. Accept the fact that if you keep going the way you are, you're going to be in big trouble." The same director recalls, "We had one retail in my district that, when we went for [our] visitation, we made our presentation, and the manager was very annoyed with us even suggesting that they should be doing something different, and as much as told the region manager and myself we would not get approval [from them]." The chairman of the board then "asked us if we would just step out and they would discuss it in camera for awhile. We stepped out of that meeting. An hour later we were still outside the doors and we wondered whether maybe they'd forgotten about us, but eventually the president came out and asked us back in, and he said that we have, board and management, agreed that we will go along with the recommendations, and if we can't do it with present management, I guess we'll do it without [that] management. Never heard a word from the manager."[51]

Probably no one experienced more frontline tension than Nick Nichol, who in 1981 went from being FCL's Home Office finance manager to regional operations manager. In his new job, his role "was to analyse the operations and finances of the retail co-operatives, to decide on ways and means of correcting problems, and to give back recommendations. In that process we had quite a team of people. Each one of our region offices had region managers, retail advisors, and finance and control managers. Part of my responsibility was to see that those groups were doing the right thing at the retail co-operatives," he says. "I also had specific assignments of a number of larger retails with serious problems. They were under my direct responsibility rather than the region's responsibility. We had to analyse, find solutions, and see that the solutions got implemented."[52] The system had tremendous difficulties, according to Nichol, in attracting good, experienced managers to go into co-ops that had such serious problems. The ones that made it—like Otter and Vanderhoof—did so in part because good managers agreed to take them on.

Nichol's position was in many ways unique. Because he was sent in to reorganize insolvent retails, his word was close to law—a far stronger position than FCL representatives usually enjoy with retails. "They were so dependent on Federated Co-op for their survival," Nichol says. "If Federated, through me, said this is what is going to happen, then that is what happened. I didn't have the same type of frustrations as region managers or retail advisors had, because I was dealing with the most serious types of problems." Co-ops that were not quite so badly off could spurn Federated's advice; but Nichol was watching them. If they didn't turn things around their own way, sooner or later someone like Nichol would come in and they would have to do it FCL's way. Nichol adds, "The frustration came when we would come in with a plan that we felt would work, and we would implement the plan and the damned plan didn't work. That was very frustrating." But he adds that it was a learning experience. "You learn a lot from making those kind of mistakes—they're not actually mistakes—but developing those types of plans and having them not work. You go back to the drawing board and come up with something different that hopefully will work. So over the years you see a lot of different ways of attacking these same problems."

By late 1982 or early 1983, FCL and many retails were implementing painful decisions. There was one more group that had to be persuaded to take a hit as well: the co-operatives' creditors. FCL wrote to eight co-operative-sector lenders on 16 February 1983 to inform them of the financial problems facing about thirty heavily indebted retails that were running large losses. The implication of Treasurer Wayne Thompson's letter was that while FCL wanted to work with them to help ensure that retail debts were paid, the lenders might have to make some concessions on interest or repayment terms in order to get their principal back.[53] The CEOs and CFOs (chief financial officers) of all eight creditors met on 30–31 March 1983 with CEO Bell, Treasurer Thompson, Vice-President Wiebe, Finance Officer Postle, and President Leland of FCL. Discussion centred on the nature of FCL's "moral commitment" to back its retail members and cover shortfalls in their debt repayment. It seems clear from the written report that FCL intended, insofar as it was able, to cover what it considered "real" losses by the financial institutions on their loans to CRS co-ops; but that it expected the lenders to do their part—to defer principal repayments, not to capitalize interest, to refinance loans at lower rates, and not to exercise foreclosure options.[54] The lenders balked initially at much of what FCL proposed. In the end, institutions such as The Co-operators, Co-operative Trust Company of Canada, Credit Union Central of Canada, the Co-operative Super-annuation Society, and the Credit Union Centrals of the four western provinces wrote off millions in defaulted retail interest payments, and restructured debt to help the co-ops through. For its part, FCL honoured what it considered to be its guarantees, putting its own money into co-ops that were being dissolved to ensure that their creditors could be paid off.

Problems... Tough times... Difficult decisions—accurate but understated words to describe what went on in the Co-operative Retailing System in the early 1980s. Everyone felt the hurt, but the co-ops that were saved helped preserve the Co-operative Retailing System and make it what it is today.

~

I MET WITH RON MCCLENAGHAN, RETAIL GENERAL manager, in his office at the Yorkton, Saskatchewan, co-op. He's in his fifties, a man with some presence, whose look is sharp and appraising. He switches off his phone, and smiles. "I love turnin' that off. I don't do it very often." As a manager, he's blunt in his assessments of people—blunt the way you can be when you've proven yourself, when you've run your co-op for twenty or more years, and when you're not looking to have to please anybody or change jobs again. He exhibits no false humility. McClenaghan was trained and experienced as an accountant before he joined the CRS, moving up from office manager to general manager, travelling through retails and FCL positions in a couple of provinces. He characterizes himself as strong on the administrative side of the skills needed by a GM. He came to Yorkton in 1982—just in time for the co-op's and the system's big crisis—and has stayed ever since. "The plan at that time was three years in Yorkton, then on to something else. That was sort of the master plan—my own and Federated's. I always say I came here for three years, twenty-one years ago."[55]

Like many co-ops at the time, Yorkton Co-op was in a mess after the recession and high interest rates hit. The co-op's line of credit was strained, "receivables were high, and inventories were out of control. We were operating several departments that were totally unviable ... and on and on and on," says McClenaghan. "I think the co-op had really failed to keep up to the competitors in Yorkton. The facilities were rundown." The co-op had, much earlier, passed up the opportunity to relocate into a major new mall. "They had an opportunity to be the anchor food store ... but they chose to stay downtown. I'm sure that happened in a lot of cities this size. When the big mall was built, a lot of things changed. That's part of the problem; our downtown department store was a dinosaur...."

"We struggled along over there with the dry goods department, the hardware department, cafeteria in the basement, the same as a lot of other co-ops had in that time period."

As a result of the co-op's rapidly deteriorating position in 1982, the new GM had to begin with some forceful measures. "The first two weeks I made several pretty important changes," recalls McClenaghan. "The position I took was that this is so bad I basically can't do anything wrong, so let's go at it...."

"We had some good people; we had some poor people, too—people who were beyond changing," McClenaghan says. There was "a lot of resistance to change, of course, because the changes were almost daily. And big things: we totally revamped the credit policy; we eliminated credit for all but those who actually had to have a credit account, such as bulk farm customers, institutional and business-type customers. We eliminated accounts for everybody else. So we cut the number of accounts on the books from twenty-two hundred to about seven hundred.... Of course there was a big uproar.... That was one of the big

things … and we did that in the first two weeks." More restraint measures followed. He reduced hours of work. He saw too many staff, too
many levels of management, and laid off middle managers. He cut the
salaries of the remaining managers by 10 percent, following FCL's guidelines—including his own, even though he had only been there two
weeks and was still paying a mortgage in Calgary. "I struggled along
with the co-op," he comments.

The Wroxton branch closed; the Kamsack lumber yard and bulk
plant closed; the co-op "thinned its lines," going out of chemicals and
fertilizer at the Yorkton agro centre. Finally the Yorkton home centre
closed—"That was the best facility we had but it was in the wrong location. The lumber sector in Yorkton was very well populated and very
competitive, and unfortunately that was what the co-op chose to spend
money on. Big mistake. So we closed it in 1983 and laid off everybody
who worked there."

McClenaghan recalls the reaction when the staff heard what he
intended to do. "Their mouths dropped open; some were mad, some
were disappointed. The best ones weren't surprised. The best ones knew
that we needed to change." Someone leaked the information about the
cuts to the local media, and McClenaghan spent weeks fielding challenging questions from members. The prevailing attitude, he says, was
"disbelief": the co-op had been showing profits (based on FCL refunds,
not its own local earnings) and allocating patronage refunds, so that
most people were not prepared for the crisis.

What followed, again similar to many other co-ops, was a long,
slow rebuilding, a steady process of winning back ground through better marketing and improvements to facilities, including moving out of
the downtown location in 1989 and numerous renovations and expansions, up to the new agro/cardlock facility in 2003. "It's been interesting," McClenaghan says. "I feel very, very fortunate to be where I am.
I don't have a university degree; I just think I've got a little bit more
than my share of common sense…. I just feel really fortunate to have
been a part of this system, and here in particular," he says, because of
"where Yorkton Co-op was when I came here and where it is now. I
don't take the credit; I take some of the credit, but I certainly don't take
it all because the system's success has a helluva lot to do with the credit: a good, solid board of directors for a long time; some really terrific

department managers; a lot of great staff. It's all those things. All that stuff has a lot to do with it, so I just personally feel very satisfied. That's probably the reason why I never left here. I love the city; it's real good to my family and I see no reason to leave."

~

WHEN YOU ASK PEOPLE IN THE SYSTEM ABOUT SUC-cess stories and well-run co-ops, they are apt to mention Vanderhoof and Districts Co-operative Association in their short list. It's no coincidence that it's one of the retails where FCL likes to send junior managers to train for jobs in other retails.

Vanderhoof is a town of about five thousand people, an agriculture and forestry service centre nestled in the valley of the Nechako River in northcentral BC. There is lush agricultural land to the north, but mixed forest flows down the hills to the edge of town, light yellow-green poplar leaves in mid-May, and dark spruce. The co-op mall in Vanderhoof stands a stone's throw from Highway 16, more or less at the centre of town. One of the first things you see as you drive down the hill into town is the long mural adorning the side wall of the co-op, a mural preserving the historical memory of trains and transportation and industries, and not incidentally, an image of an earlier, humbler, co-op grocery store. The mural is a statement about place, memory, and identity.

The co-op has the largest mall in town, with numerous other businesses as tenants. The co-op purchased the mall in 1977 from a failed developer, and has made it into the commercial hub of the community, with a drugstore, restaurant, jeweller, hair stylist, gift shop, insurance agency, and many other small enterprises. You can tell it's a focal point of the town because it has two of the essential institutions of rural western Canada—the Greyhound bus stop and the Sears catalogue office. The co-op itself has a food store at one end, a home/garden and hardware store at the other, an agro centre behind the building, and a gas bar within sight along the highway. Interestingly, the gas station adjacent to the mall parking lot is a PetroCan. The food store is bright, open, and attractive, renovated about five years ago as an early version of the system's new Marketplace store concept. Soft neon lights identify the different departments around the perimeter. General Manager Cliff Irving talks about the need for continuous investment and upgrading. There are aisles and sections that speak to local needs: toys and seasonal items, small appliances in a display case, and of course the additional floor space down the mall for hardware and garden and agro supplies. A store has to be a bit of a general store, filling in the gaps in what is locally available, if it's going to serve the purpose of saving members the longer drive into a bigger city. The co-op now shares the food business here with a new ExtraFoods outlet, but compensates for that with a rapidly expanding petroleum business—expanding so rapidly that it now makes up 70 percent of the co-op's sales volume. The co-op and the ExtraFoods between them are helping to keep Vanderhoof dollars at home. The real competition is in Prince George, fifty minutes away on the Number 16. You get a real sense that as Vanderhoof Co-op goes, so goes Vanderhoof itself.

Vanderhoof Co-op's bulk plant/cardlock facility.

General Manager Irving has a long connection with Vanderhoof Co-op. His grandfather was president of the organization. He himself started here as a teenager, working part time. Now he's a general manager, one of the most respected in the system. He talks easily, with a down-to-earth way of expressing himself. But you can tell he thinks before he speaks, and that nothing comes out that isn't based on both experience and reflection. He knows his business, knows people; you definitely have the sense that this co-op is *his* co-op. He's a GM of the old-fashioned variety, who has few airs and doesn't think much of them in others. When I meet him, Irving wears no jacket with his tie, but simply a blue-striped shirt with a CO-OP® crest sewn on—a uniform much like his staff wears. This is farming country. He says he has members—business operators—with accounts of one, one and a half, nearly two million dollars: he affectionately calls them rednecks. "I don't know how you make someone like that feel humble," he says, "but I know how you make a manager feel humble. You just don't walk through his door. He'll notice that real fast."[56]

Cliff Irving remembers coming back to the Vanderhoof Co-op as a brand-new general manager in 1982. He found himself responsible for a large, diversified co-op with one huge problem: debt. It was the mall, of course. Taking over the mall was a multimillion-dollar project by the time it was finished and stocked. Then the recession hit. "We had a drop in sales and a rise in interest rates, I would say is basically what happened," explains Irving. They were running repeated losses, up to almost a million dollars a year in 1982, with very low member equity. The first thing they did was close an outlying branch, then they shut down their dry-goods department and downsized management and the other operations. Even then, only Federated could keep the store afloat, kicking in nonrepayable grants and giving direction. Irving recalls how the lending institutions tried to foreclose on them. Nick Nichol came in and played hardball with the bank manager. Nichol explained all the steps the co-op had taken, the positions they'd eliminated, the departments they'd closed, and then asked the bank vice-president what *he* was prepared to do. "By the time we broke at lunch, I think I went to the washroom and got sick," says Irving. "I remember coming back and telling the rest of the team here that I was sure glad that Uncle Nick was on our side." He sums it up: "If it hadn't been for Federated Co-op, we wouldn't be here today."

I ask him why this co-op made it and others didn't. "I think because we had a total team effort. Management, the board of directors, and the membership got behind us. One of the things in an agricultural type of co-operative, although ... we're not what you would call a prairie co-op, when things get tough, people stay and do business at home. I guess that's human nature. When things are good we all do our own thing, and when she gets tough, we all bear down and do it together."

Getting through the tough times is one thing; taking advantage of opportunities is another. Like many co-ops, Vanderhoof's expansion in recent years has been in petroleum. "Of the $38 million that we will do this year, 70 percent will be petroleum related," Irving says. "The major oil companies, in their restructuring, have gone to what we call a spoke and wheel. They've pulled out of the smaller communities and have gone to what they call a super agent," he explains. "Now, in a resource-based industry like we have in farming or in the logging side of things, a lot of these people still want the personal contact. Within reason they'll pay a bit more for it, for the personal contact and the service on the pricing. So for us that's an opportunity. Every time one of these major oil companies has done something like that, that's become a definite opportunity for us."

~

T HE DOWNTOWN OF VERMILION, ALBERTA, IS dominated by its co-op. Its stores take up a full half of a downtown block, a large food store on one side of a parking lot, and a hardware, gifts, and farm supplies store on the other. This does not include the nearby co-op furniture and appliance outlet fronting the main business street or the prominent gas station at the top of the hill on the highway through town. It is clear that the co-op must be one of the largest, if not *the* largest, downtown retailer, and a major employer in the town. Vermilion has a bustling town centre full of commerce, and it seems the co-op is helping to keep it that way. Moreover, this co-op is not only Vermilion: Eastalta Co-op also has branches in Wainwright, Mannville, and Dewberry. By all reports, the Wainwright branch is taking off so strongly that it is increasingly becoming the second hub of the multibranch regional co-op.

The co-op facilities in Vermilion are not brand new. The hardware store reflects an earlier decade's design, though the food store is newly redone with the system's contemporary signage and décor, making it a striking store to shop in. This is a highly successful co-op that has not built any palaces, and therein is a significant part of its success.

Warren Gill has worked some forty-six years as an employee in the Co-op Retailing System, more than a quarter century as general manager of Eastalta Co-op. His father was a co-op GM before him, and his son is now a store manager, too. The co-op has had positive local earnings every year and paid cash refunds every year but one during Gill's managership. The secret to its success? It avoided expansions where possible, and with one exception, paid for them, if they were necessary, in cash. "We had a mall proposed to us at one time," Gill recalls, "but the board of directors and the general manager at the time—myself—were opposed to moving out of town into a past-the-track, poor location." Instead, says Gill, "we stayed downtown," and downtown in Vermilion is where the commerce is. "The board has the final decision on anything that does happen at the retail ... ultimately it's them and they were opposed to it, totally opposed to moving from the downtown location, which saved us." He reflects, "I think what's made this board so effective was that they weren't influenced by others; they just had a real strong feeling of what works best in our community."

The one year the co-op couldn't afford a cash refund was because of the new downtown store in Vermilion, built in 1981, for which they did have to borrow money. Gill recalls, it "was scary when we built this food store." But he is also proud of it. "That store has been added onto," says Gill. "It's had two or three renovations since that particular time. But that store still was the basis for the success of Eastalta Co-op."[57]

Eastalta, in short, is a financially strong co-op that has rarely borrowed much, has never undertaken unwise expansions, has regularly paid cash refunds to its members, and that made it through the lean years of the eighties and the growing competition with no major crises. The co-op has grown and modernized slowly, retaining and consolidating its dominant place in the community economy. Eastalta Co-op might in fact be a vision of what many co-ops in midsized communities would be like today without the miscalculations and bad luck that bedeviled many of them in the 1980s.

~

GENERAL MANAGER ALLAN MERRITT HAS ALSO BEEN around the system. Like a number of today's retail managers, he earned his stripes with the system by managing near-impossible cases, co-ops that were failing, some that couldn't be saved, and some that were turned around. After a couple of GM postings, Merritt worked for awhile as a retail advisor in Manitoba, but discovered that the crushing travel schedule—long hours, five days a week on the road—was impossible for his family. He got back into retail management, turning around the problems at Dauphin Co-op in Manitoba. "I look back on my career in the co-op and I look at Dauphin in particular and I think we had a hand in salvaging that co-op from certain bankruptcy.... As a result, I felt myself changing as a manager; the work that I did in Dauphin and the style of management that I operated under was [to] roll up your sleeves, get into the mix of things, and go fix it. I think it's easier to look at the problem when you realize it's not your problem," that is, that it doesn't matter where it came from and blame is not an issue, "and you're there with a wide-open mind trying to fix it."[58]

Merritt's fix-it attitude was tested again in his next challenge, at Portage La Prairie, Manitoba—the co-op he still manages. Portage, too, was in dire straits. "We moved to Portage to see if we could do it all over again. Now Portage has become an even larger sense of accomplishment for me.... Certainly there were two managers prior to me who dealt with a lot of the pain; had to dispense with the closures of some of the departments and the frustration and fallout with people as a result ... so it was now a matter of rebuilding," he says. "Not everybody would want to come in and have to do a lot of personal sacrifice. Our managers worked a ton of hours. They're dedicated, like not many other companies in my view.... Very few of the companies I see put in the time and commitment to an organization like those of co-op managers." As a result of proactive planning, Portage Co-op developed and renovated its facilities, including its food store, in 1998. "We saw to the fact that we got in and renovated and up to speed before our competition opened up," says Merritt, "and so that brought us a lot of credibility in the community. As a result, Portage Co-op, the following year, was recognized as the outstanding business of the year, and for the first time ever, they recognized myself as general manager as the businessman of the year," he says, while sharing credit for both awards. "The two awards collectively are a result of the positive image that we were able to turn around in the community."

Merritt also stresses that they "owe a huge debt of gratitude and moral support not only to Federated Co-op, certainly to them, but to the system as a whole for supporting us at a time when we were technically bankrupt.… Dauphin, Portage, those retails that were fighting for survival, had direct financial assistance provided to them so long as they were operating in a way that the system felt was constructive." As a special-status retail, Portage had a lot of attention from FCL region staff. "And I think at the end of the day Portage Co-op received in excess of $8 million worth of direct financial assistance from Federated Co-op. So from that standpoint there's no question—we owe our survival, quite frankly, to the system and to Federated Co-op."

The success of the co-op in Portage is apparent, and so are the signs of constant upgrading. The store is currently being renovated when I visit—a leaky roof, I learn, with a nod towards the idea that the co-op needs a new store some year soon—but there is steady business at the gas bar and the hardware is busy. A large bulletin board near the tills catches the eye. There is a Kids Club, a book exchange. Signs proudly thank the co-op for donations and sponsorships. Youth groups, the United Way, the gymnastics club, Canadian Blood Services, are all up there. Nearby are three items that catch my interest, customer feedback questionnaires that the management has decided to post. Marginal notes indicate that the general manager and other managers have reviewed these, recommended action, and put them up here to share with the staff. The first one is a complaint, though the member gives the co-op almost uniformly positive ratings in the numerical section of the questionnaire. He or she complains that advertised specials are frequently not in stock. Management's notes indicate that action is to be taken on this one. The second form is purely complimentary, an "excellent" rating in all categories. The third is similar, and adds, "We are very impressed by how it had a wholesome family feeling." Posting these in a co-op that has been through rough times means something. Long-time staff here may have suffered through abandonment by some members, mockery from others, and occasionally abuse. To see members noticing the improvements in the store must be striking.

The bulletin board also displays a series of small DID YOU KNOW sheets, dated from March to May 2003. The first reads, "Over the past 10 years, Portage Co-op has spent over $13.2 million on debt repayment, capital expenditures, and cash repayments of equity to local Co-op members." The second stresses the size of the cash refunds, more than half a million dollars in 2001. The third reports two years in a row of record sales—2001 and 2002. The fourth stresses, "Since 1991, Portage Co-op repaid over $4.7 million in long-term debt. As of Jan. 31, 2003, Portage Co-op is DEBT FREE!" The final three in the series emphasize investments in upgraded facilities and equipment, cash back of 5.1¢ per litre on gasoline, and the co-op's 75th anniversary coming on 21 October 2003. The common refrain for all seven weeks of the awareness campaign: "The more you purchase at your local Co-op, the bigger your equity repayment."

It's an impressive series of messages designed to communicate to members who have heard bad news in the past that the co-op is back—in fact, that it's booming.

JOIN PORTAGE CO-OP AND DISCOVER THE BENEFITS reads a leaflet. With a membership application form on the reverse, the leaflet lists six reasons to join the co-op:

- Share ownership in a locally owned and controlled business where savings stay in the community.
- Purchase groceries, hardware, petroleum, building materials, farm supplies and more.
- Contribute ideas and comments by talking to staff, managers, and members of the board of directors, or by using the suggestion boxes at major service centres.
- Receive cash back in the form of patronage dividends when our operation realizes a net saving.
- Guide the affairs of the co-op by participating in its membership meetings and electing representatives to the board of directors.
- Support a socially responsible organization, dedicated to the well-being of the community for over 70 years.[59]

It's a well-constructed list that pretty much sums up what people told me from one end of the system to the other.

~

I N SAANICH, BC—IN THE NORTHERN PART OF THE
Victoria urban area—I found Pat Fafard. He's a Saskat-
chewan-born co-operator who grew up with the old co-op philosophy,
but what he's discovered a passion for is entrepreneurship, even profit.
His attitude is positive and upbeat; under his direction, the Peninsula
Co-op likes to describe itself with words such as *innovative, dynamic,*
and *pioneering*. But there is no doubt that this is community-based
entrepreneurship. It's about local ownership, local pride, and service to
local people. Fafard is a GM whose real dedication is marketing. Not
that he discounts control and frugality: "We hate to spend a hundred
dollars poorly," he says. "But we're not afraid to spend a million dollars
wisely." His response to a problem is to market his way out of difficulty. This worked, some might say surprisingly, in the worst days of the
co-op system.[60]

He came in 1981 to a co-op that was virtually bankrupt, written off
by almost everyone—on FCL's "high 'A' list," as Fafard puts it. "Our
sales were declining even though we were only a few years old." Fafard
says he "received all kinds of advice not to come here because the co-
op, there was no way it could survive. It certainly wasn't an idealistic"
decision, he reflects; more just naïveté—"I didn't know better." As he
tells the story, it sounds as if what convinced him to stay was what he
saw wrong in the store: it was dirty, poorly merchandised—no marketing at all. Peninsula Co-op had failed in an attempt to launch itself as
a warehouse-style, "direct-charge" co-op, that is, one with a high annual membership fee and cost pricing.[61] The co-op had abandoned the
direct-charge part, but it kept the warehouse style, complete with dust
and dirt, until Fafard's arrival. "The attitude was, don't sweep unless a
customer complains," he smiles. He took over an unlovely store in a
poor location—an industrial area. "Our store is located in the worst
possible place you [could] ever put a store, ever."

He shut down feed and hardware departments; struggled to make a
go of it in groceries, and then discovered the co-op's salvation in petroleum, years before many other retails undertook large petroleum expansions. Peninsula Co-op renovated and expanded its gas bar, began

reselling gas to private dealers in order to increase its volumes, and eventually entered into a partnership with Save-On Gas that has result-ed in the co-op owning the chain 100 percent. The gas bars were not financially sound by the system's criteria, as the land in the Victoria area was so expensive it would take years to earn back the investment. But the earnings off the Save-On Gas chain built the co-op's capital base, and gradually they are all to be converted to co-op stations paying member refunds. It's a strategy that parallels and was based on FCL's strategy of building extra volume by selling through third parties such as Tempo gas stations (see chapter three); but it was undertaken most-ly at local expense and initiative.

Peninsula Co-op's gas bar/convenience store, located at Millstream.

Today the co-op is on track to become a major regional petroleum dealer and a growing marketer of food. "The commodities we're in are petroleum and food," says Fafard, "probably 85 percent of our volume is petroleum, be it commercial or retail." But he stresses, "Those are the *commodities* we're in; what *business* we're in, we're really in the customer-pleasing business. So, the commodities we've chosen for particular cash-flow advantages, but regardless of the commodities, really we try to emphasize at Peninsula Co-op that we're in the customer-pleasing busi-ness and that's what drives us."

O F ALL THE COMEBACKS IN THE CO-OPERATIVE Retailing System, the one that most often springs to the lips of knowledgeable people is that of Saskatchewan's Maple Creek Co-op, now called Southwest Co-op. John Pituley, retired some years now from being general manager of Southwest, saw that co-op through a remarkable turnaround in the 1980s.

Talking to Pituley about it, you get the sense that he is no ordinary manager. He is a rural person, a farm person, through and through: plain-spoken, with a committed, bottom-up approach to getting things done. Pituley remembers being invited to apply for the retail manager's job in Maple Creek, with no one telling him what rough shape the co-op was in. "I went there for the interview," he says, "and the retail advisor told the board not to tell me what it was like." The business "was basically bankrupt," Pituley says. "It was 1980 when I went to Maple Creek, and in 1982, I believe was the year, the interest rates peaked, and we were carrying 25 percent interest. We had precious little for sale and were paying out $165,000 in interest costs that should have been going to the members." The fate of Maple Creek Co-op hinged basically on three factors—the sacrifices that would have to be made by the members, the staff, and by Federated. Every one of these was a challenge to secure.[62]

One of the key steps was to appeal to the co-op's members, in member meetings and in personal approaches by co-op leaders and volunteers. "It was just a matter of saying to the members at that point in time, if you don't put some money in here, you won't have a co-op in your town," says Pituley. Co-op–minded people, as Pituley calls them, canvassed the community on a volunteer basis to convince people to put money into the co-op. "They could put in any amount they wanted as long as it was in multiples of $100, I guess it was. I had one old fellow who told me, 'this co-op is not going down,' he said. And the old fellow—you wouldn't think he had a penny to his name—but he ended up putting about $40,000 into equity, between him and his sister, and they really supported us. He got up during the meeting and told what he was going to do and everybody got behind him. He's gone now, but old Barney was the kind of guy who believed in the co-op, the pool, and the credit union." In the end the members raised about $150,000 in new equity to keep the co-op afloat. "Between equity and prepaid accounts we had $250,000 worth of new cash."

The staff, including managers and Pituley himself, also had to put something in. "We not only reduced our debt, but the staff took a 10 percent cut in pay," Pituley says. "We were left with a minimum staff, we worked our asses off, and the members in turn could see that the staff were also interested, which in turn got the members interested and everything just kind of mushroomed." Pituley remembers the 1980s as years of frugality—"You want to believe it. Big time, big time. There was a point in time if the forklift broke down, I was the guy who crawled under it and fixed it. If the roof was leaking, I was the guy who got up and patched it. I didn't want to take my frontline people away from the customers. I felt that I could disappear for an hour or two and do that work and it would save the association bundles of money, which it did. I'm not sure that I got paid for that extra activity, but I did have the satisfaction of knowing that I made the sucker work," he says now.

The final piece in saving Maple Creek Co-op was support from FCL. "Federated gave us an interest-free loan," recalls Pituley, "and I believe that was $150,000. It shocked the pants off Wayne Thompson

Southwest Co-op's new food store in Maple Creek. Photo courtesy Wayne Litke, Maple Creek *Advance Times*.

when I paid that interest-free loan off, too." Pituley has the distinct impression that some people would have written off his co-op. It was the degree of the members' commitment, and perhaps Pituley's own forceful style, that made Federated's senior leaders take a second look. "In order to make it work I had to have some very heated discussions with some of the powers that be," he says. Although he was advised to close departments, Pituley felt that in Maple Creek's situation that would be the beginning of the end. "Being stubborn and bull-headed and everything else, I stuck to my guns and told them that I went there to operate that co-op as it was, and I wasn't going to start folding departments; rather I was going to go to the members. After having gone to the members, I did in fact get some sympathy from some of the high-up people in Federated Co-op, and by working together—lots of good, hard work—we were able to make that co-op a success."

"To be real honest about it," he says, "I believe that Federated put a figure that they didn't think we'd ever collect. But we fooled them and collected it, and they had to come through with their share of the bargain, which as far as I'm concerned was a blessing, because without it we'd never have made it." Having said that, he adds, it was also a matter of "saying to Federated that we had to be worth something to them with the purchases we were making. So it was a matter of using common sense, laying the cards on the table and deciding that this place is not going to go down the tubes."

"Things just started to flourish," he recalls. Sales multiplied from $3 million to $8 million when he retired. "In '96 when I left there, all the bills were paid, the facility was fixed up—they weren't new by any means, but they were fixed up—and members were receiving cash back. So going from bankrupt to that in sixteen years, I felt, was an accomplishment on my part; but by the same token I have a lot of people in the directors and in Federated to thank for the support they gave me."

~

A T THAT TIME JUST BEING A CASHIER" IN THE 1980s, one co-op employee told me, "you could tell things were really tough.... Co-ops or managers and staff were taking a roll-back, a salary roll-back, a benefit roll-back, and they didn't know how many co-ops were going to survive through that period. I remember, you know, being aware of that type of environment."[63] More than one retail manager told me about hitting the road before payday, visiting members who had not paid their bills. The managers *had* to collect the accounts receivable, or the co-op wouldn't make payroll and employees wouldn't get paid. That's part of what "really tough" means.

It is impossible to understand the Co-operative Retailing System today without appreciating what it was like for those staff, leaders, and managers to have peered over the brink and faced the fact that co-ops could fail. And then, to see the financial success that followed.

As the preceding stories make clear, co-ops learned lessons in the 1980s, and from that learning came their growing success through the 1990s and beyond. It was not simply that FCL told co-ops what to do. The message from Federated's leaders and managers might be summarized as follows: cut costs and start marketing. But ultimately this was a message that depended on the willing co-operation of the retails, without whom Federated could not make any money. It was a viewpoint that retails had to take to heart, and while they increasingly did so, it came in different ways and at different rates in different retails. The stories of Maple Creek and Peninsula show that managers had considerable autonomy in their co-ops, while also needing FCL's help to succeed. Co-ops could do surprising things, could reject or partially reject the advice Federated representatives gave them, and could succeed through sheer bull-headedness—as long as it was accompanied by frugality, good marketing, and member support.

"In the eighties, when we hit skid row, as I call it, when everything was going the wrong direction," one general manager told me, "a lot of people dug down hard to make it survive, and we did a lot of things that nobody thought we could do. That was a big step.... We made it through the eighties ... most of us made it through the eighties, and Federated became very strong as a wholesaler," he said. Thinking back to those years, he recalled, "Federated had a plan and the retails bought into the plan because Federated told us where we were and how bad off we were—and we all knew it, too.... When the plan worked, they gained a lot of credibility. During those eighties, a lot of the managers who didn't buy into the programs just didn't make it, and the ones who did were hungry and aggressive." The new managers and the ones who survived "know what it's like to be broke or on your own and not to have the buying power, and we know now, today,… that we're all individual co-ops but we have to work together for a common goal. Competition, retailing, is the slimmest, toughest business to be in because there's not much for margins. It's the most competitive business in the free world. It's a very, very tight industry. We've had to learn that if we're going to survive, to fight off the big companies, we have to act together in a lot of ways."[64]

The system's answer, led by Federated, "was to remember, first, that we're a business, right, and that if you're going to be a business, you have to be a healthy business, financially, marketing-wise, the works," he said. "In the early eighties we were off track, we were unproductive, we had lots of ideology and not much practicality to go with it, so we had to cut away all the ideologies to survive," he says. "We stuck to the things that started to make us money, and we did a lot of price-slashing for a lot of years. That went on," he told me, "all through the eighties and early nineties. We slashed expenses, we cut back, and then in the nineties we started to become successful. We knew we could make it financially, and then we decided we were going to have to become a marketing company. And that's when we started to market."

~

FCL's CEO, WAYNE THOMPSON, COMES FROM A BACK-ground in financial management, and it was certainly his finance and administration skills that FCL looked to in 1982–83. But when explaining the system's success after that time, Thompson does not talk primarily about cost cutting or about Federated's change of direction: those were just steps along the way. Instead he says, "I'm going to start at the retail. Federated has to set the example, but you've got to start with the retail. Part of what the retail has to do is really focus on the fact that they need to be the best in town. They also have to be the friendliest. They also have to realize that every time somebody comes into their store, they're comparing the service they get to the experience they've had anywhere else, whether it's a direct competitor or not, or a completely different kind of business." He goes on: "People travel so much these days they rate everything to how they've been treated. So you've got to create a friendly atmosphere, good service, good image, cleanliness, good merchandising, create an image of competitive pricing, all those things. Now in terms of Federated, everything we do *must* either be designed to increase sales at the retail level, to improve marketing programs, or to improve efficiency. We have to make sure that we're in the position that we're buying at the best price all the time, which includes belonging to buying groups and taking advantage of all the opportunities. Being very, very efficient. Lowering our costs as much as we possibly can. Generally speaking, we've been maybe on the soft side when it comes to marketing costs. When it comes to straight overhead, we've been very, very tough in controlling the overhead."

A December 1983 report by Federated's Marketing Division put it as follows:

> Our main objective in the future is to be a *marketing organization,* bottom-line-oriented, rededicated to provide excellent service to our member customers (getting closer to our member customers in search of excellence), *to be competitive,* which means getting back to our original purpose of being able to maximize the economic benefits to our members.[65]
>
> As we look back over the past number of years, we can see with great clarity how we erred in the past. The great majority were caught up with growth, expansion, and increased market share at whatever cost. As a result, the System was dealt a tremendous blow when the real world surfaced, one we are sure many of us will not soon forget.... The lesson has been harsh and the costs to the CRS simply horrendous.... [To avoid a recurrence], the total marketing team will become *sales* and *service* driven.

FCL buyers would look for better deals from suppliers; there would be more promotions; regional sales meetings would be held to motivate sales staff; "spiffs" would be used as one-time incentive programs to encourage staff to move product; there would be more use of coupons and flyers; there would be changes in image; there would be more attention to development of people, "particularly as they relate to *sales, service, and productivity*"; and both Area Development and Growth from Within would continue.[66]

One example of the new marketing thrust is especially close to the heart of Lynn Hayes, today FCL's senior vice-president, Corporate Affairs, but then involved in the Agro Division. "My whole background in agriculture has taught me that if you're going to be successful in marketing to farmers, you better understand the farmer and you better be comfortable on his turf," Hayes says. "Co-ops weren't strong in that area." The idea of the new Farm Contact Program of the mid-1980s was to get co-op petroleum drivers, petroleum managers, and agro managers out talking to existing and prospective customers on their farms. FCL used a combination of outside training in professional selling skills and inside training-the-trainers to develop new marketing courses for employees. "Now ten, fifteen years later, we are probably gaining market share faster than any other marketing organization in western Canada because we're the ones who are left in the rural community, we're the ones out in the rural marketplace who are attracting new business from Esso, PetroCan, Shell. But it doesn't happen overnight." He remembers Elmer Wiebe and others in 1983–84 who began developing the company's attention to marketing: "That's when I said to myself, now I know I've made the right decision" to join the co-op system, says Hayes. It meant the end of the bad old days of lacklustre marketing.

It used to be, according to Hayes, that there were those who felt their job was to stand there and hold up the counter and wait until a member came in. *My job is to serve the member. My job isn't to go out and make a bunch of farm calls to people who aren't members and grow the business*—that was the attitude at the time to the service role of co-ops. Hayes smiles, perhaps a little grimly. "Well, we wouldn't have grown the business and the profitability if we had kept that attitude forever, and we wouldn't be half the organization we are today."[67]

"We found managers managing from behind a desk instead of on the floor," one retired retail and FCL manager recalls. "One of the things we said to the managers was, you cannot manage from an office hidden … in the back. You manage by being on the floor, and you concentrate your efforts on everything that has to deal with operations and service, even if it means, to some extent, not being as involved in some community activities or Federated committees. Your first responsibility is to restore the health of the co-operative. And when it's strong, then there's time to do some of those other things," he says. "Once the retails recognized that they could improve the bottom line, they could improve their financing, they could pay patronage refunds in cash to the members ... the incentive was so strong that we had tremendous support." Because FCL staff made more effort to visit the retails, to help them, to provide tangible assistance, "they also realized that Federated was not there to lord over them."[68]

An FCL region manager agrees. "I think we learned to do only those things we can do right and not try to be all things to all people," he says, repeating one of the system's mantras. "We also realized that all of us had a role to play and each one's role was not independent of the others'. We had to work together to make the system work. We"—now he means Federated itself—"we had to become more retail oriented," and that meant Federated had to focus in on doing just those things that made a difference to retails. "The turn wasn't immediate; sure, '82 was a tough year, '83 was better ... and '84 got better yet."[69]

One reason Federated managers and staff earn respect and loyalty from the retails—apart from results—is because many of them come themselves from backgrounds in the retail co-ops. "It is valuable in our system," reflects former Senior Vice-President, Corporate Affairs, Al Robinson, "that at least some of the senior people do have both retail and wholesale experience, I believe. This is from my standpoint. You get the very best of background and training with the people who have been both retail and wholesale." This gives them the ability "to quickly adapt to a new kind of an environment." Robinson himself comes from this mould. In the early 1980s, he had been working as a retail general manager, was pulled back into Federated's home office to become "a sort of super RA [retail advisor]," as he describes it, working with problem retails. After that he became region manager in Regina, a job that again had him working with the retails that were on the front lines, before returning to Saskatoon as VP, Agro, and then corporate secretary. "People who have been general managers in the retail scene and then either move up in that area or into the wholesale side ... carry a lot of credibility with the system as a whole,"[70] he says.

More of a retailing orientation, more personal contact, and a softer personal style made all the difference, to judge by how former Marketing VP Wiebe talks about relations in the system. "You can pick up the phone and call [VP, Retail Operations] Ken Hart or [Region Manager] Larry Rupert or ... any of these people, you can say anything, and it can come out wrong or whatever it is, and they're not going to take it for something that is the end of the world," says Wiebe. I suspect he means you can shout at them when you're upset, and still apologize later. The new style is patience, tolerance, and practicality. "They're going to say, well, let's just take a further look at this thing. What's really bothering you, let's get down to what's really bothering you, and that's what they like, you know, so now you're getting the emotion out of the scene and you can talk about anything you'd like to talk about. And you say,... [I'm] really concerned about ... and what happened to be a great problem becomes some minor little irritant, but you resolve it, whereas you could very easily hang up the phone."

~

As a result of FCL's growing credibility, the retails voluntarily picked up many of the wholesale's policies, even though they don't apply automatically to them. Federated has built up a kind of normative or standard-setting function over the years. Many retails that want to develop their human resources policies, for example, literally take pages out of FCL's HR manual.

In the 1980s, the wholesale began to develop performance incentives for managers. A resolution at FCL's 1983 annual meeting mandated the organization to develop performance-based compensation plans that could be made available throughout the CRS. As a result of the resolution, Federated's personnel division prepared background papers on communication with employees, performance appraisal, normal salary administration, "gain sharing" with employees, "spiffs" as sales incentives, and nonfinancial incentives for employees. These were discussed at the regional general-manager conferences and at the Fairmont Conference during 1983.[71] Putting these ideas into practice seems to be one of the accomplishments of which Senior Vice-President Zakreski is proudest.

"Prior to that time, if you had mentioned the word bonuses in co-ops, the walls would have crumbled, the buildings would have fallen down, the whole place would have come to a stop," Zakreski smiles. "Well, I still remember in 1984, saying to Wayne [Thompson], you know, we went to these employees in the time of need, and I think we should maybe reward them by way of some form of bonus program, and he agreed." It turned out that there were advantages for both sides. "Now the thing it did for us, it gave us an opportunity to focus on the bottom line and to focus on a key number—return on equity—to the point where [we could] say, the board has an objective on return of equity of 20 percent.... If we achieve or do better than that, then, yeah—we'll go to the board and recommend that they consider some kind of a bonus," Zakreski recalls. "I think we probably gave a lesson in economics better than any university class has done, better than any text book has ever done, better than anybody else has ever done, in terms of the importance of having your return on equity in your business." And the lessons were not only for management. "At the same time," Zakreski continues, "we took our nonmanagement [staff], and particularly in those places that helped us out, and we said, why don't we give them $200 cash at Christmas ... so we took it to the board and got that approved. Well, that $200 has subsequently grown. But that first year, I can still see the employees, how appreciative they were of what we did. But I think it says something about the management of this organization. You never forget when somebody does you a good deed. You remember." It's a practical expression of Zakreski's approach and of FCL's culture since the 1980s.[72]

Another FCL manager comments, "I think that at one time prior to the tough years of the 1980s, people thought that the co-operatives were in business for philosophy reasons only." By philosophy he means providing community service, doing good things simply because they were thought to be needed, and that "nobody should make money in a co-op." In the eighties, "I think we all learned that unless you make some money, you could not exist on philosophy; and I think that was a very valuable lesson for all of us, that we had to be profitable, and we made this company, this organization, a very profitable organization. And with the profits and the earnings that we do have, we can afford to pay back dividends to the consumers, and that's what co-operatives are all about, is paying back a patronage refund to the people who use the services in a co-op," he says. "It's just like finding a new way of doing business.... We'd go into planning sessions, and I'd be saying to our group ... You've got to sell something before anything else can happen, before you can have a margin, before you can pay the expenses." He adds, "There's a real message there ... for the people coming after us, that [even] if they had twenty good years, there's always that period of time when they might have to bite the bullet like we did."[73]

Patronage refunds are an old principle of co-operatives, but one that has found a new, central place in the philosophy of the Co-operative Retailing System today. When customers get back a share of the profits, they have an interest in the store. When that share is paid as a percentage refund on their purchases, the way co-ops do it, they have an interest in purchasing as much as possible. In many co-ops today, this principle is the bedrock on which member loyalty is based. The patronage refund is a tangible expression of why the co-op is advantageous for the individual as well as the community. But more than that, it is also a key part of the relations between the local co-ops and FCL. Independent local co-ops receive refunds from Federated in much the same way individual members do from their co-ops. The flow of patronage refunds in the system links it together from top to bottom.

According to CEO Thompson, the co-op refund is "absolutely huge. Now, you can try and explain co-op theory all you want," the system's top manager says, "but the minute you give that member a cheque, they all of a sudden start figuring out how it works pretty quickly. So at the retail level to the individual member, we find that as soon as retails start consistently giving patronage refunds back, they consistently start getting more support, which of course then provides additional money for them to develop their retails." In other words, give profits back to the members continuously, in order to reward loyalty and grow the business; that way, you can *earn* the additional capital you need to pay for future investments and expansions, without borrowing. It's an approach that does things the hard way, the gradual way—no quick fixes—but that keeps co-ops in control of their own destinies. "Going back to Federated," Thompson continues, "the more money that we make, in total, for the system, then passing it through to the retails, gives the retails the funds to build the kind of facilities that they need ... and to do all the things that make them look successful and look like a winner and so on. And that also helps to provide the money that flows to the members," he explains.

It isn't self-evident to everybody that co-ops need to concentrate on paying cash back to their members. Some co-ops don't, or can't, for shorter or longer periods of time. There are many other demands for capital: debt to be paid down, renovations, new facilities, expansions. It would be easy to do without the refund, and invest in new facilities instead. Sometimes, it would be tempting to lower prices to get consumers' attention—to give them the refund up front, so to speak, and in so doing, lure them away from the competition. So why does the Co-operative Retailing System's marketing stress patronage refunds rather than other strategies? To answer this, it's helpful to think about patronage refunds as more than a mechanism for distributing cash. They are that, but they also convey information, serve as incentives, bring attention to different product areas, and help guide investment and development decisions.

CEO Thompson explains that each department of FCL has, potentially, its own different refund level. "We measure every department. We start with sales, and we go right down to the specific incomes of that department. We allocate all costs, including formulas for allocating overhead and interest costs" of the company as a whole to each unit. "So every department has their own bottom line. Each individual bottom line is allocated based on earnings for that department, so there are really not a lot of decisions that are made in terms of the allocations once we determine the bottom line for each department." If gasoline earns more margin than food (it normally does), then the patronage allocation on gasoline can be higher.[74]

I asked the CEO why the system wouldn't pay a higher refund on some commodity it wanted to feature or encourage, as a kind of promotion. I expected he might answer, because it gives an improper incentive; it leads to inefficient or unproductive allocation of purchases; it gives the wrong signals for growth. But his answer was very interesting. "I think it's not fair," Thompson says. If FCL paid artificial refund levels to its member co-ops—paid a lower refund on food and a higher refund on something else than those commodities actually earned, for example—it would be "taking part of the earnings that were generated by the retails in food and giving them over to a retail that's not in that business. It wouldn't be fair," he says. "It's like an individual customer at a retail co-op supporting the food store, for example, and the other department is losing money; and when it comes down to the refund, you don't get your money back that you've helped generate—you give it to someone else. It's kind of like a distribution of wealth in an unfair manner. As you earn it, you spread it out. And the other thing at the retail level (and it's the same at Federated, but more so at the retail level), if you're allocating earnings through a department that is consistently losing money, that retail maybe would continue in that business. Then when you have to close that business, the member will say 'Why are you stopping that business when I've been getting a refund?' If there is no benefit to the members of that department existing, that department should really not exist, because the only purpose of co-ops is to enhance the value for the members." So refunds represent both fairness among people buying different things, and serve as a yardstick for where the co-op should be in business.

Given widespread sensitivity to gasoline prices, it is, of course, especially on petroleum products that patronage refunds attract attention. People like getting five cents (or in some co-ops, seven cents or more) cash back from what they paid for every litre of gas. Periodically, people complain to the co-op about gas prices, too, since co-ops generally have a policy of matching competitors' prices. But the difference in a co-op is, at the end of the year, if gas prices really did enable the company to earn a large surplus, it will be refunded. CEO Thompson has heard it before. "Well, I always said, why don't you shop at the co-op? The extra amount [the co-op makes] by you buying your petroleum, you'll get it back. It won't be given to some other department or retained by a company for their shareholders; it'll go back to you as a co-op member," he says. "That's another reason why you allocate the money that you earn," he explains, rather than have the co-op give back less or more than it actually made. "If you're buying from the co-op, you know you're buying at, basically, cost," he says—the actual cost after allowing for the fluctuations during the year, and for needed reinvestments.

This is the reality behind the argument that co-ops are nonprofit. It's not that they don't earn surpluses (what many people call profits); it's that those profits get returned to the consumers. Normally, the refund isn't all in cash. Part of it is "allocated," as people in the co-op system say, to share accounts. Members usually get back part in cash, and part in shares that give them increased ownership in the co-op and which they get back later in their lives. But ownership is more of an abstraction; it's the cash back each year that members notice most.

The co-op system is certainly more financially successful than it was in the 1980s, and perhaps more co-ops are smarter, too. That's why they stress cash refunds, even though there are many other uses for surplus earnings. Patronage refunds are, essentially, investments in member benefit and member loyalty, which have been every bit as important to the co-ops' success as other investments, in image, facilities, products, and marketing.

⌇

T HE SYSTEM'S GRADUAL RAMPING-UP OF ITS MARKET-
ing effort began in 1983 with the new stress on finan-
cial management and payment of patronage refunds, with the strategy of concentrating on what co-ops do best and paying attention to earn-ings and margins, with the reorientation towards sales and retailing, and with the performance incentives for managers. Other steps fol-lowed, in a sustained and methodical way. Beginning in the 1980s, CEO Thompson, Vice-President Wiebe, and others began speaking of mar-keting success as something like building a pyramid. "History tells us that progress can only be made in stages, one level at a time, in the proper order—like building a pyramid," is how a 1988 planning session put it.[75]

In the mid-1980s, as financial desperation began to ease a little, the next level of the pyramid involved greater attendance to the physical image of the co-operatives. Image was identified as an important focus in 1985, ranging from exterior signage, colour schemes, and grooming of grounds, to interior shelving and neatness, staff uniforms and atti-tude, clean washrooms and tidy warehouse space.[76] An "awareness cam-paign on image" began. Retail-wholesale study groups were formed on various related topics. This was also the time when FCL began to place a growing emphasis on food and petroleum as the key products at which it excelled and for which it wanted to have a reputation.[77]

Long-time FCL VP, Distribution, Al Roden has a blunt way of describing co-op facilities before the 1980s. He remembers that in the eighties, "I was so bold as to suggest that our image was terrible … we needed a real wake-up," he says. "One of the first things that I did was put together a very vivid slide presentation and I called it the good, the bad, and the ugly. I took that slide presentation to all of the fall conferences that year, and I started out my verbal presentation by suggesting that our image 'sucked.'" Some people suggested Roden could have used more polite language, "but I certainly got everybody's attention … it was an awareness campaign. And I can remember at a number of those fall conferences, general managers coming up to me after the presentation and literally saying, you know that particular slide you took of our fertilizer shed, I can't believe it looks that bad…. It started a process by which everybody got on the bandwagon."[78]

Many co-operatives had to shake an image of being "the farmers' store," where bare-bones retailing, a bit of dust on things, and some equipment lying around the property were acceptable because members didn't expect too much. Some older members were comfortable with this low-key approach, but lack of margins, volume, and loyalty were signs to the system that things had to change. At first, the co-ops might not have been able to afford much more than cleanliness and a coat of fresh paint, but from there an attitude of pride and professionalism began to sink in. The result was much more careful attention to buildings, rolling stock, equipment, and more. Sure enough, at a number of co-ops I visited in 2003 I discovered that directors had policies of undertaking periodic image checks of their facilities. It's now become a regular part of the job.

"The standards we had with regard to cleanliness and orderliness,… the new attitude towards merchandising and staff uniforms and training and attitudes, everything, really turned the Co-op Retailing System into what it is today, an absolutely first-class organization," Roden says. "Even today in many rural communities where there's virtually nothing left but the co-op, they operate the best facilities anywhere."[79]

A growing pride, especially in how the system handles food and petroleum, was another part of the new co-op culture. The man to talk to about the system's food and general merchandise is FCL Vice-President, Consumer Products, Norman Krivoshen. A pharmacist by background, Krivoshen joined the Prince Albert Co-op as drugstore manager in 1965, came to FCL in 1973, and has been in his current position since 1980. He has seen a lot of changes in that time. "The one word that would best describe the last twenty-four years ... is, simply, *maturity* in the system," says Krivoshen. And he adds: "The biggest thing, or turning point, was the tough years in the early eighties. Along with those tough years, some very strong leadership emerged in Federated Co-operatives. Along with that strong leadership, the rest of the system just matured." Part of the lesson is about focus. "There's no question that in our organization there are two commodities that drive our business, that is petroleum and food," says Krivoshen. "And in a number of locations, we had to downsize in the other commodities because we were not as good as our competitors in those categories of product. We believe that we are very good in marketing food products and petroleum products, and that's where we shine."[80]

The system's ambitious approach to marketing is evident in one of its new initiatives of the late 1980s, which has now become fixed in the annual cycle of the co-op system and provides an important meeting place for co-op managers. It's a marketing gala held every five years known as Expo. Ken Hart, FCL's VP, Retail Operations, who chairs the co-op Expo, explains that "in 1988 ... we could see ourselves coming through the eighties getting better operational results, but still wanting to drive marketing, marketing, marketing; so we created this new event in '88. We called it Marketing Expo '88. We took food and petroleum as the two key commodities, and said, let's see what we can do with those; and then ... to a little lesser degree ... we also involved the crop supplies, feed, and general merchandise departments." The 1988 Expo stands out in his mind as the place where the first presentation was made to launch what became FCL's corporate bulk-fuel program, discussed in chapter three as an example of innovation in the system.

"We found that Expo '88 was so well received that ... we decided we were going to do it every five years, not that we did away with any other clinics, food shows, general merchandise shows, or anything," Hart says. "So five years later we did another one and decided that we were going to start making these an exciting but also an informative and educational experience." As Hart describes it, the philosophy was to educate, inform, and perhaps entertain retail personnel, but not to sell.

"Retails didn't have to worry about coming in here and buying products; we weren't trying to sell anything; we were trying to launch new programs, new interior décor packages for our stores, new equipment, how we're going to merchandise product differently now.... Whether that was trucks to haul fuel, decals that we were going to put on these trucks [discussed later in this chapter], that's what we focussed on and not with an order pad saying, well, how many of these would you like to buy? We didn't do any of that.... We wanted retails to learn and ... to ask our suppliers questions."[81]

As a result, Expo has become a high point few managers miss. It's a place where they find out what's going on in the system, what new promotions or features are available for their co-ops. The system's suppliers—the companies that supply what the system markets—turn out with hundreds of representatives, setting up displays and events for the retail co-ops that are the purchasers of their products. Big companies and universally known brand names are there as part of a wholesale/retail showcase that fills the halls at the exhibition grounds in Saskatoon, with social and entertainment events at the Sask Place arena. By all accounts, Expo is an eye-opening experience, especially for new retail department managers who have little experience of the system. "They had no idea that our system was as big as what it was," before coming to Expo, Hart explains. "They, and rightfully so, sort of focussed in on their retail, their district out there." Suddenly they are immersed in marketing that expresses the system's buying power and sophistication. Top motivational speakers, sports figures, and so on fill out the program and contribute to an atmosphere that is both celebratory and energizing. "So that's what we built that whole Expo theme on. We've had some great entertainment for them over the years.... We've had beach party nights, carnival nights, and western nights where everyone can let their hair down a little and enjoy themselves, and have lots to eat and socialize, and maybe even do some dancing. We try and create a whole package for a weekend of learning."

The attendance, which runs into the thousands (3,031 in 2003, according to Hart), includes on average a delegation of five to seven staff members from each of the nearly three hundred retails in the system, in addition to all the suppliers and exhibitors and FCL's own staff. Going by the number of suppliers who participate, Hart figures it's likely the second-biggest marketing show in North America. And what really suits the cost-conscious culture of FCL: it doesn't directly cost the wholesale much money as the costs are covered primarily by the suppliers themselves, who are eager to have access to the system.

~

FACILITIES AND PRODUCTS DON'T SELL THEMSELVES without staff. The people of the system had a critical role in improving the co-ops' marketing. They were supported by personnel policies, evaluation and performance policies, and training supplied and encouraged by Federated; these are discussed further in chapter two. The system made a number of strategic choices in the 1980s that emphasized the importance of staff. Most co-ops, for example, committed to only full-service gasoline pumps. Customers could do self-service at competing gas stations, but for the same price at the co-op they would get personal service from increasingly well-trained and attentive staff. In the late 1980s, FCL developed a marketing program around the slogan "Value ... Service ... Guaranteed!" Retails could adopt corresponding signage and policies, including the "No-Hassle Guarantee" for returning products previously purchased. Service was also the theme of CEO Thompson's address to the 1993 FCL annual meeting. "In our Co-operative Retailing System, we have an extra incentive for service," Thompson reminded delegates. "Not only is that person walking through the door a potential lifetime customer, he or she likely is now, or could be, one of the owners of the organization."[82] Increasingly, co-ops promised a level of service and satisfaction that would exceed what was available from many competitors; and they were putting in place training and programs to deliver it.

The system's marketing ideas were developed further with the launch of the Co-op Membership Benefits marketing program in 1994. As explained in FCL's *President's Newsletter,* distributed to officials in the CRS, "Our cash patronage program was the original loyalty program but was not effectively marketed. Our Membership Benefits program focusses on four themes: cash back, personalized service, quality CO-OP® products, and our role as a community builder." With signage to hang from ceilings, lay on floors, or post in parking lots, the program was meant to convey that "co-ops have a vision. We are dedicated to something more than selling products. Our vision is much larger. The co-op vision is about giving people power and control, creating wealth, providing a needed service, and holding communities together. This is a very current and compelling vision."[83] FCL officials mention today that they have thought of developing new marketing programs, but instead have continued to work with Membership Benefits because it is so successful and has been so widely adopted among the retails. In particular, Membership Benefits helps highlight, for marketing purposes, some of the differences between co-operatives and their most important competitors.

There is no doubt that the co-ops have faced tougher competition in the last twenty years. The new competitors included, first (in many areas), Superstore and various warehouse-style retailers, and more recently, with a growing business in food and in some cases petroleum, WAL-MART. There are, of course, many small communities where the co-op is the only retailer, but one shouldn't be fooled into thinking that these co-ops have no competition. Their competition, too, consists of the large urban retailers down the highway, who increasingly have pulled in mobile customers from the surrounding region. Besides being large national or transnational companies, one thing these retailers have in common is an emphasis on low prices. Looking at their advertising, one might get the impression that price is the main thing, or perhaps the only thing, consumers care about. It is in this context that the co-ops have developed a type of retailing based on personal service, a friendly atmosphere, and convenience, as well as prices that are competitive but not necessarily the lowest. There is still some anxiety in the system about how well the co-ops can make an alternative approach work, but the results seem to provide grounds for growing confidence.

"I think there are two types of shoppers," says Vice-President Krivoshen. "There are those shoppers who are price shoppers, and I would suspect that about 25 percent of all the shoppers are focussed solely on price. These are the type of shoppers who would perhaps shop the WAL-MARTs, the Costcos, the warehouse clubs of various companies, and so forth. But there are those shoppers, the other 75 percent, who are value shoppers, and we go after those shoppers who go after value—value being a combination of price and quality; and that's where we focus in on, is the value shopper."

In the last number of years, the system has moved its food marketing up a notch. Vice-President Krivoshen says, "We took a look some years ago, back in about 1997, at how we were going to market our food products, and we very quickly realized that we would not be able to be a wholesale club, a warehouse club; we would not ever be the world's largest retail, like a WAL-MART; we would not have stores like the Superstores. But we said to ourselves that we could be the very best conventional supermarkets in the towns or cities where we are located," he says. "And I think we have proven that today with our stores like Attridge here in Saskatoon, Kindersley, Wadena, Carstairs, Calgary, and the list goes on and on. We are the very best supermarkets in most of the communities that we operate in," says Krivoshen.[84]

Kindersley Co-op's new food store grand opening celebration, held 20 June 2002.

To be "the very best supermarket" today means investing in attention-getting new store designs that go far beyond anything co-op members would have imagined twenty years ago. "Retail theatre," for example, is one of the ways the new co-op stores differentiate themselves from low-price competitors such as WAL-MART. As explained in a 2003 grocery-trade publication, "The central idea is to give customers a better shopping experience by making improvements to retail design, décor, store equipment, merchandising, product selection, and customer service." This means "an upscale, fun environment with touches that might include murals, stained-wood bunkends,* upscale bistros, working model trains, all surrounded by the smell of fresh-baked bread."[85] Today in co-op Marketplace stores you can experience thunderstorms, herds of mooing cows, and other novelties in the relevant departments. Big pictures and signs, but also cooking and product demos further liven up the atmosphere. The new stores in the co-op system are not just clean and bright; since 2000 they particularly emphasize freshness and ready-to-eat foods. "When a consumer walks into our store," Krivoshen explains, "we want that consumer to feel that they're not just buying food, but in fact, they're buying a meal.... We know that our consumers are time-starved, so we try to focus on providing a meal for consumers that they can put on the table in a very short period of time," he says. "We had to convince our retailers that they had to be a one-stop shopping centre, and rather than a provider of food, they had to be purveyors of meals.... Consumers can go into our stores and buy barbequed chicken, potato salad, a fresh baguette, ready-to-eat fruits and vegetables, and then go home and enjoy a very healthy meal."[86]

The new stores and the merchandise assortment are designed to achieve this effect. "When you come in the front door," Krivoshen describes the concept, "you're going to see whole-meal solutions and the deli, both hot and cold; you're going to see an assortment of bakery products that are just fresh out of the oven; you're going to see ready-to-pop-into-the-oven, value-added meat products; and you're going to see a great assortment of fruits and vegetables." Originally this approach was designed to appeal to double-income families, people who "are taking their children to perhaps soccer or football, or whatever activity it might be; they don't really have time to prepare their meals," says Krivoshen. But along the way, co-ops discovered that many people, young and old, rural and urban, value the same kinds of prod-

---

* "Bunkends" are display units at the end of aisles, typically featuring special products in three directions.

ucts and advice. "Many of the seniors ended up buying these products," he says, because of their experiences in the Great Depression of the 1930s. "They were brought up to not to waste product. So when they see that these products can be bought in smaller portions, or that they can consume them in a relatively short period of time, without waste, they end up being very good customers of these value-added products."

Co-ops are a little sensitive to the perception that they are old people's stores. There was, perhaps, a little truth in that in the 1980s, when older members stayed with some co-ops out of loyalty while younger consumers went to old or new competitors. This has to be a concern for co-ops, because while they value the loyalty of long-time members, the dollar volume that they need in order to provide efficient service to all members can only come if they get the patronage of younger people with families—hence the strong emphasis on family-oriented marketing. As it turns out, co-ops today generally seem to have no difficulty attracting younger members while keeping older ones. An example is Saskatoon Co-op. "We've kept track at Saskatoon Co-op because we were kind of curious about that," says General Manager Larry Rupert, who is also the region manager for FCL. "We had the feeling, and were often told, oh, we're the store that caters to seniors. And so we looked at that; and I've personally kept track over the last fifteen years, and the Saskatoon Co-op now gets about three thousand new members a year." This is an impressive total, and it means a younger membership. "For the last twelve to fifteen years, about 65 percent of those new members … are between the ages of twenty-one and forty-five," says Rupert. "So it looks as though the co-op's appealed to new members for the last decade or more. It's pretty much in line with the demographics of the community."[87] Statistics I have seen for other urban co-operatives suggest similar patterns.

"The important thing about the stores that we have today," Norman Krivoshen says, "would be the pleasant atmosphere that we're creating in co-op stores. People want to shop in stores with a great ambience, and today we're providing them with a great shopping experience. We're providing them with top-notch products and with a huge product selection. Our presentation of the merchandise is second to none and really, what the local co-op has left to deliver on is service. And if we get those four things put together correctly, I think we're quite unbeatable: that is store ambience, product selection, product presentation, and service at the local retail."[88]

The new generation of co-op stores stands out a bit even in the most competitive large urban markets, but they make the biggest impression in smaller centres where no competitor has anything remotely as well designed or new. Rural people are no less time-pressed than urban people, and in any case they often shop in urban stores, so the competitive standard is really the same. The difference is that the co-ops will put those new stores into the local community, investing and keeping services and jobs there, so that rural co-op members can have top-quality stores right in their local towns. "It becomes a real community store, it's a community centre, and in many communities, it's the last business in town," says Krivoshen. "It just does my heart good to go into communities like Wadena or Kindersley or Meadow Lake or Davidson or Watrous or ... many similar communities [where] we are the best store in town and provide all the services that consumers would get in the larger stores in the urban centres. Today, we're providing, for instance, fresh baked goods in about 120 of our stores, which a few years ago ... wouldn't have been thinkable."

As for price competition, the co-ops haven't given up on that. The system's latest large food-marketing innovation—launched in February 2003—is its VALUE PRICED *Every Day!* program. Krivoshen explains that the program "is, simply, one where we know the top items that consumers are aware of relative to pricing. It's the Tides of the world, the Cheez Whizes of the world, and so forth. What we have done, rather than being a high/low dealer—where in fact one day we might have, in the consumers' eyes, a high price on an item, and the next day, on a sale, a low price—[is] we've flattened that out. What we've done, on an everyday basis, [is to be] competitive on all of the most popular items that you would find at any supermarket, warehouse club, or wholesale club." People liked the program so well, Krivoshen says, that when it was first introduced they started stocking up on the value-priced items, not realizing that the price was going to stay the same from day to day. Retails liked the program as well, and quickly picked up the advertising and signage. "You've seen the signs on the shelves, you've seen them on the store floors, you've seen them on the trucks," says Krivoshen. "We introduced the program with a big bang and it's gone over very, very well."[89]

With the Marketplace stores and the VALUE PRICED *Every Day!* program, and other new programs and strategies, the Co-op Retailing System has changed its face completely since the 1980s. At FCL's annual meeting in March 2003, CEO Thompson reviewed the progress of the system over the last twenty years. He pointed out that from 1982 to 2002, retail co-ops' long-term debt had fallen from more than $260 million to less than $55 million, besides which, retail co-ops had cash invested in FCL of $82 million. This was after having paid out more than $739 million to members and investing $700 million in fixed assets. Their equity ratio now exceeded 77 percent of assets. FCL, in the same period, had reduced its long-term debt to *zero* and had $237 million cash in hand. FCL's equity ratio was 58 percent in 2002, and the wholesale company now regularly returns 80 percent of patronage refund amounts in cash to retails. Further highlights included improved retail facilities ("more often than not ... the best in town"), bulk-plant consolidation, shared services among retails, retail managers working with FCL through the Executive Management Committee, and improvements at Calgary Co-op. (A number of these topics are singled out for attention in chapters two and three.) In total, "the relationship between retail co-operatives and FCL has probably never been better."[90]

∽

I F YOU WANT A WALK THROUGH THE RECENT PAST, present, and near future of co-operative food retailing, you can see it all within the City of Calgary. With some twenty stores of many different designs, Calgary Co-op has a wealth of experiences within a single organization.

In 2003, Calgary's Village Square store was considered "stale" and in need of renovation. I visited at about the time the board was voting $4 million to transform it, and found the store large, spacious, and clean—modern by 1980s–90s standards. The store has a functional exterior that blends into the mall to which it's attached, without the imposing pillars or attention-getting entrances of the new designs. Inside it's a standard, large urban supermarket, rectilinear in layout. The view is dominated by straight, utilitarian aisles. The frozen-goods aisle has old freezer units, open, L-shaped, with no doors. These aisles didn't seem narrow a few years ago, but they don't make a statement of spaciousness like the new ones do. On the far end of the store are aisles full of hardware, toys, and dry goods, with a certain neglected air. The produce department is low-ceilinged and a little dim—it's at the very back of the store. The cafeteria is the old kind, also relatively low-ceilinged, walled in on three sides. At one end is an old chrome self-serve lane; the tables are reminiscent of utilitarian small-town restaurants. It has only a handful of people in it at 11:30 A.M., when the food court down the mall is getting busy. The store has a cozy, neighbourhood feel. A poster announces "Clinic Day: Are you at risk of heart attack?" A pedestrian outside stops while crossing the street to pick up debris and carry it to the curb. It's a comfortable community supermarket, with nothing really wrong with it, except that it's not up to today's co-op standards.

The Southland Oakridge Store is larger. Most of the mall is co-op, shared with a First Calgary credit union branch and a CIBC bank; also co-op travel and co-op liquor. This store has been recently renovated. You walk in and are faced by a display of fresh flowers opposite the door; a huge produce section expands off to the side, inviting entry. The ceiling is high, creating a sense of openness; suspended lighting makes the whole area bright and uniformly lit. Beside the produce section is a large deli counter combined with a fast-food line; nearby is a café seating area. In the deli line, a middle-aged woman in co-op uniform explains that the store was renovated in June 2002. They very much like it; yes, the new design is good, "especially for us in the deli, eh. We used to be in the back corner of the store, behind the meat." But (she fixes me with a look) "they closed the cafeteria, too, you know." Replaced it with fast food. Sitting in the café afterward over a plate of perogies and French beans (I passed up CO-OP® grilled panini sandwiches, CO-OP® cappuccino, and much else), I notice that the other customers are a mixture of seniors and young mothers with children. The seniors seem a little tentative in the slope-backed chairs, handling their food carefully on the round, glass-topped tables as if afraid of it falling off. The young mothers and the children look a lot more relaxed. Bright signs all around the store proclaim messages such as "Value Plus Savings" (a members' savings card), "Meat Manager's Sale On Now," "Members

Saved 6.5¢/litre on Fuel Purchases," "Voted Best Grocery Store" (by *Calgary Herald* readers), and "Interfaith Thrift Stores"—one of the local projects the co-op supports.

The Macleod Trail store is new, the cutting edge of co-op retailing as of summer 2003. The outdoor signs promise Deli, Bakery, Travel, Pharmacy, 1 hr. Photo. Across the parking lot in a separate building are the co-op liquor store, Co-operators insurance, and (in two other separate buildings) the credit union and a bank—businesses clustering around the co-op as the hub. The foyer features, across from the shopping carts, a community bulletin board, a book exchange for members' use, and recycling information. The store actually looks smaller than some of the older ones, but much more open. You enter into a wide, bright produce area, with a café on the left. Fresh food dominates the view. Behind all this are broad aisles. One, towards the middle of the store, features popular magazines and greeting cards. This store still has some toys, stationery, hardware, and so on, but it seems to be integrated throughout the store. Food is everywhere. Beside the checkouts and offices is a bright, prominent, enclosed Kiddies Korral, a Calgary Co-op innovation that has stood the test of time and remains in the newest stores. I can tell there is attention to design and appearance when even the men's washroom has fresh-cut flowers.

So is this the be-all and end-all of co-op retailing? Well, not likely; it's merely the current stage. It's the commitment that lies behind it, to innovation and improvement, that really counts. As one manager tells me, "The members will choose. If they decide they don't like this, we'll have to try something else."

Calgary Co-op is more than just an example of a successful co-op. It's in a league of its own, by far the most successful food retailer in the system. In point of fact, it is the largest locally based consumer co-operative in North America and one of the biggest in the world.[91] Calgary's board chair Barry Ashton comments, "When I go to the [FCL region] fall conferences or when I go to the … annual meeting … it's amazing the interest amongst the other retails in what's happening at Calgary Co-op. They sort of look to us … we're kind of a weather vane on the CRS if you like, as … by far the largest player in the system," he says. "It's interesting that they always are very keen to know how we're doing, and the latest word, and what … issues we're dealing with." Ashton stresses, "I don't mean to be critical of the CRS, we're not. We're an integral part of that. It's in our interest to remain an integral part of that. We have no intention of doing otherwise, we co-operate and so on, but I think in many ways we are leaders in the CRS because we are larger … not always the leaders but often the leaders."[92]

It does sometimes startle people to discover that the system's largest co-op is in Calgary, a city renowned for its free-enterprise orientation, for the influences of cowboy culture and Texas-style oilmen, and for right-wing politics in provincial and federal elections. Usually they ask what it is about Calgary that makes the co-op succeed, rather than wonder whether there really is any conflict between co-ops and any of the other things named. Long-time Calgary (and former FCL) board member Alice Brown says that she can't count the number of times people have asked her, "'How did Calgary Co-op become so successful in the most capitalistic province in the country?' 'Why wasn't it in Saskatchewan?' … and, 'How can *you* be involved'" in something like that? Brown is not a shy person; you need to see the gleam in her eye and hear the tone in her voice as she says, "I tell them co-operatives are the freest form of free enterprise." She explains that "It's a group of people, pulling together, forming their business, investing their money, and sharing in the profits, if they're lucky, and that's all it is. Where you go into the social issues and the other sides" of co-ops, Brown says, those things "are fun, but they're not what it's about. That's not what the folks in Rochdale did"—Rochdale, England, where in 1844 working-class activists created the first consumer co-op of the modern type. "They did it to beat the company store. They had a purpose. The folks in Saskatchewan wanted their coal and they wanted to ship their grain better, and that's all it was. They were mad. [It was like in] the movie, I'm mad as hell and I'm not going to take it any more." And she looks at me pointedly again. "Ralph Klein's wife worked for us thirteen years in the accounting department," she says.[93] Everyone in Canada knows Ralph Klein, one-time mayor of Calgary and currently the Conservative premier of the Province of Alberta.

Board member Brown is a local person with deep roots near Calgary, but Calgary Co-op CEO Milford Sorensen has been in the West and with the co-op system for only a few years. Sorensen explains it like this: "There's a huge commitment to local business. I would not overlook the fact that part of the reason we're successful in Calgary is because we're a strong local business, and we happen to be a co-operative. It's not gone unnoticed that there are a lot of western businesses that are very successful here." Sorensen mentions a sporting-goods chain that has gone national, and the banking system—"They've got that American flair. Local banks, local businesses, support the local." He says that "Albertans like to support their own. They don't like the profits taking off to the United States of America or to Toronto. They like the profits to stay here in the community, and I think that is something that is of significant benefit to us. Being a co-operative is also important, but I think the two of them together are largely responsible for Calgary Co-op being where it is today." Along with its local character and co-operative structure, Sorensen also mentions a third strength, the neighbourhood strategy developed under former co-op leader Gordon Barker, which helped ensure that Calgary Co-op sited new stores at key points in districts throughout the city. "We have great locations. We're a local company; we support the community in a big way. There were times when it was suggested that the big national organizations were going to put Calgary Co-op out of business. We've been able to withstand that and I think the combination of the good locations, being a local business, and being a co-operative … works extremely well for the Calgary Co-op."[94]

Sorensen sees the needs and experience of a co-op like his own as important to the future of the co-op system. "There are many things that Calgary Co-op does, because we are an urban co-op, that are benefiting Federated," he says. "They're adopting a lot of the things we're doing and then rolling them out to other stores." In particular, he sees retails like his own helping to drive FCL to be more efficient. While Calgary Co-op is focussed on providing value and service to its members, "at the same time, we're putting pressure on Federated to implement systems so that we can be more competitive at retail, and now I'm talking about the supply-chain management system, as you can only do so much at retail. WAL-MART and Superstore are able to run discount stores because they are more efficient in the distribution system. I can't affect the distribution system, only Federated can; but I can work with Federated in sharing my information so that they can make better decisions and lower the cost in the distribution system and ultimately lower my costs at retail." No matter how good a job the local retail does of marketing, "we need to improve our efficiencies to drive costs out of the system so that we don't have what I call insult pricing." This is the source of the VALUE PRICED *Every Day!* program. "What we've done is," Sorensen says, "we've taken a lot of those items that our members buy every day and we've reduced the price substantially. We're negotiating with our suppliers to get a lower cost on those items so there isn't as big a gap between the price they're paying at a discount operation versus what they're paying for ours. I'm talking about the Tide, the sugar, the milk, flour—those things they buy every day that they are extremely price-conscious about." The program is one example of how Calgary is "focussed on working with Federated to do whatever they can [to use] technology to drive costs out of the system ... as they drive their costs out of the system, that means my patronage refund from them is going to be stronger or my costs are going to be lower, and I'm going to be able to compete more effectively in the market-place," Sorensen says. "So it's a dual approach."

As Sorensen makes clear, Calgary Co-op is linked into a larger system; it does not stand on its own. The ways in which the system has helped Calgary Co-op withstand its own difficulties are examined in chapter two, but for now our focus is on the system's drive for improved marketing. Because of the way the CRS works, innovations aren't limited to individual local co-ops. They are developed, tested, and can spread throughout the system.

~

THAT'S WHY WHEN I VISITED BRANDON, MANITOBA, in early June 2003, I found a brand-new store reminiscent of Calgary's leading-edge designs. This is all the more striking because Brandon is not an upscale, large urban market like Calgary. It's a sizeable city, an important service centre for western Manitoba, but people there have never seen a store like this before. When I visited, it was barely three weeks old, the newest store in the system. It epitomizes the new design. Outside is two-tone brickwork (tan and reddish-grey/black) with black upright pillars supporting overhanging low roofs that provide a homey feel. There is also a huge entrance portal. Left of the door are outdoor tables and a door out from the deli area. You enter—of course—into a long sweep of "fresh" departments running to the back of the store. A huge U-shaped deli counter, with indoor tables, is right there in front of you. Behind that, to the left, is a baked goods area, with a bakery counter and visible work area and warming ovens, to emphasize the freshness. To the right is fresh flowers, and produce, running along the whole length to the Butcher Shoppe visible at the back with red and white awnings over its windows. Nestled in between the deli and the baked goods is a kitchen area; General Manager Barry McPhail explains that food and recipes are demonstrated here. Chefs and students from a local college come in to learn, test, and put on displays. The floor catches my eye—a brown concrete floor, polished with a high-sheen finish; in the fresh area it has a yellowy alligator pattern. There is a huge aisle of big freezer units in about the middle of the store. Large photo murals of Brandon dominate the view lines. A nice touch is electronic games on the sides of the checkout tills, located at the right height for small children to amuse themselves while mom and dad are paying the bill.

Behind the tills are a Westoba Credit Union branch, and a Co-operators insurance branch, reflections, I am told, of the good working and personal relationships with both financial co-ops, and of the credit union's encouragement of the new store and determination to have a branch inside it.

Heritage Co-op's new food store, located in Brandon, Manitoba.

All this represents the ambitious re-entry of the co-op system into a food market that had been lost. Brandon had had its own independent co-op, shut down in 1982. The old co-op store and lumber yard were sold; with FCL's help and encouragement, nearby Minnedosa Co-op saved the petroleum business, taking over Brandon's co-op service station. "There was very little money that we had to put out, you know," says Barry McPhail. "But what we got, really … was the business. Those petroleum customers, the farmers in the Brandon area, were loyal to us. I mean, we hardly lost any fuel customers in the early eighties when Brandon Co-op dissolved and they lost all their equity.… They stayed with us, in large part, you know. I think that was significant." From that toehold, Minnedosa—renamed Heritage Co-op in 1990 to reflect its regional growth outside Minnedosa, with branch operations and services in various communities—has now re-entered Brandon in a big way.[95]

The new Brandon store is made possible by the combined success of Heritage Co-op and Federated Co-op. The food-store facility is owned by Federated and leased to Heritage (the site also includes a gas bar and c-store owned by Heritage Co-op). The local co-op has to be profitable and not constrained by debts, but it doesn't have to front the cash for the store; the system does that. It's the kind of wholesale-retail partnership that has driven explosive growth in the system in the last couple of years. Ultimately, it's made possible by the good finances of the local retail combined with the powerful flow of earnings and investment through Federated.

The new store is a huge leap for Heritage Co-op. Its staff doubled when the Brandon store opened. Co-op membership has grown by twenty-eight hundred—30 percent in one month—to make a total of eighty-five hundred members. A large majority of the co-op membership now lives in Brandon, even though the main co-op office is still in Minnedosa. Staff were signed up from other co-ops, from among university students looking for work, and from competitors. Rumour has it that a meat manager came from a competitor and brought the whole meat department along. These staff members, according to managers and directors, are often attracted by a store where they have more autonomy, flexibility, and voice, where the manager who makes the decisions is available to talk to personally and can be reasoned with—

not far away in Toronto. (This is a theme we will revisit in chapter two.) Integrating these staff and making them a co-op team is an important job. And then there are the members. Thousands of people in Brandon—older people—remember what a co-op grocery is about. Do the new members understand? Or do they simply see it as a kind of discount scheme, where the co-op patronage refund is just like the incentives of competitors? If they are motivated by attractive facilities, then they are sure to respond positively, because Brandon now has a co-op food store as good as any, anywhere. And the re-entry into food in Brandon marks an important step for the system, the reclaiming of the kind of market it ought to be in.

"The city was certainly behind us to open this new facility," says McPhail, "and the press has been good. I think there's a lot of member education that has to happen yet—I think some of that's been lost. But I think the older generation … certainly knew the difference between a co-op and WAL-MART. The person in Brandon here who's thirty years old, they're going to have an education on what's the difference between us and the other guys; and that's up to us. We've got our work cut out for us, educating new members, and it will take a while to do that." But in the meantime, he says, "Brandon people are very happy we're here."

The Brandon store is only the latest success. McPhail has managed Heritage for over a decade of continuous growth, renovation, and expansion. (In fact, he was familiar with the co-op before he became its GM, since he used to visit it as Federated's retail advisor before that.) "We've had a lot of fun in the last ten years," he says. "We've seen some big changes in this organization. In fact it doesn't resemble anything [that was here] when I first started in 1992 and it's totally changed, the organization. But it's been a lot of fun, a lot of growth, I've learned lots, and it certainly keeps me entertained from day to day." McPhail makes it sound easy: "We've made $1.5 million to $2 million in net savings each year in the last ten years," he says. "Roughly half of that was given back to the members … roughly $1 million per year in cash back to our members, and the other $1 million we're investing back into assets. And both have helped, you know—[if] you put money into the assets, the members like that; they'll come and support the stores better. And they also like the cash they're getting back at the end of the year, too. So both have been strong factors in our growth."

E<small>VERY TIME A MEMBER PULLS A PRODUCT OFF THE SHELF</small> in one of the new stores, the purchase is the end point of a long chain of wholesale purchasing or manufacturing, handling, warehousing, and trucking. Every time members pull up at the gas pumps, they draw on a petroleum distribution system that leads back to the Co-op Refinery in Regina. Similarly, agricultural supplies are backed by the system's feed mills, lumber yards by the sawmill and ply-wood plants at Canoe. The logistics of manufacturing and distribution are complex and not always directly visible to consumers, but they make a huge difference to the system's success.

When I asked Elmer Wiebe about the highlights of the system's recent history, the first thing he mentioned was Calgary Co-op, in its heyday, as an example of what co-ops could become. But he also mentioned topics that would not be so obvious to an outsider: consolidation of warehouses and bulk plants; expanding the system's volume by selling through new channels and acquiring new subsidiaries (see chapter three); and generally the growing emphasis on marketing, image, and sales. "Marketing ... started to take over ... everything we did," Wiebe says, and led to the wholesale and the retails having to work closely together, the boards and the managers.[96]

It's worth taking a closer look at some of what goes on behind the scenes in order to make the system's marketing successful and put products into consumers' hands. Let's use the refinery and the warehouse system as examples.

I mentioned in the introduction that while Federated's refinery subsidiary, Consumers' Co-operative Refineries Limited, or CCRL, is important, it is not a licence to print money. There are other co-op refineries in North America, and not all those co-ops have made money. So we have to ask *why* this refinery works the way it does, and one of the best people to ask is CEO Thompson. "We have to go back to where it really starts," Thompson says characteristically, "and it really starts at the retail. If the retail does not sell the product, the refinery does not make the money. The refinery is a production facility. The role of the refinery is to produce the product at the lowest possible cost. They have done a very, very good job at running a very efficient operation and making it a very low-cost refinery," he says.

Growing petroleum volumes as well as the need to meet new environmental standards have contributed to a refinery expansion project, which was completed in 2003 at a cost in excess of $400 million. "The expansion process," Thompson says, "has really come about because of the job that our marketing people have done at FCL in terms of developing a marketing program for retails, and the jobs that the retails have done in marketing petroleum. There's a huge increase in volume, and the increase in volume comes from the retail system. That makes for further expansion. So the expansion doesn't make the sales; it comes the other way."[97] Thompson is describing a demand-driven marketing strategy that links the refinery to consumer support, not one that produces things and then looks for a way to sell them.

The refinery's manager, FCL's senior vice-president, Refining, is Bud Van Iderstine. I met Van Iderstine in his office beside the Co-op Refinery in the north end of Regina, Saskatchewan. On his office wall he has pictures of his predecessors, men who managed the refinery through seven decades. The pictures are spaced on his wall roughly to reflect the length of time the different managers served. The message they are meant to convey is a historic continuity of mission and purpose. There is the president/manager combination of Harry Fowler and O.B. Males, 1935–47. There is Ben Pawson, who led the refinery for twenty-seven years, and Bud Dahlstrom, who led it for twenty-three.

"He's Bud Wiser," Bud Van Iderstine comments. "I'm Bud Light."[98] But somehow, I don't think Van Iderstine's staff would ever use the word light to describe him.

Van Iderstine says that when he has a decision to make, "I look at that wall and say, I wonder what those guys would do? Would they approve? And if they wouldn't, I have to ask myself, am I beginning to move away from the values, vision, and culture these men were trying to secure?" This isn't a culture Van Iderstine grew up with. He's a professional engineer who worked with other companies before coming to CCRL in 1989. The co-op system is something he has learned about. There is still something of the engineer about Van Iderstine—perhaps the partly rolled-up shirtsleeves and the dark, formal tie. Or perhaps it's

his manner, rooted in professional competence and authority, combined with a relaxed and slightly folksy way of relating to people.

Van Iderstine confirms that the purpose of the refinery is to supply
co-op members with their fuel, and this is what has driven the recent
expansion, the most expensive in the refinery's history. He goes right
back to the beginning. "Really, the concept back in 1935 when those
original retails banded together and decided they didn't want to be
ripped off by the Imperial Oils or the big oil companies of the day, and
said we're going to build our own refinery to serve our needs, that principle has never changed," says Van Iderstine. "It will always be the reason for our existence in the system. And one feeds the other," he says.
"The system is better because of the refinery, and the refinery is better
because of the system." As the co-ops experience success, moving more
product, "so does the refinery." And of course the refinery benefits from
FCL's massive investment—more than $400 million—money that comes
ultimately from the retail co-ops that are selling the refinery's fuel.

The investment in the complex refinery expansion does reflect cost-
mindedness in that it efficiently serves several purposes: it meets higher environmental standards for desulphurization of fuel that will come
into effect in 2005–06; expands the refinery's output by nearly 50 percent; modernizes the plant; and enables it to take in a wider variety of
crude oil as input (see chapter three). The expansion also shows that the
co-op system is willing and able to make very large investments when
the business case is convincing. These investments are selective. The co-
ops have also modernized their BC sawmill, though not nearly in so
expensive a fashion; they have kept up their feed mills; whereas in the
1980s, FCL got out of formal participation in fertilizer production altogether. The refinery expansion is an example of the system concentrating on what is successful.

When I talked to him, Van Iderstine pulled out the speech he made
to the FCL delegates in March 2003 as an illustration of what he believes
CCRL is all about. Here is the excerpt he chose:

> There are now fewer refineries and the remaining ones
> are becoming larger and much more sophisticated. This
> trend will continue. Also, as I have indicated, fuels are
> becoming cleaner-burning and this trend will also con-

tinue. From a very humble beginning your CCRL refinery has had to adapt and evolve in a constantly changing and demanding petroleum business. This spring is
the completion of the large and valuable refinery expansion project. We created a second train of processing
and significantly increased the sophistication and flexibility of our complex. Your refinery will be processing
over 85,000 barrels per day of the most difficult and high
sulphur crudes in the world, and producing some of the
highest quality, lowest sulphur gasoline and diesel in the
world. CCRL will then be elevated to one of the world's
higher, value-added petroleum refining facilities on the
basis of complexity, sophistication, capability, and flexibility. CCRL will continue to adapt and evolve as required. We will, at the same time and most importantly, continue our mission of service to the Co-operative
Retailing System. Our total dedication to this goal will
not change as we move proudly forward into our future.
Becoming one of the better refineries in the world has
been the result, never the goal. Serving you and serving
you in the best way we can has always been the goal.

It's hard for co-op delegates not to applaud a speech like that one,
because it presents the refinery not as a technological marvel or a venture that is an end in itself, but rather as a service directly tied to the
needs of members.

A refinery dedicated and optimized to meet consumer needs is an
example of the way the system is linked through to individual members'
transactions at the pumps, in the store, on the farm, or wherever they
may be in western Canada. To take another example, the same philosophy increasingly drives the Federated distribution system.

~

AL RODEN STARTED OUT WORKING IN FEDERATED'S
Saskatoon warehouse in 1959, and during a forty-year
career ended up serving twenty-one years as FCL's vice-president of Distribution. It was a period of relentless change, new systems and tech-

nologies, and pursuit of efficiencies in moving and storing products. The system's business is selling things to members, not running warehouses and keeping inventories for their own sake. These latter functions, in today's retailing environment, need to be continually made more efficient or pared back to just what is needed to get the products members want into their hands.

"When I first took over the Distribution Division in '77," Roden recalls, "I think we had approximately 2.3 million square feet of warehousing." Then "our mentality started to change because we had this thought process that if you can't measure it, you can't manage it." This was the beginning of a more organized approach of tracking "tons per man-hour ... where we knew the productivity of all of our people and everything," and of "the crusade, if you want to call it that ... to continually address those costs ... reducing them, by getting your productivity out of ... all of the infrastructure you needed," Roden says. "Buildings were a major component"—improving and modernizing them—but so were automation and added shifts. "For many years we ran those buildings as we would run a retail store. We opened at eight in the morning and we closed at six in the afternoon. Well, we started to run those buildings as if they were trucks, because everybody in the trucking business knows that if a truck is standing idle, it isn't making any money. If a building is standing idle, it's costing you, and so we started to run the buildings twenty-four hours a day, and that made a major, major difference in our costs."[99]

"When I retired," he recalls, "we had reduced the amount of warehousing space we needed by a significant amount.... I think we have it down to about 1.7 million square feet," despite the system's huge growth in volume in the intervening years.

A related piece was inventory consolidation. "When I first started, every region had a warehouse full of food, full of hardware, full of lumber products; in the case of Winnipeg, we had dry goods, all our clothing, etc., and today in Federated you have one hardware inventory, which is located in Calgary," and other product lines have also been consolidated where possible. "Eventually, we got to a point where we could service our entire system from Calgary [for hardware] as compared to having five separate inventories as we initially had." Along the way, the BC warehouse closed in 1979–80—with strong opposition from the local union—so that retails in BC have since been served out of Calgary and Edmonton. FCL's Regina warehouse closed later. Roden continues: "We've been able to increase sales, increase tonnage, increase throughput, and do all of that … not by adding space but by making better use of what we had, getting more turns with our inventory, making better use of equipment inside the warehouse" through automation. "And so we took away a lot of infrastructure costs, and at the same time we were able to increase our sales and our throughput." Similar consolidations around the system, each of which took two to three years to plan and implement, have reduced the system from five multiline warehouses to just food warehouses in Winnipeg, Saskatoon, Calgary, and Edmonton, and a hardware warehouse in Calgary.

"I can tell you that the consolidation process, which … took a considerable period of time, had a significant impact on Federated's bottom line," says Roden. It directly contributed to the high levels of earnings and refunds that have flowed through the system. "Initially, it was somewhat difficult to convince our retailing system," he recalls, due to resistance from retails that did not feel they would be well served from distant warehouses. "I can remember on many occasions … having to answer very, very tough questions in front of our board, because our retails, although they were very supportive and accommodating, still had to have product on a regular basis." The savings achieved by Roden and the warehouse managers and staff were part of what has made the retails competitive. They also set the stage for more recent innovations such as the new computerized warehouse management system introduced beginning in 2002–03.

The man in charge of logistics modernization today is Roden's successor, VP, Logistics, Terry Bell. Bell has been working in the co-op system since 1970, first at the retail level and since 1984, with Federated. He comes from a co-op family—his father, Pat Bell, worked thirty-three years for FCL and ended as its CEO. "I think that it's one of the few companies where you can definitely start at the bottom and work your way up, one of the few companies left [where] you can do that," says Terry. "It's an organization that number one, can't be bought out by a competitor and you don't get major shake-ups all the time; and secondly, it generally doesn't have major structural changes." As a result, you can see people who have spent long careers in the system. The main difference from the competition is that it's the locals who own the central and the central has no automatic authority to give orders. "It's a family," Bell says, "and it's different, there's no doubt about that, compared to the WAL-MARTs of the world."[100]

The different character of careers and relationships in the CRS is the subject of chapter two, but Bell's reference to WAL-MART is a reminder that while the co-ops may be different, they are called upon today to compete against the largest corporations in Canada and the world. Warehousing and trucking might not sound romantic, but they are critical to how the co-ops put products on shelves in a way that is sufficiently competitive for consumers to choose them.

Bell is the one in charge of the warehouses and trucking fleets. "One of the things that the food division really started pushing a number of years ago," Bell explains, "is taking costs out of the system. Anything you can do to take costs out of the system makes you more competitive at the end of the day. So that's our objective," he says. "We look at ourselves"—at logistics—"as a cost, and what can we do to keep those costs down?" In recent years this has meant introducing new technology, such as electronic buying systems and a computerized warehouse management system. "I would say that we as a system have kept up to the technical [standards] in the industry," says Bell. "A lot of people sometimes think we're not leaders in technology, but they don't understand if they think that—because we are."

A case in point is the new warehouse management system introduced in 2002 in Saskatoon and being phased in during 2003–04 in the other locations. "By the end of the day, it'll probably be a five-year project from the time we started working on it to its completion," says Bell. "It's an over eight-million-dollar project with a payback of about two years."

Bell explains the new system. "If we go back," he says, "we used to pick product in the warehouse based on [the following system]: a picker would be provided with sheets of labels that would be attached to products as they were picked. So, if you can imagine picking product with all these labels—first you'd read this sheet, then go find the product, put the label on, put it on the pallet, and then move to the next one. And there could be ten of an item, so you had to pick ten like that.

Then at the end, putting them together and calling it a day." All that has changed so that computers co-ordinate the orders as well as the locations and restocking of bins in the warehouse. Computer software sorts orders by retail and sends the orders to the warehouses. "Then the picker," says Bell, "instead of going to this sheet of labels, puts on a headset and follows the directions of the computer, which gives the picker voice commands. So it will say, 'Go to aisle such and such, bin such and such, and pick two,' and the picker will go to that bin." The software also requires the exchange of "check digits" that confirm the product is correct for the order.

New warehouse management system introduced in the Saskatoon warehouse in 2002.

"So what we've done is gone from [a] manual system, and now you've got a picker [who is] hands-free, taking voice commands," says Bell, "to the point where it is virtually impossible to pick the wrong product.... We can get well over 99 percent picking accuracy; we think it's closer to 99.8 percent. And on top of that, we are giving a much better service level to the stores, because of the fact that this system is also giving commands to the forklift operators to replenish those bins when they are getting close to running out."

"So we've improved our service level in Saskatoon alone by .7 percent," explains Bell. "That translates into over a million dollars in extra sales for not only us but for the retails, because now they're getting that product" more quickly, reliably, and at a lower handling cost. Moreover, by managing space flexibly in the warehouse—assigning products to whatever spots are free and keeping track of where they are—the computerized system makes more efficient use of facilities. "It should cut back on our having to expand the facilities as quickly as we have in the past," Bell says.

Further efficiencies are gained by working with suppliers to increase speed and accuracy of orders and deliveries. In many ways, it's all about information. Vendor Managed Inventory, or VMI, is a system whereby FCL's procurement group partners with suppliers, transmitting information to them on co-op sales, inventories, and promotions. The suppliers analyse the information to determine more exactly what the system needs. Another program is Direct to Store Deliveries, or DSD, which creates authorized lists of products set up in FCL's system to make it easier for retails to order them and work them onto the shelves. Then there are Advance Shipping Notices, or ASN, which allow each supplier to update information on the status of purchase orders, such as quantities and projected delivery dates. These kinds of procedures are critical to the warehouse-management system.[101]

All this, once again, is the logic of linkage. Every function in the system has been more closely linked to the purchasing decision made by the member.

~

MEMBERS ALMOST NEVER SEE THE SYSTEM'S WAREhouses and likely don't even know where they are. Trucks are different. Trucks are a visible sign of the commerce that ties the co-ops together. In recent years, they have also become emblems of the system's success.

No aspect of the Co-op Retailing System is more visible than its trucks, which cover nearly 38 million kilometres per year, and which for a number of years have been decorated with attention-getting and award-winning designs. The trucks have become a point of pride and identification for people involved in the system. When I comment to Terry Bell that everyone seems to be interested in the system's trucks, he nods—"Yeah, that's the truth."

The Quality Fresh Products graphic launched in 2002 won the Tractor-Trailer Graphic Award from the Private Motor Truck Council of Canada.

"Our objective is to be the number one trucking company in western Canada," says Bell. "We want to generate an image for the co-ops that they want to portray to their customers.... We've got some very sharp-looking trucks out there." Co-ordinated with the system's marketing priorities and products, the logistics department works with FCL's commodity departments to develop one new graphic design per year for the trucks. In 2001, the CO-OP® Gold Ice Cream graphic was a hit; the 2002 Quality Fresh graphic won an award and supported the system's marketing thrust in fresh products; and 2003's new graphic, unveiled at the FCL Marketing Expo, promoted the system's VALUE PRICED *Every Day!* program.

Bell explains that the system really has three separate trucking fleets. There is an FCL merchandising fleet carrying the CO-OP® designs, as well as a TGP (The Grocery People—see chapter three) fleet flying different colours; finally, there is the petroleum fleet. The merchandising fleets consist of 225 trailers based in Winnipeg, Saskatoon, Edmonton, and Calgary; 90 of these are TGP trailers. "Last year [2002] our merchandising fleets travelled 20 million kilometres and [delivered] 575,000 tonnes of product," says Bell. The petroleum fleet consists of 76 tankers, which hauled 1.8 billion litres of fuel and travelled 17 million kilometres. "They're going all the time," says Bell, supplying the system's rapid expansion in petroleum products. The trucks are symbols of the commerce that flows through the Co-op Retailing System, and of its present-day marketing success.

~

THIS CHAPTER HAS EXAMINED HOW FCL AND MANY retails turned around their fortunes in the last twenty years by focussing on marketing, by relinking the entire system to the purchases and needs of members. Two important pieces of this story have been touched on only in passing and are examined in greater depth in the following chapters: first, the roles and relationships within the system, the jobs performed by members, staff, and managers in making the co-ops work and in making their basic messages understood; second, the processes of adaptation and innovation that have allowed the system to develop new ideas and new approaches from the community level on up. Before turning to those topics, a few concluding remarks are in order.

One question I asked many interviewees had to do with how the co-op system reflected or was important to western Canadian regional identity. Most people seemed to have trouble putting into words what being western meant, how it differed from anything else, or how co-ops were related to it. But one who had a ready answer was Calgary CEO Milford Sorensen, a westerner by recent choice rather than by birth. "I guess the West always intrigued me," Sorensen says. "We absolutely fell in love with the West immediately, and with Calgary. There's a sense of free-wheeling spirit, entrepreneurial spirit, here in the West. A you-can-do-it attitude; full speed ahead, damn the torpedoes; let's not wait for the bureaucracy; let's get things done. It's very refreshing and something that I would sum up by saying, I wish I had found the West a little earlier in my career. I wish I'd been here sooner."[102]

There's little doubt that the co-ops' recent history reflects that aspect of western culture. And with the increasing urbanization of the West, a co-op like Calgary is worth paying attention to. Sorensen reflects that Calgary Co-op, like others, has had to learn to overcome tired stores, unimpressive image, and an aging membership. But today, he says, "our vision is to be the premier shopping destination in the communities we serve," and adds, "That's no different than a strong regional player," i.e., a locally based supermarket chain of any kind. "There has to be value; you have to be able to provide value to your members, your customers, in those communities. We have spent huge amounts of capital changing our stores" to be what members want. "If you want value, if you want service, if you want quality, you want variety, you want freshness, you come to Calgary Co-op because [it has] the best overall value, and there's always a place in the market-place for that." This message is reinforced by the co-op character, the patronage refund, the community orientation—"We support the community; we're focussed very heavily in that area," Sorensen says. The walls downstairs in the Calgary Co-op administrative offices reflect this, with numerous plaques, awards, and thank-you letters from school groups and others for the co-op's charitable donations. The selection by local newspaper readers as the number one local business is part of it as well. But Sorensen leaves no doubt that marketing is at the heart of it all, and with it, the need for co-ops to work together through FCL to improve efficiencies and drive costs down.

For a view from the wholesale side of things, Art Postle has been involved with FCL since the 1960s, when he was an articling student with Deloitte & Touche, as it happened, working under Wayne Thompson, who was with the same firm at that time. Since 1987, he has been senior vice-president and treasurer of FCL—the money man, so to speak. He is conversational and well spoken, with a certain dapper sense of style. Not surprisingly, the treasurer is also an advocate of co-ops making money.

Co-ops are unique, Postle explains, because of working through local boards of directors, always having to persuade them and demonstrate that your plans are the right ones. This adds discipline, soundness, and quality to decisions. But otherwise, "in terms of business acumen, in terms of conducting business, I don't think we're any different than if I was working for another organization. I mean, we're in the business of being profitable, call them savings if you want, but we still have to be profitable. We still have to give the customer the goods and services they want, at competitive prices, the choices that they want, and so on. So, from that perspective, we're like anybody else," Postle says. "Of course, as the treasurer," he explains, his position is that "if we

don't make money, we can't do any of the other things" that are important to co-op members. "We've got to survive, and money is the lifeline
for any organization, including a co-operative."[103] This doesn't mean a
co-op organization eliminates all unprofitable or less-profitable activities, he points out. "I think there's nothing necessarily wrong with it,"
he says, when co-ops maintain money-losing services, "if they can show
[that while] we might have a bit of a loss in this particular area … it's
integral to supporting another area of the organization to grow very
profitable." What co-ops can't afford to do is say it's okay to lose a little bit of money here or there, because it's a good thing to provide the
service. "If there's no connection to another part of the business that is
profitable, then I'd say … that's a waste of money," the treasurer says.
"I don't have any problems with absorbing some losses; I guess, at the
same time, I'd want to say you want to *minimize* those losses as much
as you can."

What retail co-ops have had to do in the last twenty years is the
same thing Federated has done. Postle says that FCL "has identified
what its core business is. Our core business is petroleum and food. And
that's not to belittle or downplay the other businesses; they are vital to
the overall success of the organization.… We've said what are the core
businesses we're in, and those are the areas," he says. And that drives
investment. "If you had to be restrictive in terms of resources—whether
that's financial or whether that's human—they would be the ones to get
it first," he explains. "Now, fortunately," Postle continues, "we've had
success over the last eleven or twelve years that has enabled us to do
everything that we need to do. But if [we ever got into] a situation
where we said we've got to start pulling back, I know that we'd be
pulling back in other areas first before the core business. Food isn't necessarily the most profitable. Petroleum is; there's a lot of money to be
made in petroleum, but there's also a lot of money to be lost in petroleum because things can go against you just as much as they go for you,
and it takes much bigger investment, and so on." The products FCL
handles today are those it feels it can do well; others over the years it
has relinquished—manufactured homes and vegetable processing, for
example. "Maybe that's speaking against vertical integration," he concedes. But FCL doesn't feel it needs to integrate diverse operations unless
there is a clear benefit. In a sense, it's simple marketing.

S O WHY DOES IT MATTER HOW FEDERATED CO-OP and the Co-op Retailing System rediscovered marketing between 1983 and the present? Is this any different from what any other company would have done? It *is* different, and there are three reasons why it matters.

First, it may sound like common sense to return to the basics of good financing and good marketing, but it is surprising how few companies actually do so. What else could the system have done, starting in 1983? The wholesale could have cut back, concentrated on its own success, found other lines of business to make money in, and let more of the retail co-ops decline or fail. The result would have been a smaller and less integrated system, with less community presence. Or, it could have swallowed up retails, becoming a centralized and totally integrated organization—a drastic change, to be sure, but one that other co-op systems in North America have gone through or are going through. The result would have been a more monolithic organization, with less local autonomy or sense of local membership. Or, the system could have sought an infusion of outside capital from a private-sector partner or from the stock exchange, an option that would have decreased the extent of member ownership and also promoted centralization. Those are three alternative choices the system might have made; there is nothing inevitable about the path it took. The actual path was influenced by the vision of the management group and by the structure, culture, and history of the system.

Second, FCL's success illustrates distinctive features of business success in co-operatives. The strategy followed by FCL and by most successful retails was one of concentrating on services that were needed and demanded by members, to the point where the co-ops could earn a surplus on those lines of business. Activities that members did not adequately support or demand were reduced, in line with the approach Postle described. The result was a retailing system more integrated with or linked to what members were actually purchasing. At the same time, the insistence on paying patronage refunds, promoted at the FCL level by Thompson and other leaders and carried down through many local co-ops to individual members, meant that members benefited directly from co-op surpluses, and in proportion to their purchases. Member benefits were linked to system success. Financing and investment policies ensured that the system remained member owned—in fact, that its degree of member ownership deepened over time. Adaptation to member needs, interlocking benefits, and member ownership are examples of the ways in which the system as a whole, from top to bottom, became better *linked* to the pocketbooks of members. Then, especially in the 1990s, investment in image, equipment, and new facilities promoted member *identification* with the system—another kind of linkage with members and communities.

Third, the path FCL chose is the one that preserved and maximized local ownership of co-operative enterprises. If local ownership matters to people in a globalizing age—as Sorensen and others have said it does—then this is a significant choice, and one that demonstrates the potential for local autonomy within a context of economic efficiency. The CRS chose a *federated* solution in an age when experts are saying organizations must be *centralized* to survive. One important US study of agricultural co-operatives recently concluded that the "cooperative of the future is likely to be relatively large, centralized, and market driven." Apparently, it is typical for "federated cooperatives to see the locals as ungrateful and somewhat disloyal," as averse to business alliances, as opposing change, as "dinosaurs bound for extinction."[104] While these comments were made about agricultural co-ops, few analysts see the general retailing industry as being any kinder or gentler. Federated Co-operatives and the CRS disprove such assertions—in spades. They show that a federated system, one based on a dynamic balance between local autonomy and centralized efficiency, can be astonishingly effective in marketing, in capital formation, in providing service. It can do so because of the way in which different elements and levels of the federation work together.

CHAPTER TWO

Transparency

Management, Governance, and Trust

I WAS DRIVING ACROSS TOWN TO VISIT THE ADMINIS-
trative offices of Calgary Co-op when the radio played
an interview about corporate scandals in the for-profit
world. The program was CBC Radio's "The Current" with Anna Maria
Tremonti, who was interviewing Sherron Watkins, the executive who
blew the whistle on Enron Corporation's world-famous scandal in 2001.
I was struck by the contrast between what I had been hearing from co-
op managers, and the me-first attitudes that sucked Enron down into a
cesspool of blame and evasion of responsibility. Watkins described a
doomed corporation with a culture built on competition among the
employees, scratching and clawing each other for bigger pieces of the
pie—with the whole thing held together only as long as people found
creative ways to make the pie grow, or appear to grow. Those involved
seemed to view life as a game where the goal was to extract all you
could: big houses, cars, stock options; retire rich as soon as you could
get out—once they were wealthy, they were gone. There was no loyalty. So-called "aggressive accounting" kept the whole thing afloat for
awhile. Critics were bullied into silence.[1]

The Enron culture was one kind of corporate culture. The Co-op
Retailing System (CRS) has another. People in the co-op world do similar jobs to people in other businesses; they strive to meet high and

increasing standards; but, at least where system management is best, they do it by building people up and working as teams, not by elbowing each other aside. Co-ops are not the only businesses that highly value team management and teamwork among staff, but the co-op framework gives them an advantage in doing so. This is partly because the co-op system is decentralized, based on local autonomy, and accountable within a democratic framework of member-elected boards. But having said that, the co-op system mirrors all of the mysteries and complexities of modern democracy and organization. Many people in the system today are not sure what it's for, how it works, or why it works. There are lessons in it others can learn from. Not the least of these is the way organizations sometimes work better *because* of the unresolved tensions and ambiguities, checks and balances, in their structures.

One of the most important tensions in the CRS is the tension between local autonomy and centralized control or efficiency, which can come out sometimes as tension between the retails and the wholesale.[2] While such tensions were evident and often negative in the 1980s, the reverse is the case today—they appear to have been converted into strengths. One might speak similarly about tensions between members and boards, boards and managers, staff and managers, and so on.

This chapter takes a look at people and relationships from one end of the co-op system to the other. Along the way, we'll meet some real individuals and also eleven composite characters who will help illustrate different roles in the system. Traditionally, organization charts of cooperatives put the members at the top, so we'll start with them.

~

WHAT DO MEMBERS LOOK FOR IN A CO-OP? WHY do they join? While members undoubtedly do a certain amount of calculation of costs and benefits from time to time, most people, on a day-to-day basis, have to go by their gut feelings. So we can also ask, why do members *think* the co-op is beneficial to them? What makes them *trust* that the co-op operates in their interest?

The connection of members to their co-ops is easiest to see when the co-op is relatively new or when its location is isolated. When a co-op is new, many people remember what was there (or not there) before, and why they disliked it enough to form a co-op. Also, when a co-op is in a remote place, far from alternatives and with few other competitors for peoples' hearts or their purses, the significance of the co-op remains clearer, longer. So for a clear-cut case—almost a throwback to the early days of co-ops—consider Hornby Island, a co-op on a small coastal island three ferry rides and half a day's travel away from Vancouver. On a sunny afternoon in May I chatted under the trees in the outdoor coffee shop with two long-time co-op members, Hilary Brown and Muriel Rogers. These two remarkable women have been leaders in multiple roles in the co-operative and in the community. I asked them how they first became involved, and why Hornby Co-op is important to Hornby Island.

Rogers was born in rural Saskatchewan and soaked up the support for co-ops that has been so deeply rooted there. "I guess I was born that way," she says. "My folks were … Saskatchewan farmers, and were members of the Wheat Pool and co-op grocery store. After I was married, my husband and I were members of the credit union that was started up … in the little town where we lived." It was natural to become involved in the co-op in about 1970, a few years after she came to Hornby. As for the co-op, "Well, it's the only store we have," Rogers says. "I mean, that's almost reason enough" to support it. "It's also … pretty much the social centre, certainly, of the island," she comments, and adds, "Almost every organization is getting help from the co-op store."[3]

Hilary Brown was there in the 1940s when the local credit union was created, and in the 1950s when the co-op was set up—"No, I didn't start it," she says, "I co-operated with other people." She remembers when the island consisted of a dozen or so families eking out an isolated living, fishing and farming, without regular ferry service, long before the influxes of young people, artists, nature enthusiasts, retirees, and others who have since transformed the island. "The interesting thing is that it has become the habit now on Hornby" to co-operate, Brown says. "First of all, people try to organize something, then they ask for government assistance. They don't get it; they get turned down, so then they stick together and say what they think about the government.… And then after that they say, well, damn it all; we have to do this. We need that thing, so … let's do it ourselves. So then they start thinking, how can they do it? Then they start scratching their heads and saying, well, maybe we can try [something along] co-operative lines and, in fact, that seems to be the solution a lot of the time."

Hornby Island Co-op's general store sells everything from groceries, gas, hardware, and housewares, to crafts.

In places like Hornby Island there is an organic connection between the needs of the community and the creation and activity of the co-op. In more complicated communities, there is no such organic relationship. The connection between members and the co-op, between community needs and co-operative action, is not so clear or so obvious. This is the situation to which most co-ops in the system have had to adjust, to greater or lesser degrees.

To many in the system who have lived through the change, it seems like a loss of member loyalty—though not everyone agrees. It is certainly a change, from ingrained or presumed loyalty to loyalty that is contingent, that has to be earned all the time, all over again. One who has seen the change is long-time elected member representative "Frank Stefchuk."* Stefchuk was brought up to be loyal to the co-op in his rural community in Saskatchewan, and when a position came open on the local board in 1976, he ran and was elected. He has been on the board continually ever since, through all the difficulties of the 1980s, except for one three-year term he sat out. He has participated actively in FCL district, region, and annual meetings.[4]

Stefchuk describes how his father came to the prairies as an immigrant from eastern Europe, and how the faith shown in them by a co-op manager helped get them established on the land in the 1920s. "I was just a young little punk at that time, but I remember my dad going to town with a wagon and a team of horses.... He came back with a load of lumber" for their new home. "He said, 'I went to the co-op and the manager ... gave me credit for this load of lumber.'" It still surprises him when he thinks of it. "What trust!" Stefchuk says today. "Dad had to go and ask a complete stranger, and this man, who was a manager, had the trust to give this man the credit.... It was probably just a handshake." He remembers his father saying they had to do everything they could to repay the loan. Afterwards, "whenever we went to town ... we never went anywhere to shop but the co-op," whether it was for tack or fabric or food or tools. "We bought everything at the co-operative. I remember once, I had a younger brother, and we'd say, well, dad, can we have this? Or mom and dad, can we have it? And dad would say, well, if we can afford it and [if] we can buy it at the co-op, we'll buy it." With his father's example, "you wouldn't even think of going anywhere to buy anything but at the co-op. I have two daughters and I've tried to train them on the same principles," Stefchuk says. "They have different ideas now and you can't argue with them; they seem to have a point, but by the same token, you know, you don't like to see it that way because all that our parents and grandparents tried to bring to us and give to us, that is sort of being erased now. It's being lost."

---

* Co-op director "Frank Stefchuk" is the first of the eleven composite personalities used in this chapter. Each name is introduced in quotation marks to indicate that the name is not a real one. Each composite represents three to six different people I talked to who had relevant similarities of gender, position, age, career path, outlook, and/or type of co-op. Geographic and ethnic characteristics are generally fictional. When the text reads, "Frank Stefchuk says...," this is equivalent to "a number of long-serving rural co-op directors I interviewed who were active in FCL generally agreed, and one of them says..."

The other composites are staff members Alicia Acland and Emily Freund, junior managers Nora Hurley and Mark Thrane, general managers Bill Haas, Jim Mitchell, and Jean Derone, presidents Abe Greenwood and Bill Maclure, and director Trish Potter. For more about the composite personalities, see the appendix.

Co-ops have adjusted to the fact that members are different. There are still "many people who will do business with the co-op even if it happens to have higher prices simply because … their belief is concrete, you know, their philosophy is strong," Stefchuk says. "There are the others who will, for a very small differential in price, go to the competitor because for them it's bottom line," he says. "Ultimately what happens is people who try … the other side, the greener pasture …, they may stray to the competitors and they may look at their prices and everything else … but many of them will come back because they say they're always willing to pay a little more for service, quality, and they understand that we are locally owned" and that the co-op is a good corporate citizen. This is a much more complex appeal than the stark necessity of Stefchuk's father's time.

One thing that has stayed the same is the appeal of patronage refunds, an old co-op principle that has new life in the CRS. Payment of cash to members at year-end had become less common as co-ops undertook expansions and perceived themselves to be short of capital in the 1970s and early 1980s; but as noted in chapter one, patronage refunds (both from FCL to retails and from retails to members) have been a cornerstone of the system's marketing strategy. FCL estimates that in 2002, more than 90 percent of retails were paying out equity to departing members, and more than 80 percent were making general cash repayments. Part of the refund is allocated to the member's equity account, which they begin to get back only when they turn sixty-five or leave the area; it is the cash portion, in particular, that has been increasing and becoming more common. In the last ten years, retails are estimated to have paid out $739 million in cash to western Canadian co-op members.[5] Cash back on purchases, in addition to quality and service, is a strong marketing device.

Urban co-op director "Trish Potter" is younger, likely the age of Stefchuk's daughters. Potter joined the local co-op in her city, where she operates a small accounting business, in 1985. She served on member committees, then was elected to the board of directors in 1991 and has served ever since. "The older members, I think, generally have a better understanding of what it means that this is a co-op," Potter says, "and that's why there's a much higher percentage of them at the annual meetings and that sort of thing," she says. "I think there's a lot more loyalty among those members too, but the younger members, you know, middle-aged and down, I don't know. I don't think that's very good." At the same time, Potter is part of the demographic group the system is now trying hard to appeal to: younger people with families. Creating a sense of attachment to this group of members, through quality and innovative services, does seem to be working. "As a parent myself and for other parents, there's a big convenience factor in having wonderful Kids Clubs," she says, which have been "phenomenally popular ... it's quite family oriented for the most part."[6]

FCL Region Manager Larry Rupert (who doubles as general manager of Saskatoon Co-op) says that changes to appeal to members like Potter have been successful. "Maybe if anything, some of the younger members were probably ahead of where we were, to be honest with you, but the older members have accepted the changes, too." The marketing changes are based on input. "As an example, here in Saskatoon where I'm most familiar, before we built the new store in the northeast corner [of the city], the Marketplace on Attridge, we talked to people. We had focus groups in that area asking what kinds of services they were looking for, whether they were familiar with co-ops. Some were, some weren't, but they advised" that the co-op's basic plans were appropriate: food and gas close to where they live, to save them time. "There were a few things that we learned from them that we didn't know, too, so we incorporated those into the store and into the adjacent buildings that we're building now" to house tenants and additional services. "What we found is that they were saying they needed a network of family services, so we got a hair dresser in the strip mall and a tan franchise, a dry cleaner—a dry cleaner is one they mentioned that didn't occur to us, we don't have it in our store; they mentioned a flower shop: we put a flower shop in our store as a tenant. So those were some of the things that we didn't think of necessarily because we are primarily intended to be in the food and gas business," Rupert says.[7]

~

OF COURSE, ANY KIND OF BUSINESS CAN RUN FOCUS groups and find out what people think. The difference in a co-op is that the members also *own* the business, and as a result, elect its board of directors, and share in surpluses or (up to the amount of their investment) in losses. As Trish Potter indicated above, one of the concerns in today's co-op movement is that too few members, especially younger ones, know about and make use of these rights.

Frank Stefchuk sighs and says, "Well, we need fifty for a quorum, and we really have to go to get fifty. The last two years we've been fortunate to get enough, but it's a real struggle. We've offered prizes, up to two tickets to a dinner theatre in [the nearest big city] … we've got some nice door prizes we give away to people. [But] unless there's … something going wrong," people stay away. "If things are going smoothly, they['d] just as soon let it; don't get involved."[8]

"Abe Greenwood" is also an elected member-leader in a rural co-op. Greenwood has farmed in northcentral Alberta since 1957, and became a member of his local co-op as soon as he started farming. He was asked to run for the board in 1968, was elected, and has served on the board ever since—thirty-six years. He has been president of the board for twenty-one years, and member participation has been on his mind. "Meetings are [a] little problem that we have," Greenwood admits. "I can't say that we've been too successful [at] having a big turnout at meetings." As a result, it's hard to "[know] where our members stand in what we're doing." Greenwood's co-op has more than forty-five hundred active members, "and we get eighty or ninety or a hundred out to a meeting at the most. Usually around eighty, which is perhaps not that good. We've put supper meetings on," he says. "People come for supper and leave when the meeting starts. So." What do you do? He remembers when the co-op was smaller and a couple of hundred people attended, filling the town hall. "Now it seems as we become more successful, we seem to have less interest." "They must think things are going pretty well … [that's] the way that we read it, anyway," he says.[9]

It's not generally different in urban co-ops. For a comparison I asked "Bill Maclure," who has been president of his urban co-op for the past eleven years. He first became involved with the co-op, as a member, soon after he moved to the city in 1970; and through involvement in various issues and co-op committees, he ran for the board of directors and was elected in 1982. Since his retirement as a schoolteacher, he has been able to devote himself to his role as president.

"I do believe there is a responsibility as a citizen of the country, as

a member of a co-operative, to be involved in some way in the democratic process," Maclure says. "When we only have about .35 of 1 percent of members … actually participating in the democratic process,
there's always the risk that small interest groups can take control," he
worries. "One of the goals the board's taken on is to try and stimulate
interest," he says, "through telephone and/or electronic voting, trying
to find a new format for our annual meeting that might stimulate
greater interest … make it a family event, bring families out somehow.
We're going to do it on a Saturday" at a large facility instead of a weekday night at a meeting hall.[10]

Co-ops are struggling, like all democratic institutions, to find out
what democracy means to younger people today, and how to make it
interesting. With all the hand-wringing, the co-ops may be too hard on
themselves. The simple truth appears to be that members take democracy, at least in its traditional forms, for granted. According to polls and
anecdotal information, they like transparency and accountability, but
that doesn't mean they have to be in there all the time voting—worse
than that, many have become alienated and suspicious of voting
processes. The democratic framework has to be there, but democracy
seems to have become a kind of commitment or value statement of the
organization rather than an actual mass-participatory procedure.
Whatever the resolution to these issues, co-ops will need to focus on
some significant pieces that make important differences to their operations. How to keep particular interests from influencing the co-op, as
President Maclure asks. How to find the capable directors, community
leaders, and representatives that the co-op needs for its governance—a
key concern of many directors I talked to, such as Stefchuk and Potter,
Greenwood and Maclure, who spend a lot of time networking and
recruiting and grooming successors. And how to educate members better about the importance of their choices.

Deficiencies in member education are most glaring in one, potentially dangerous, kind of circumstance: when members demand the
impossible or expect contradictory things from their co-operative. This
is why consumer information, business information, marketing programs, and patronage refunds are among the most important forms of
co-operative education, because they signal connections between
actions and consequences, choices and impacts. What's important in

any co-op is the trade-offs involved, economics being about what you do with scarce resources. Woe to the co-op whose members don't intuitively or consciously grasp the trade-offs they face as a group and as individuals.

"There are frustrations, yes," concedes Maclure. "You know there are some people you could never please no matter how hard you try; they're just never going to be pleased and you have to live with that.... The fact is, the customer is not always right, and sometimes you have to have the courage to tell them that"—even when the customer is also the owner.[11]

It's quite possible for members to abuse co-operatives.

"I think there's an expectation of customers that co-ops should be able to compete with the biggest and the best that the industry has to offer, not realizing how large in scope some of these competitors really are," says General Manager "Bill Haas." Haas is one of the system's relatively younger general managers. A bit over forty years of age, he started work for the co-op with a part-time job when he was a high-school student. He stayed after graduation, worked in lumber and hardware, became a department manager, did his GM training, and had his first posting at a small rural co-op in the late eighties. He managed three, successively larger retails, before arriving at his current assignment in 1996.

Haas says people expect co-ops to offer the same cut-rate prices as their huge competitors, and at the same time, they expect extra from the co-op. "I think the reason that co-ops have a tougher time," he says, "is that we're so personally connected with our customers in a way that perhaps private business or a corporation isn't. If I was to use the example of Eaton's as a company, when they started to shut their stores, while there were certainly those who were outraged by the decision and disappointed after many years of being able to support them, I don't think that that disappointment ever rose to the level of criticism, perhaps even abuse—personal abuse by members who felt betrayed by [a] co-op for closing [a] department." Haas has been through that. When he had to shut down a department, he faced numerous complaints from members, especially old-timers upset that their co-op was shutting something down. They took it personally. But then he asked, have you noticed the new competition in town? You've been there? And your friends have too? It's that busy? Well, how long did you expect us to last?

Haas doesn't blame the members for this, but he does say it is important for co-ops to conduct careful strategic planning, signalling to their members where they are going. "We plant seeds well in advance of things that we want to do," is how Haas puts it.[12] If members aren't carefully prepared for what the co-op needs to do to make money, they may demand unrealistically low prices or maintain pressure for other policies the co-op cannot sustain.

Frank Stefchuk sees not only a pressure from members for lower prices, but, in his rural retail, a tendency to exploit accounts receivable with the co-op. They think the co-op will be softer on them over unpaid bills just because it's a co-op. "It's really dealing with people they know," he explains. They think they "can maybe get away with a little more; where the bank says, well look, if you don't do it, we're going to do this and this.... And I think that the co-op is probably the last one that gets paid, well maybe not the last, but we see it as that."[13] This is a complaint I heard from many rural co-op members.

What's the problem with members wanting low prices, their favourite departments kept open, generous credit policies—when all the while they themselves are shopping down the street or over in the next town? Well, in one sense there's nothing wrong. They are within their rights, and it does put pressure on the co-op to be creative and efficient. But it is shortsighted. When members don't pay their bills, they are, in the long run, cheating themselves. When members demand low prices—beyond a certain point that depends on the co-op and the business it's in—they are threatening to starve it of the margins it needs to operate well, invest in new facilities, and do other things that members like. They are beggaring themselves, getting a quick benefit today—low price—that jeopardizes years of benefits they could get in the future. That's why co-ops charge market prices, as best they can, and distribute surplus after revenues and costs are known and funds have been set aside for the business's future development. Such problems are not questions of co-op philosophy or old-time morality; they are common sense. Typically, co-op members need some education, somewhere along the way, in order to draw out and strengthen their common sense. Typically, this happens when they interact with other members—or with co-op staff.

President Greenwood says staff make "all the difference in the world." That's the thing "that avoids conflict with our members.... Poor staff members can create more problems than, I don't know what else; but providing good service and being pleasant, and understanding where the members and customers are coming from ... that's something that's immeasurable," he says.[14]

But it's more than treating members well. "Jean Derone," another of the younger general managers in the co-op system, is one of many people who spoke to me about how staff can communicate the co-op's message to members. Derone grew up in a rural community, where she started working for the co-op while she was in high school. She moved through several departments in the 1980s, also acquiring training in marketing and management from FCL and from postsecondary institutions. She became a general manager in 1999. Derone recalls how her receptionist "was talking to one mom about local businesses and how we should support them," and made the point that her children were going to want to have jobs. "[If] you don't support us, how are we going to support your child when your child comes in for employment?" Derone's co-op, like many others, makes a practice of employing local students, often giving them their first work experience and helping them develop skills and habits that literally change their lives. The receptionist was making a pretty powerful argument for why local people should support their store.[15]

I was reminded of this when visiting a co-op and chatting with a staff member about her work as a cashier. She mentioned "co-op principles" and I asked her what these were. "Local ownership," she said. "Co-ordinating fundraising," like having the union executive and the board of directors out doing fundraising together. "You're making a difference in the community and strutting your stuff" at community events. That's a co-op in a nutshell, as explained by a nonmanagement employee.

~

THE PROFESSIONALIZATION OF CO-OPERATIVES IN THE modern era has meant a growing importance of staff, not only for the technical operations of the co-op, but to animate its relationship with its members. Staff in retail co-ops today require a standard of training and proficiency far beyond what was needed two or three decades ago. In addition, every staff member is also, in effect, a member-relations officer of the co-op. Even those who work in back rooms interact during their off-duty hours with friends and neighbours, spreading good or bad impressions of the co-op, and pursuing involvements in community activities.

Staff come to local co-ops or to FCL for a variety of reasons. Rarely is it a philosophical commitment to co-ops. But at the same time, if the organization were not a community-based business, the job might not be there for them, in their town or neighbourhood, at all; and sometimes they know that. Once they join, it seems to take a few years for the sometimes subtle differences of co-operative work to sink in. Over time, the people I talked to say that the wider co-operative structure and environment make a difference to their work, especially at the retail level. Not one person I spoke with thought the work relationships in co-ops were the same as those in competing organizations. They thought they were, in general, better. This was particularly true of people who actually had experience in other companies. The sample of people I spoke to is not large enough to be representative. It reflects mainly those who stayed in the co-op system and who found something exciting in it, who have gotten ahead or who want to. I talked to only a few people who had left co-op employment, but even then, I was struck by how much goodwill they retained towards their former employers as institutions. Clearly, there is something going on in co-op employment that is contributing to the system's success.

"Alicia Acland" has been a co-op employee for eight years in a Saskatchewan city. She is a young woman in her twenties who sees the co-op as a good job, is proud of the work she does, and is beginning to see there could be more possibilities for her in the system. "I applied to [the] co-op. I was encouraged by my mother. My parents have been co-op members for years," she says, explaining how she came to be a co-op employee. Acland is a young woman, not tall, but she gives an impression of some strength or toughness. She has a short, direct style of speaking—a bit clipped and to the point. She talks about the physical challenges and unpleasant aspects of her work, but says, "I like the people. I like the manager. I like the way people are treated. The benefits are awesome." When I ask, she says what impresses her is the 100 percent coverage: students, young single mothers ... "They don't discriminate against anybody." At a large oil company where she also worked, "there was no raise, few benefits, no prospects.... You can work your way towards something better with co-op. You're not stuck." She would like to see herself in a more responsible position one day and has started taking some courses, at the co-op's expense, to improve her skills.[16]

"It's kind of like a family," Acland says—using a phrase I heard many times, from new employees right through to forty-year senior managers. "We work together as a team ... we know how each other works. You can go to your boss and talk about something and know it won't go to anyone else. They're very professional that way.... They care about you." What makes co-op different? I asked her. "Friendliness, customer care, helpfulness." And, she says, "People go to other departments to help out, and can fill in for each other." She describes being rudely treated by staff at a large-format competing store, and comments that she doesn't think that would ever happen at her co-op.

Like Acland, "Emily Freund" came to her co-op simply because she was looking for work, but it has become more than just a job. She is in her late thirties, with twelve years experience working for the retail co-op in her home town in Manitoba. She did other work and had a family before joining the co-op. "I shopped co-op before I started working. I originally decided to work for just one year, to make money for a family vacation," Freund explains. She began work part time as a cashier and stock clerk. "The money was *good*. It got me out of the home. The staff was good. Co-op was really respected in the community.... I couldn't leave—it [would have been] like leaving family."[17] As she has gained experience, she has become a supervisor (senior staff, but still in-scope of the union) in her department. She's considering the possibility that she could be department manager one day.

"What I love about it is the people," Freund stresses. "There's the customers coming in, you get to know the customers who come in everyday; and I like the people I work with, and that's a big part of it." There is a comfort to the familiarity. "Everybody knows each other," she says. "I guess [if] you've started at an entry level, having done stocking, cashiering, and working in the different departments, it gives a really broad look at how the store functions. Having that time to get to know how the store functions and the customers and the community" is what makes the job meaningful. "One thing that comes to mind is with the co-op [customer] being an owner or a member-owner ... the customers do become more involved," Freund says. "I think they just feel more, I don't know, they feel a sense of pride [and a] sense of caring what happens in the store." Chances are that if members see something they don't like, they'll tell her about it rather than just leaving.

"My role as a supervisor is, first of all, to ensure we have excellent customer service," Freund says. She describes her co-op's customer-service system, which involves supervisors rating staff every two weeks on the service they provide, weekly for those on probation. The staff have to sign off on the evaluations, "so they're in the loop," she explains. "Our primary focus is customer service"; beyond that, she tries to ensure that all staff understand their jobs in the broadest sense, so that, for example, they know the full range of co-op services and can answer questions about other departments.

In different ways, Acland and Freund describe a work culture that features stability, teamwork, individual self-improvement, and an emphasis on quality. It exhibits these characteristics in part because of the relationship with the customers, who, in a co-op, are also member-owners. While these characteristics are undoubtedly not universal or evenly developed in every co-op, they say something about the system's strengths, and about the secrets of the more successful co-ops in the system. As you go up the hierarchy and talk to people in management, they become more precise and more articulate in explaining what is different in co-ops.

"Nora Hurley" and "Mark Thrane" are junior managers in the co-op system. Hurley began working in her home town co-op in Alberta soon after she left high school in 1982. She worked part time in the administrative office as a secretary, gradually developed her skills with data processing and accounting, and now serves as office manager. Thrane worked in the private food trade before he joined the co-op system. He was an employee at a for-profit specialty food store before he moved to a new community in western Canada in 1995. Since then he has worked in co-op deli and produce, and in 2001 became assistant store manager.

"I've always been very fortunate in the jobs I've had, to work with great people," Hurley says. "A lot of them have been mentors for me as well." She credits FCL's training programs and employee assistance family policies with helping her get ahead. "Federated ended up paying 75 percent of all of my costs," Hurley explains. "So I was working, got an education, didn't have any student loans, nothing like that," and ended up qualified for a professional management position. "If I was working for a [for-profit] business, I probably wouldn't have had the opportunity to advance. There are opportunities within the CRS to move up into more responsible positions," she says. She stresses this to applicants for entry-level positions. In doing the interviewing, she has discovered that her co-op has a reputation in its community as an excellent employer and a good place to work.[18]

Unlike Hurley, Thrane worked for other businesses before he came to the co-op. It was a conscious decision based on a straight-up comparison of what they offered. "What [seemed] most interesting to me," Thrane says, "was the commitment to both the members, as opposed to, say, shareholders, and the commitment to the community that they were involved in, and how [the co-ops] were very integrated into the communities that they served." The role that the co-operative plays in the community "becomes like a tool that you can use for marketing, marketing our actual company and stuff, which is very interesting," he explains. "Well, with my previous employer, the environment was a little bit more corporate." In the co-op, "it's a totally different dynamic.... The management team seems to be able to move a lot quicker to take advantage of specific things that happen in the industry that are [relevant] to such a small market ... as opposed to ... a North American market, which is something that a larger company would have to deal with." In a big corporation "it was very difficult to move in a direction when something presented itself very quickly." In a co-op "you get to hear from your members as often as you want to. I think it's one of those things that we do a very good job of, but we could always do better.... Our members, they are vocal, they want us to succeed, and if we listen to them, they'll continue to shop." But local character is also important in another way. Thrane explains that his spouse has a good job and they are rooted in their community. The co-op is one of the only companies where he could advance to a position of such responsibility without transfers that would uproot his family.[19]

The role of retail co-operatives in providing local employment and developing local people struck me when I visited Yorkton Co-op. As I walked through the busy Marketplace store, a block south off the main thoroughfare—crowded with customers at 10 A.M. on a weekday in June —I picked up a copy of the Yorkton Co-op *News*. The cover featured the co-op's new agro centre and cardlock facility, as well as the co-op's new website, explaining, "Unlike most retail websites, its purpose will not be to sell product [at least, not yet]. Its purpose will be to inform people … about our Co-op. It will include a quick tour of our facilities, our mission and objectives, information about our Kids Club and what we do in our communities. Visit us … at www.yorktoncoop.com." Inside there is a feature on "The Co-op Team," stressing the employment created by the co-op for local people. It's a good representation of the role co-operatives like Yorkton's play in their local communities.

"Your Co-op provides employment for 124 people in the communities that it serves," states the newsletter. "One of the Co-op's objectives is to develop and reward employees who effectively utilize their abilities for the benefit of the Co-op." The co-op stresses competitive salaries, statutory benefits, and added benefits for all permanent employees, including part time. "Another important benefit of Co-op employment is ongoing training and skill development which can lead to excellent opportunities for advancement in the Co-op Retailing System or at our own Co-op. Nine of our Co-op's twelve department managers began their working careers with the Yorkton Co-op and grew into their present positions. Several other employees got their start with us and then moved on to bigger and better things within the CRS.

"Co-op employees, together with their families, purchase or rent homes in our communities, pay taxes and use retail services and facilities. They volunteer their spare time with service clubs, minor sports, church, school and other community groups. Your co-op and its employees help to make your community a good place to live." A sidebar advertises

"OPPORTUNITY ... SUCCESS ... CAREERS WITH A DIFFERENCE"

~

THE STAFF CULTURE AT FEDERATED ITSELF IS A little different. In the region offices and even more so in home office, the environment is further from the individual members—they aren't coming in off the street looking for service. But still, a number of FCL staff come from backgrounds in retail co-ops, and in any case it is all integrated into the same network, so it's not totally divorced from the retail environment. One of my interviewees, who formerly worked in FCL, told me, "I suspect that a lot of the staff in Federated don't really view their job as much different from their counterparts across the street. I think in a retail co-op they do tend to.... As you move up the levels of the staff, there's more identification with the company than there is at the first levels." But, he adds, "there's a certain satisfaction in working for an organization, whether it's in [a small town] or Saskatoon, working for an organization that ... you know [is] not going to go bankrupt tomorrow, and it's not going to get sold tomorrow, and it's not going to disappear." At one time, "that maybe would have been kind of a hollow thing, but not in the last ten or fifteen years," when so many other companies have restructured, changed ownership, or closed their doors.[20]

Working in FCL is not for everyone. "So-and-so is really well suited to working in a retail," someone commented. "They would be stifled in the wholesale company, where they would have to work with procedures, hierarchies, approvals, policies to follow." The more free-wheeling environment of a retail co-op is better suited to managers who need that autonomy to exercise their creativity, who need daily contact with members to stimulate their thinking, who need to use their people skills with the general public. FCL has a specialized purpose, which it sees as efficient delivery of services to retail co-ops. As one senior manager put it, "Federated's role is to provide goods and services to the retails at a competitive level, and provide expertise, and derive the maximum amount of profitability from doing that. And then to move that profitability back to the retails based on their support through services and the goods. So what we're really saying is, we're a wholesaler and we're behind the scenes; the retail co-ops are the front line. Federated doesn't really want to be on the front page of the newspaper."[21] The comments of half a dozen interviewees can be summed up as follows: Since the cutbacks of the 1980s, FCL has become more bottom-line driven, more hard-nosed or choosy about decisions, and more determined to hire and promote people who suit the company's style and purpose.

Three stories, each told to me by several different people, illustrate FCL's approach. First—a small thing, but indicative of the emphasis on economy—when the home office's records threatened to outgrow the filing space, as happens eventually in any organization, the directive was to weed the records to fit the space, rather than let them grow by providing new storage. Similar economies are evident in use of equipment and support staff. If it isn't *needed,* the money isn't spent—with need rigorously interpreted. Then there is the company's policy on vacant positions. Just as every major spending decision requires justification, so, too, do hirings—no one is automatically replaced. Each vacant position is scrutinized. In effect, the company tries to do without positions, reassigns essential work, and sees what can be dropped before it resorts to hiring. Finally, there is the interview policy. Each new employee in Federated is interviewed by multiple levels of managers. While lower-level interviewers narrow the field to those who have the required skills and qualifications, senior managers look at each candidate for what some call corporate fit and others call simply attitude. No employee is hired without being interviewed by a company vice-president, or in the case of regional employees, by the region manager.

When I asked CEO Thompson, he told me his advice to new employees would be, "You go out and work with a good attitude, a positive attitude, and you work hard, and you have some fun.... Attitude is critical." The company looks, above all, for the right attitude, "because attitude you can't correct, you can't change. You can develop people and anything else, but if you have a negative attitude, guaranteed, you can't change those people. I always have a saying that a positive attitude builds—a negative attitude destroys." Skills, he says, the human-resources people will take care of. Attitude is the key. "How I measure that is this way—if somebody asks me about an employee who works for Federated, I never want to be ashamed to say, that employee works for Federated. I always want to be able to say, that's a great employee we have, with a great attitude; because that really makes a lot of difference out in our communities as to what people think about the co-op."[22]

The result is a tightly integrated culture that can look a bit mysterious to outsiders. One senior manager put it this way: The culture is "to be a winning team. We all want to be a part of a winning team." Integral to this are clear guidelines and open communication. "The vast majority of our employees understand and they appreciate that there [are] guidelines; they appreciate [that] there's leadership; and they appreciate [that] there's communication," he says. "We encourage our departments to have monthly meetings," make sure they have discussions of new policies and directions, and in general encourage what he calls an "open-door, family kind of policy.... I think that's a bit of our culture, for sure: a full-family atmosphere, and the trust and the direct leadership that's there, and understanding, and the encouragement of communication."[23]

Another manager contrasts the co-op system with large corporate workplaces. "What I find with the co-op people is they don't get stagnant," he says. "I think part of the reason is because there's so much opportunity here; you can go so many ways. You know if you find yourself in a position that you're maybe not happy in, you can use it as a training and a learning position and an opportunity to move up [or] laterally. And that's another thing I talk to the young people about. Just because you're coming into this company as an agrologist or a feed sales rep, that doesn't mean that's what you're going to be for the rest of your life.... The company has so much to offer because of its complexity of retail and wholesale and manufacturing and distribution." The other difference that strikes him is that "people are very easy with each other. People ... act and react naturally. I mean, there [are] not people carrying false façades ... you don't see that kind of stuff around this company." Everyone is on a first-name basis.[24]

There are certain common features across the system, whether employees are in retails, FCL offices, or subsidiaries. Stability, continuity, and the feeling of family are among the things many system employees told me about. The importance of attitude, of being a people-oriented person able to work as part of a team, was mentioned as well by almost everyone. There is also the consistent theme of opportunity and personal development for those who fit. Finally, the system has achieved a blending of hierarchy, personal roles and responsibilities, and informality in the workplace. It is striking to find frontline employees referring to their CEO or general manager by his or her first name, as they did almost everywhere I went. This doesn't reduce the manager's authority—quite the contrary.

~

ANOTHER CONVERSATION: WHILE WAITING FOR MY debit-card transaction to go through, I listened to the two young co-op gas-bar attendants chatting behind the counter. The young woman was evidently thinking of looking for different work elsewhere, something besides pumping gas. "I'm not planning on being here forever," she said to the other attendant as she handed me my debit slip. I lingered for a moment, curious. Her colleague shrugged noncommittally. "You think you'll stay forever if you're over there?" he said to her.

It was her turn to shrug. "So, what are you doing tonight?"

I was tempted to tell the young woman that her boss, the general manager of her whole retail, had started off at her age pumping gasoline for his local co-op.

In fact, of twenty-three people I interviewed for this book who are or have been co-op general managers, sixteen had started off working in entry-level jobs in retail co-ops—most of them as teenagers. They had been gas-pump attendants, stock clerks, cashiers, secretaries, truck drivers, produce clerks, and so on. While this pattern is changing somewhat with the professionalization of the system and the growing importance of formal education, the fact remains that the system's culture, especially at the key level of retail general managers, has been shaped by people who worked their way up from within the system. Of the seven other GMs I interviewed, five were basically hired right out of postsecondary education into accounting or management positions in the co-ops. The people I interviewed agreed, generally, that it is rare, and difficult, for anyone to transfer from outside into co-op management at the GM level or higher. The job of a co-op general manager is simply too difficult, and there's almost nothing outside the co-op system that can prepare you for it. As I listened to people talk about their jobs as GMs, it occurred to me that these people were the purest, likely most creative, and certainly most multitalented entrepreneurs in their communities. They were on top of everything their co-ops were doing. They knew their communities. And they knew FCL and the co-op system inside out, or most of them did. They are the system's key links, the people who connect the local community to the wider co-op network, the people who make marketing happen, and more than any other individuals, determine the success or failure of their co-ops.

~

I N THE PRECEDING PAGES, WE'VE ALREADY MET A couple of composite characters based on co-op general managers:* Bill Haas, who's been a GM for more than fourteen years, and Jean Derone, who has nearly five years experience in that role. One of their senior colleagues in the network of co-op retail managers is "Jim Mitchell." Mitchell worked part time at the co-op when he was in high school in Saskatchewan, and subsequently got a job in the co-op food store in his home town. He worked his way up the ladder, from senior clerk on the food floor to produce manager. That was when he noticed the note in the coffee room about FCL's general-manager training. He did the training, gaining experience in larger and more diversified co-ops, and became a general manager in 1980. He also worked for FCL for a year as a retail advisor, until he became a GM at his current co-op in 1984. With nearly a quarter century of management experience in the system, Mitchell has seen it all, from the tough times of the 1980s to today.

---

* General manager, or GM, is the most common term for the top manager in a retail co-op—the person who doesn't report to any other supervisor, only to the board of directors. In the wider business world, these people have come to be known as chief executive officers, or CEOs, and some co-ops (notably Calgary) use that terminology. It is also common within FCL to refer to them as retail managers, to distinguish them from managers in the wholesale. All of these terms are used interchangeably in this chapter, and all refer to the same people.

When I asked him about the job of a retail manager, he almost chuckled. "It might be easier just to say what he doesn't do." There's the administration, management, and running a store. You have to have all the commodity knowledge that your competitors' managers have. There's labour relations and bargaining, which would be done for you if you ran a store in a bigger company. There's watching the finances, the balance sheet, the capital and debt. There's planning and developing new initiatives; relating to the board of directors; relating to Federated and knowing how to use their strengths; being involved in the community. It's quite a job description. "I believe that you need initiative" to deal with all this, Mitchell says. There are "so many things that we have to be," he goes on to explain. "We're not like a lot of the other businesses," where "you're spoon-fed so many things," where "everything comes down the line to you. You basically just do whatever [they lay] on your plate. In the co-op system it's so different because you're almost running your own store." You have information and advice, but that's all. There's no one else to make it happen. "The dedication that we have as managers and employees, I think, has definitely helped the co-operatives grow and succeed.... There are people who have put a lifetime in, and that is our life.... I always say we should run it like we own it, but stay within the guidelines [and] the policies that are laid out by the board of directors. Lots of times those policies are already directed by management because we're involved" in the planning that goes into them—"Democracy in action."[25]

Performance is what counts for a retail manager. That's one reason there are different styles of management in the system, because anything that gets results may be acceptable, and anything that doesn't, ultimately isn't. "I always maintain, and to the people who I've trained over the years I always say, you're only as secure as your last month's financial statement," is how Mitchell puts it. You can't ever let up. "If at any time the development of our co-op slows down because of my health, then I better get the hell out of there, and I firmly believe that. Move over and let someone else do it. Lead, follow, or get the hell out of the way."

Within that overall framework, Mitchell sees two different areas of responsibility. "One of them is to service the business that you have and see that the rapport is there." This is the management side of the job—

administration, building a team, keeping it working, watching the finances, relating with the staff and the board. "And the other is, in somebody else's failure or somebody else's ability to change how they've done business, is always an opportunity. So we have to be always aware on an ongoing basis of opportunities ... that are created for us." That's the entrepreneurial side of a retail manager's job—the creative opportunity to make new things happen, to find unique things to do that are suited to the local community, the co-op's market opportunities, and its members' needs.

Haas agrees with the picture Mitchell paints, and adds a few more strokes. "As a GM, you're responsible for every aspect of the operation, be it people, be it the assets, be it the financial balance sheet, the cash flow, everything. Even our department managers are much, much more in tune to manage their departments as a business. And, as a comparison, I've had a chance to go [to] courses and [meet] people from different companies, vice-presidents of other organizations, and they do not have the control or the expectations that we have of our people," he says. Co-op department managers have some autonomy, depending on the GM's style, but the retail manager himself or herself has no immediate backup, no superior to report to. "Sometimes you feel a little isolated," Haas says. "You learn very quickly, after you've been around awhile, to get a network of people together who are doing the same job as you are. We network a lot," he explains, bouncing ideas off each other to find out how others have handled the same problems.[26] But while there are courses, trainee positions, mentoring arrangements, conferences and so on set up by FCL, retail managers generally have to learn the most important lessons by experience.

Jean Derone recalls that "sometimes you feel like you're out there without that support, without anybody understanding what you're going through." She remembers very difficult things she had to do, and mentions calling people who had families to support into her office to tell them they were being laid off.[27]

Then there are the day-to-day challenges. "Well for me, anyway," Derone continues, "it's a lot more like being general maintenance. If there's something that needs to be done, whether it's mopping out a bathroom or looking at a compressor and trying to figure out what is happening, it just seems to fall on my shoulders. It's a case of well, it's

got to be done, so let's do it. After awhile, I suppose, you do get a few
notches on the old axe handle [and you] know who to call, or have seen
the same problem before; but I swear there's so much that you have to
know! I'm glad I don't have my Class 1 because I know I'd end up driving truck," she smiles. "If you've been in a locale for awhile, people start
to expect that, with your position, you know everything" from the latest prices to the best ways to handle personal problems. "Customers
and staff think you're a minister, a financial advisor, a commodity
expert, a merchandising expert; and in reality that's just a jack of all
trades and a master of none," she says. "You never know what's going
to be on your plate from one day to the next."

"I've heard [that] if you are a co-op manager, so many more doors
are open" at the competition, Derone adds. They would love to hire
people with experience as co-op managers, "because you not only
understand about the merchandising, about stock rotations, but you
also have all the bookkeeping aspects down pat. For a lot of the major
food companies, larger home centres, and petroleum outlets, so much
is done by a head office. In the Co-op Retailing System, it's all done at
your own doorstep." The system is "kind" to managers "because you've
got a lot of resources out there to help you whenever you need it. But
it can also be very harsh when it comes to a situation where it is considered that you should know better. With all the information a GM
must know and continually maintain, it can become overwhelming. To
say the very least, life as a GM is one of constant learning … it never
gets boring!"

The creative side of a GM's job means that some of them have come
up with unique and intriguing innovations, small or sometimes not-so-
small ways of meeting local needs. Some of these have subsequently
spread to other co-ops. The innovation process in the co-op system is
the subject of chapter three, but for now, let's just say that one significant part of co-op innovation is the result of the relative independence
and autonomy of retail managers—and that jack-of-all-trades job
description Derone refers to.

"When you look back on some of the things you did or that you
were called to do, especially when you were very young, you kind of
wonder today how you ever got through them," Bill Haas says. "You
remember the lessons [and] maybe now when you look back, you say,

I sure should have done this differently, I sure learned a lot by doing it the wrong way," he says. When I ask him for details, he replies, "Oh man, maybe sometimes how to deal with people a little better." I get the impression that the so-called soft side of management, the people skills, the tact and diplomacy—which he displays in striking measure—are things he learned over the years. You wouldn't know it unless he told you. "Or you learned little things, like you get things when you first become a GM of a very small retail," he says. Like many of today's co-op managers, Haas had the opportunity to learn lessons on a small scale, in a small rural co-op, before he moved on to bigger organizations. "Lots of weird things happen in small towns. And they happen to you, and you have to make decisions on them. You go back after and you say, you know, maybe if I had handled it *this* way I would have had a little less trouble with it, or maybe the board would have bought into it a little better if I had done it *this* way. You learn some really basic skills."[28]

Managers such as Haas and Derone are typical of many co-op GMs who learned their trade in the last twenty years. Most started off in very small, usually rural, retails, and then went through a succession of progressively larger or more complex retails until they arrived at their present-day assignment. This process is an interesting one, and critical to the system. It is generally facilitated by FCL. Managers in the wholesale monitor the performances of retail GMs, keeping an eye on people they consider capable of taking on bigger things. When a vacancy comes up, there may be a figurative tap on someone's shoulder, perhaps a quick phone call, to alert the prospect to the vacancy for which FCL considers them suitable. Or perhaps the vacancy is simply posted and distributed within the system, inviting applications from anyone who is interested. Despite Federated's role, all the people involved make their own decisions. The managers choose where to apply, and some of them prefer to stay put. The co-ops decide whom to interview and whom to hire.

This process exemplifies the way that retails and FCL work together, and the tensions between them. Co-ops, especially small ones, sometimes feel as if they're being raided—they get a good manager who achieves results, and the person applies for a job somewhere else and is gone. Other co-ops have found a niche as, in effect, GM training grounds. This assures them of a steady stream of good, bright, young managers, even if no single one of them stays for long. Formally, the co-ops call the shots. FCL operates in the background, facilitating, co-ordinating, a nudge here and a word there. Not all co-ops like having FCL do manager searches for them, or hire the people FCL representatives recommend. But over the years, a good deal of trust has built up, perhaps grudgingly at first, as many retail boards have recognized that this system provides them with good, well-trained managers who are suited to their destination co-ops.

One of the most demanding aspects of the manager-development system lies in the seemingly inescapable requirement that people who want to be GMs must be mobile. As department managers, as trainees, as young general managers, they may move through a succession of co-ops—more than a dozen in the cases of some people in the system—often for only a year or less in many postings. This presupposes a special commitment on the part of the managers in question, and their families.

When I ask FCL Human Resources Senior Vice-President Zakreski about his advice for aspiring managers, his jesting answer is, "Don't get married. I'm kidding." But then he goes on in a more serious vein. "No, it's mobility that is our biggest problem. No question about that. And, of course, society has changed, and with the changing society you get into two-career families, and then you get children who become more attached to the community and have more say in terms of what happens in the family than what perhaps they had in the past. So mobility is a key issue.... We have all kinds of people who could move up higher into more responsible jobs, but [lack of] mobility is preventing [it], and for the right reasons." It's not just consideration for spouses and children, but also increasingly care for aging parents that keeps people rooted in particular locations. But more generally, in some cases "you become ingrained in the community, you become, through your work in the co-operative ... very involved in the community, and you just don't want to give that up, and so you develop a quality of life." But, he adds, "we still manage in any given year" to move people through the system. "We're well over two hundred placements" per year (employee transfers of all types, not just GMs) in the system's approximately three hundred co-operatives, "so that's quite substantial."[29]

Some old-timers suggest that there is less moving and transferring today than in the past, that the jumps are fewer and the stays are longer. But even young managers today remember that their early years, especially, were hard. Derone comments, "My family was more like Gypsies" than a family that stayed in one place. "We didn't unpack boxes for years at a time. We'd just leave them packed up because soon we'd be moving again." At the same time, she adds, "I've never found any pressure within the system that you have to move at all. I guess it's just based on your own motivation or your interest, because the more that you move around, the greater your experiences and likely, I would think, the better the opportunities" for advancement in the system.[30]

A number of managers move around the minimum amount, then aim for a good retail opening in a community that's good for their family—and stay there. Other people worry, though, that managers don't move when probably they should, from the point of view of developing the system's talent and getting the best people in the co-ops where they can make the most difference. Some are worried that the system is losing good people altogether, people who decide to make their careers in some other organization. It is noticeable that there are relatively few female retail managers in the system. Since those I spoke to reported no particular barriers or hindrances within the co-ops, the discrepancy is likely attributable to the fact that husbands have been less likely than wives to make sacrifices with respect to their own careers and incomes.[31] As the system, through sheer demographic transition, begins to require more and more younger managers, it is questionable whether it will be able to afford anything that reduces the available talent pool. With the changes in people's lives, long-time General Manager Jim Mitchell thinks "we may have to look at the moving policies that we have and make that a little easier."[32]

Given the challenges and responsibilities, you might wonder why anyone would want the job of a retail general manager. But the challenge and responsibility is likely what attracts them. In most western Canadian communities, there is no other job like it—to run what is often a large and diversified enterprise, in the face of stiff competition, to develop new initiatives to meet local needs, doing this without taking orders from head office, but still as part of a wider network, and knowing that what you are doing is important for the local community. And the job is not without status; co-ops and their managers stand out in their communities. General Manager Haas comments, "I won Kinsmen of the Year. I've won different accolades, but I couldn't have done it without the support of where I work. When you do community stuff, they view you as the co-op," he says. "Very rarely do I get introduced as [Bill Haas]; it's always [Bill Haas], the manager of the co-op. And I'm proud of that. And my children, they're so proud of it, Dad works for the co-op."[33]

What retail managers do today is a far cry from what their predecessors did twenty-five and more years ago. The expectations are higher. The skill sets and the professionalism are much greater. But perhaps most importantly, the way managers talk about internal team building (among their staff, boards, members, and community) and external team building (with FCL and the wider system) is different from what you hear about old-time co-op retail managers. Managers' independence used to mean they could run their co-op like a fiefdom, with, shall we say, sometimes less-refined human-relations skills than those displayed by today's managers. Management in the CRS, at least at the retail level, seems to have become softer in style, yet with higher expectations about results.

An FCL veteran talks to me about hard-slugging, old-time retail managers who had total control of their local co-ops, were fearless about not avoiding or perhaps even pursuing confrontation, and were happy to give both barrels to FCL managers in public meetings. When they tore a strip off you, you remembered the experience. But these older managers were also willing to walk the floor, to pitch in with their own hands, to do whatever needed to be done to make their store, their co-op, a success. They were like lords in their fiefdoms, with a style that was perhaps authoritarian but also down-to-earth populist. "Very independent, but also, in most cases, very, very successful," this FCL official recalls. "To be honest, I didn't always agree with their style, but, you know, I always appreciated input from a manager whether he was right or wrong, if he had a good operation.... They attacked you, but you know, it wasn't personal." And then there were the old-style FCL managers who fought right back, and he mentions one of the region managers of the day as an example. "Sparring" is how he describes the exchanges. Late 1970s CEO Bill Bergen was plagued by what my interviewee called "an army camp of aggressive managers."[34]

Today you notice that many of the younger managers, the ones who move around and upward in the system, have a softer personal approach. They stress teamwork. They deflect credit to others, or include them in the spotlight. They wear the same uniforms as their staff. Some of them take turns on the sales floor when the office is quiet—take a close look next time you're in a co-op store. The person bagging your groceries might be the CEO. They speak in measured tones. They keep their emotions in check, and have learned to *listen,* to devote their whole attention to the person in front of them. They always begin from and affirm points of agreement when they talk with you. But they still have to be keen judges of people; they are perceptive, intelligent; they see quickly what's inside things, because that's how they have to be to do their jobs. They are careful about expressing dis- agreement and choose their moments and methods to do so, but they do make themselves plain. You don't take a co-op general manager lightly. Increasingly today, they are "system" managers, who are depen- dent on FCL and its networks for their career advancement. For this rea- son alone, they are much less likely to stand up in a meeting and tear into senior FCL managers while colleagues watch. Differences of opin- ion there may be—there certainly are—but they are discussed in less public settings. You walk on eggshells when you are around the senior FCL people who have influence over your career, according to one retail manager.

The transition is complete—from give-'em-hell management to soothing, nurturing management; from fiery confrontationalists to dedicated team players. Co-op GMs have changed, but so has FCL, and the two things are related.

In the last couple of decades, FCL has become more retail-oriented, more marketing-driven, as described in chapter one. In many ways, the retail managers in the system are the people FCL is serving and support- ing. While there are still conflicts—particularly between retails that want individual attention and the wholesale's desire for uniform and standardized programs—most people, GMs and FCL managers, say the whole relationship works much better than in the past. There are like- ly several reasons why this is so. The fact that FCL appears to provide better service, as well as year-end patronage refunds, likely smoothes things over quite a bit. Some FCL managers are former retail managers, and for this reason may be easier for current GMs to talk to. In addition, commodity and other specialists in Federated have skills and expertise that retail managers want and need access to; retail GMs see Federated as a resource to help them in their jobs. FCL has regional offices, a primary point of contact for retails, but people also know the personalities in FCL's home office and by all accounts feel free to call them up to explain a grievance, right up to the CEO himself. When I asked general managers about whom they talk to, whom they network with, they mentioned different people in region and home offices of FCL, as well as other retail managers and groups of retails within regions. It seems as if everyone finds some avenue, some person or place, for the communication they need.

There is also formally organized communication with retail managers. There are marketing meetings starting in January, June regional conferences with managers, and then FCL's fall region conferences, which are attended both by elected directors and by many managers. In these venues, managers hear about new initiatives that are under development or being introduced. They can discuss them among their peers and provide feedback. There are issue-specific committees within FCL regions or centrally, formed, for example, to review training or to study new ideas for marketing programs. The managers who participate on these committees provide input that helps FCL refine what it offers. FCL leads study tours of managers to the United States to look at marketing ideas (see chapter three).

There is also a permanent Executive Management Committee (EMC), which meets with and advises Federated's senior management four times per year. The EMC consists of retail managers elected by their fellow GMs in each of FCL's five regions (Winnipeg, Regina, Saskatoon, Edmonton, and Calgary), the CEO of Calgary Co-op, plus a BC representative. BC was historically an FCL region, though the retails there are now served out of Calgary or Edmonton. The managers come from different types of co-ops, different ages and levels of experience; and what they are exposed to is a system-wide perspective, the way FCL managers see it. The members of the EMC advise the CEO of Federated; act as liaison between retail GMs and FCL senior managers; act as liaison between retail GMs and FCL region managers; serve on region committees; and help plan spring managers' meetings and fall region conferences.[35] "We bounce various ideas about the programs [off] them," says FCL Consumer Products VP Norman Krivoshen. "Sometimes we'll reject the program; sometimes they will provide us with very good advice on how to enhance the programs that we have, and that is very, very much appreciated. They're on the firing line with their members and customers, and they see things that we perhaps may not see, and hear of how consumers react to a certain program, and that is very, very beneficial for us."[36]

It's also beneficial for the managers. "Oh, that was exciting!" one manager told me when I asked about the EMC. "Talk about an eye-opening experience. You had to go to Saskatoon and sit on a panel with the managers with lots of years of experience and dialogue with the CEO and the vice-presidents.... It's ... an eye-opening experience of being in a big picture." This manager, who joined the EMC when fairly new in the job, remembers being amazed at the knowledge and information of the senior executives and more experienced managers. To be able to interact with them, to discuss issues and programs with them, was a huge developmental experience. And with it went the opportunity to make suggestions that could influence how the system does things.[37]

A highlight of the year, for all the managers I interviewed, is the annual Fairmont Conference, which is open to GMs of retails with more than $5 million in annual sales. Interestingly, the meeting is not actually run by FCL, but by something called the Co-operative Managers' Association (CMA). The retail managers themselves are in charge, and technically, FCL senior executives—even the CEO—are there only by invitation. Bill Baumgartner currently serves as secretary of the CMA. Baumgartner retired in 2001 as FCL's Regina region manager, following a forty-three-year career in co-ops that also included teaching at the Co-op College of Canada, working as deputy minister of Co-operation and Co-operative Development for the provincial government, and serving on multiple credit-union boards. Within the Co-op Retailing System he was an accountant, a retail general manager, a retail advisor, a finance officer and director, as well as region manager. Today—in supposed retirement—Baumgartner works with a committee of six general managers (one from each region and BC) and with FCL Vice-President, Retail Operations, Ken Hart to organize the annual conference.

A function of the Fairmont Conference is to provide training. "We bring in very high profile people," Baumgartner says, "people who are recognized in marketing, in leading people, in motivating people, in being able to work with boards. This year, for example [2002], we had a session on development of business plans," he says. Another session was on dealing with different ethnic groups because of the changing population mix that's taking place in western Canada. The retail managers pay $175 to be members of the association, and $225 to attend the conference—this covers virtually all the costs. Like the big, once-every-five-years Marketing Expo discussed in chapter one (another major event for managers), the Fairmont meeting is basically self-financing. There's a message in this about the system's way of doing things. "We have about 95 to 100 managers attending the conference of the 127 that we will have invited," says Baumgartner.[38] Most of the ones I interviewed make every attempt to be there.

But besides the formal training, the Fairmont Conference is also about dialogue. This includes an annual bear-pit session with the CEO of Federated. "That's the highlight of the conference," Baumgartner says. "The CEO always makes a report on the trend for the year; what new programs we introduced; how other programs are working; what innovations the system is contemplating; the probable results for the year, which everyone, of course, waits for; and then there's a question-and-answer period. It is very, very casual and very frank, and you can ask him whatever you like and he will respond honestly."

Annual Fairmont Conference for the Co-operative Managers' Association. Photo courtesy Sue Crowley, Crowley Photography, Invermere, BC.

A retail manager told me, "We have for years now taken one agenda item and worked through it as a group, as a manager group" at the Fairmont meeting. "Whether it's petroleum, whether it's [the] administration side … we all deal with the same question and really analyse" it and discuss it in small groups, he tells me. The managers are free to say anything they want to, and discuss it with the CEO and other Federated representatives. "That has really helped a lot."[39]

The value of the Fairmont meeting has something to do with its exclusivity: *only* retail GMs (and invited guests) are there. By all accounts, it is a remarkable opportunity to make connections, even friendships, and to share problems. Having met people face-to-face, having chatted with them after hours, managers feel freer to phone each other for advice, to talk through issues. It creates mutual support and cohesion among them. A long-time manager told me, "It seems as though when you get to know somebody on those kinds of terms, you make friends who last forever. For instance, I get a newsletter from the retirees and it tells what all the different managers are doing," he says. "[The] majority of those people, I remember."[40]

In short, FCL promotes good relations with retail managers not only by offering service and communicating with them, but by *involving* them in the development and design of services. This helps the wholesale avoid mistakes and develop good programs, but also (again, see chapter three) helps ensure that new programs have a measure of support and acceptance among the GMs even before they are introduced. This is more than communication; it's participation.

None of this changes the fact that retails have different interests, managers have different opinions, and they almost never see eye-to-eye with Federated on everything. People I talked to made this plain. Few were as blunt as the GM who told me, "My background is such that I never did work for the wholesale; I've always been on the retail side of things and I feel no animosity, even when I'm on their shit list. I understand why it's there and I've been there."[41] The basic relationship is one of independence—rooted in the autonomy of the local co-ops—in which the possibility of disagreement is always present. You can't understand the Co-operative Retailing System without seeing this underlying tension. That army camp of aggressive managers could still be there, in latent form. The authority FCL has is generally earned through its programs; its credibility is developed through dialogue and participation by retail managers. The system works together by voluntary recognition of common interest, not by force, or just because people are nice. At root, co-op people tend to be aware of common or divergent interests, are blunt in talking about them, and pragmatic about dealing with disagreements. The harmony the system exhibits is by no means an absolute unity. It is an interactive balance where the tensions—like local autonomy versus central programs—are what make the system work.

Which brings us to boards of directors.

~

IF RETAIL GENERAL MANAGERS ARE FUNDAMENTAL TO today's Co-operative Retailing System, then what do co-operatives do when the GM is a poor manager? Or conversely, how can they make a manager better? A key to both questions is the board of directors.

In a co-op, the board consists of elected representatives of the members: consumers, in other words, in the case of the CRS. They are volunteers, community leaders, perhaps just people from different walks of life, who play a distinct and critical role in the co-op system. While boards have many functions—they bring member interests to decision making; they connect the co-op personally to the people and organizations they know; they recruit new volunteers; and they may in some sense "represent" the membership—their most critical role in today's CRS is that they hire and fire and work with general managers. All of these latter functions are important, but while hiring and firing are clear enough, the "work with" requires a little explanation.

What do managers say they want from their boards?

General Manager Jim Mitchell says he expects his board to be "basically, overseeing management—making sure management isn't screwing up. Being involved in the long-term, big-picture plan and then stepping back and letting it happen. That's what my board does." Mitchell was one of a number of GMs who told me that it is important for their board to show confidence in them. "I think all general managers look for a supportive role. I think that your board of directors has to provide a strong support for the general manager and show that support, [though] not blindly," he stresses. By support, he doesn't mean that they agree with everything. He wants a sounding board, a place where he can try out ideas and get reactions to them in total confidence, where he can get suggestions for fine-tuning or starting over, where he can trust people. He also means emotional support, encouragement, confirmation. "Your general manager doesn't really have anyone else to give them support. The general manager provides positive support for his department managers so that they can go out there each day and rally the troops," Mitchell says. "When a department manager runs into a problem or gets down about the problems that he's got, it's the general manager's job to pick him up and give him direction and positive encouragement so that he can go back out there and do his job on the front line. I think the general managers need that too. They need someone to give them back the same kind of support, and as we're not a corporate organization, there isn't a district corporate manager who's doing that. The only [people] he's got really for that is the board of directors."[42]

Mitchell appreciates that his current board is "very stable.... The president of the board has been on the board for twenty-five years." He also likes a clear-cut division between board and management matters. "I'm very strong that there is a line down the middle and they should not cross over on the management side," he says. "They should be involved in the policy area and setting ... the things that are important to the members and let the management manage it." Mitchell appreciates stability and clear authority because he's been burned before. Although he is a long-serving and successful GM, he left one of his previous co-ops as quickly as he could. "I did good work, but the president continuously interfered with my work," Mitchell says. "When I got to work in the morning, he'd come in the back door and he'd be sitting having coffee with the employees. Phone me the night before and say, 'We've got to have a board meeting tomorrow,' and you know, it just drove me crazy." To add to this, "the board always bickered amongst themselves." Mitchell felt things eventually became too difficult for him to function properly. "So it became a nightmare to me and when an opportunity came to move, I moved. I thought, I don't need this.... I can't manage properly. It's going to hurt the co-op."

Bill Haas—our younger manager—also looks to the board to provide stability. "I think of some co-ops where they've had an extremely strong board of directors for years and years, and the co-ops have been successful because of the board," Haas says. "There was quite a flow-through of managers in these retails. It was like a stepping-stone in their careers; yet because they had such a strong board, the co-ops remained very strong." If he could pick, Haas says, "I would pick a board that's pretty diversified in nature. You know, young, middle, older. I would pick a board that is diversified a bit in gender, a range to match your business market, so if you have a very farm-related [co-op], you might have a stronger farm presence, but if you have a very diversified [co-op], you'd have a much broader mix. It's good on a board to have very grass-roots people. People at very opposite ends of the scale, even on the education side. A lot of educated people on the board, degrees, postsecondary educations, are good; it doesn't hurt to have somebody who has none, because it represents the whole works. But the biggest thing on the board of directors," Haas concludes, "is that you get ... directors who are open-minded, willing to change, willing to listen, hold their manager accountable for what he's telling them, and are willing to see the big picture and not make decisions based on their personal preferences. And a board that ... when [they come] out of the boardroom ... they're unified. That's real important."[43]

Co-op boards have become considerably more diversified, by and large, during the last twenty years. This is especially noticeable in terms of gender, one of the points mentioned by Haas. Gender isn't the only aspect of diversity by any means, but it's a highly visible aspect, and one in which co-ops have made progress. Women, of course, long made up a majority of the consumer-members who were making spending decisions, particularly regarding food and household goods; and they are well represented among staff in the system. They have been rarer at higher levels, and elected board positions are one of the places they have broken into, or been included in, system leadership.

A good person to ask about this is director Trish Potter, who has experienced some of it herself, and has heard about the experiences of others involved before her. In her view, the CRS was traditionally male oriented, "definitely, because it was started in the male world, you know. The word farmer is supposed to be male, I mean it's supposed to have gender," she says—which raises a whole other set of issues.[44] It is still true that when I asked rural managers and presidents how many farmers were on their boards, they generally, at first, only counted the men, but then, as they thought about it, also mentioned farm women (oh yes, she's a farmer too), or gave them a secondary identification as a farmer (there's one other who's a teacher, but she's married to a farmer). Most co-ops have outgrown their roots as farm organizations, but it still appears true that farmers, mostly men it seems, are overrepresented on boards, perhaps simply because they are interested, have large accounts, and have business skills from running their farms. There are lots of women, though, who could also be on boards, and increasingly are.

The first women who did join co-op boards generally reported a range of reactions, including other directors wondering why they were there (why her husband let her out, and whether he couldn't control her, as one of them put it); not knowing how to speak in their presence; having difficulty looking at them or paying attention to them; or generally being nervous or afraid of saying the wrong thing to them. They had trouble noticing higher voices and people with smaller builds, especially in a tumultuous meeting. They were taken aback by people who wore brightly coloured clothing. Some directors were willing to argue with other male directors, but would not argue with women, which got in the way of discussion. All this, it is said, was years and years ago. The two things that made the difference, for the first wave of women directors, seem to have been attitude and numbers. "If you're nice to them and you treat them with respect…, then you can become a buddy," Potter also says. "You just have to teach them that you're one of the guys, and that you're willing to be there, and your goals are the same as theirs."[45] All this became much less of a problem once there were several women on a board at the same time. Once that happened, the barriers became much less awkward.

There are different opinions about the effect of having women on boards. FCL, which had multiple women on its board before many retails had accomplished this (of course, it has a larger board), provides a mixed example. One male FCL director told me, "no," there was no difference on the board once women were involved, "and, you know, several people have remarked about that, and I personally didn't feel that we really changed at all. And I asked some of them … if they felt that they were out of place at all, that we'd left them high and dry or whatever, and I don't think there was ever a complaint about that."[46] But one of his male colleagues contradicted this, answering, "Oh yes. It cleared up the language a little bit" during the meetings, he said, but at least as importantly, it changed the after-hours socializing. Instead of people meeting in various separate rooms (perhaps to be able to smoke), this was no longer considered appropriate with a mixed group. Instead, the board all socialized together in a single room. "We could have a lot of interaction between the board members, and it also added to the unity of the board because you didn't have one clique in one room and another clique in another."[47]

Having women in the boardroom is one respect in which decision making has been opened up to include people drawn from a wider total pool of the membership, instead of coming only from certain segments of it. It may have improved the professionalism and quality of board interactions and decision making, which is generally one of the purposes of pursuing diversity on a board. The goal is quality discussion, lots of input, insight into different points of view and member interests, and as a result of all this, better-quality decisions. Co-op boards always need this, because they have some difficult jobs to do.

The balancing act for boards is that they have to both support and work with their managers, and also sit back in judgement on them. They need to judge performance, improvement, and the possibility that the manager isn't good or isn't right for the current challenges—because there is no one but the board that can fix things if something goes wrong with the manager.

Compared to their counterparts in for-profit corporations, where directors are different kinds of people, co-op directors bring one huge advantage and one large disadvantage. The trick, of course, is to maximize the one and minimize the other. In a co-op, the advantage is that the directors are normally independent of the CEO or GM, in an important sense in which the term is used in today's discussions of good corporate governance. Members of a co-op board should be beholden to no one, certainly not to the manager they are supervising. Because they are elected by members on the basis of one member, one vote, and share no substantial employment or investment interests with the GM, it should be difficult for the manager to influence them improperly.

Related to this, co-ops traditionally keep the office of board chair or president separate from the position of GM or CEO, as is now also recommended for for-profit corporations. However, the co-op structure brings a disadvantage, too: directors are rarely experts in management, marketing, finance, or any other specialty. They lack *information,* and it is lack of information that most threatens their ability to do their job. A board fails when it hires a bad manager or fires a good one; but it also fails when it becomes controlled or dominated by its manager. Typically it is through use of information—sometimes also through exploitation of factions among directors—that managers control boards.

This is why co-op directors need to be perceptive, need to be quick at understanding what is in front of them, and need to be trained. President Abe Greenwood puts it this way: As a director, "you need to listen to your members, and I think just be willing to take some training, to be open-minded and to be receptive to some of the points that are brought across in training." But training isn't the only thing that will make a successful board member, he says; you also need "good judgement, horse sense, shall we say." It's also good, he says, not to have directors who all think the same way, who come to a consensus too easily. "I like to see people who come up with, shall we say, strange or different or controversial ideas."[48]

Co-op leaders can't control whom the members elect to the board, but they can persuade people to let their names stand. Personal networking and encouragement is one of the only things members and directors can do to help make sure the board gets the people with horse sense and diverse points of view that Greenwood is talking about. There are also other devices. Some co-ops have districts for director elections, ensuring some geographic diversity, typically in multibranch co-ops. A few have instituted designated youth directors, people of senior high-school age who ensure a youth perspective is present at the table.

Perhaps the biggest thing is training, because it's the thing that the board can control, by policy. The Co-operative Retailing System puts tremendous effort into director training, as it does into staff training. Currently, the system has two certificate levels for directors. A number of co-op presidents I talked to expressed the commitment of their board to its job by telling me, for example, that six of the nine directors had the level-two certificate; the others had only level one because they were new and hadn't had time to complete the advanced level. So, besides attending board and committee meetings, talking to members, looking at the co-ops' facilities and using them, directors also have to take courses. Beyond this, there are the district and regional meetings, taking turns as delegates to FCL annual meetings, and other events that help directors understand what is going on in the system, and allow them to compare their co-ops to others. It takes more time than just going to a meeting every month or so; and of course, time is in short supply for many people. A couple of co-op presidents expressed their frustrations to me that they couldn't get more of their board members to do the training or attend FCL meetings.

Directors need knowledge in order to do their jobs and contribute to the success of their co-op; but this process has a side benefit. It develops civic leadership in western Canadian communities. Director Frank Stefchuk told me, "If I look at myself, I started out with not much knowledge of a co-op." Based on his experience, he says, "you have to be prepared to get involved in their [FCL's] training programs. I think they're very important; they're good programs and it's because of those programs that I was able to go into something else.... I had a yearning for local politics and ran for [municipal] council and got elected," he tells me. "I probably wouldn't have done that without the training and experience that I got through the co-op system."[49] Other directors I spoke with had gone on to serve on hospital or health boards, boards of voluntary associations, and so on.

An example of how co-ops provide opportunities for leadership would be Saskatchewan's mid-1990s finance minister, Janice MacKinnon—the first female finance minister in the country. MacKinnon, who did not grow up in Saskatchewan, became involved in public life through Saskatoon Co-op during a tumultuous phase of its existence. When she presented a petition to a mass public meeting of more than a thousand co-op members in 1983—a petition, incidentally, to impeach the board of directors—she was also launching a career in politics. One of the people who was impressed by her speech was Roy Romanow, the future premier, who would one day appoint her to cabinet. But there's more. When MacKinnon became president of the co-op in 1986, she realized that the organization desperately needed restructuring to survive. She had to learn to sell the tough medicine to the members of the co-op. Her experience foreshadowed her budgets as Saskatchewan's finance minister years later. She was the one who balanced the budget and eliminated the province's deficit. She came to appreciate that good management—and she cites FCL as an example—not idealistic philosophy, was needed to run a co-op, a lesson she subsequently took with her and applied to government.[50] In short: the experience of responsibility and accountability in co-ops develops leaders and teaches the importance of practicality and management.

It does this, of course, for people of all political or nonpolitical stripes. As an aside, it is important to dispel quickly any impression that a lot of co-op leaders go into politics, or only with certain parties. Co-op directors are active in all sorts of municipal governments, health-care institutions, service organizations, and other groups in their communities—you name it, and there probably has been a co-op person involved in it somewhere. Only a few go into partisan politics, and those few include people across all political parties.

MacKinnon's story is particularly interesting because she says she didn't, at first, appreciate the importance of good management or of FCL's advice to local co-ops. This is not uncommon for people who become involved locally. Directors naturally identify with their retail co-op; it is their job to defend and promote it. In the absence of information, or if they are fed selective information, this can easily shade over into suspicion and hostility of Federated. There are, of course, times when boards should criticize the wholesale, advocate improvements in its policies, make plain their unhappiness with bad service, and so on. But it's something else when the opposition to the wholesale is generalized and not attached to any specific complaint. Such attitudes are not widespread in the system today, but there are always some co-ops that are not willing supporters of the wider co-op system, and it's important to realize that FCL can do almost nothing about this. Federated staff generally don't go into stores if they are not welcome. The system really is voluntary.

Anti-FCL sentiment becomes dangerous when it is combined with a manipulative or insufficiently competent retail manager. One way or another, Federated is the main source of information for directors that is independent of their own manager. Federated supplies the training about what boards should do and what managers should do. Federated publishes the retail statistics, divided up into size categories so that all co-ops in the system can compare themselves to how others are doing. If a co-op is failing to earn the margin on particular product lines that other, similar co-ops are earning, this may warrant some inquiries. FCL staff can also be invited in to facilitate board reviews of the manager's performance. Plus, of course, the Federated network is the prime pool from which a replacement manager might be drawn. It is easy to see why, if managers want to control their boards and protect their own positions, they might be averse to FCL having access to their boardroom. This was, indeed, the case in stories I heard. In every example of incompetent or corrupt management, this went together with a hostility to the wider system.

People in the CRS are generally public-spirited and motivated to do what is best for their communities; but people are people. I heard of staff members who were caught stealing, directors who ran up accounts they never paid, and various other forms of abuse of positions, no more common than you would expect in any organization—likely less so. But the staff members were fired by their boss; the directors were pressed into resigning by the president, or de-selected by the members. It is a different thing when general managers abuse their positions, because they can intimidate staff and misinform boards. Given the responsibility of a general manager's position, it is noteworthy how rare such stories are; but people who have been around the system tell them—the manager who had a load of lumber delivered to build a cottage, and no one knows whether any bill was paid; a staff member assigned to walk the manager's dogs; personal favouritism in hiring and firing; and so on. You could call it sloppy procedure and unclear compensation policy, or you could call it corruption. The point is that directors need to know that such things can happen, because they, personally and collectively, are the real safeguards against such problems, and the means to fix them.

I noticed a difference of opinion among my interviewees around this, related to how much information board members collect from staff. GM Jim Mitchell feels that it's a violation of his authority if directors talk behind his back to staff members. Director Trish Potter, on the other hand, has always made a practice of chatting with staff, inviting them to talk to her, and hearing their complaints—even when the manager expressly forbade her to do this. Everyone agrees that if a director does anything with this information, other than bring it to the attention of the GM or perhaps other directors, that's stepping over the line. Directors don't supervise; they don't fix problems; they don't propose solutions to detailed operational and supervision issues. But collecting information isn't necessarily interference. Some directors, however, agree with Mitchell. They don't want anything to do with staff complaints and won't even hear them.

The best hope for directors to find out if something major is going wrong in their co-op is to network in the wider system and take advantage of information from FCL. For their part, Federated staff, managers, and FCL's own directors increase the chance of this happening by visiting retails and talking to people. Cultivating networks and connections in the system is not only a social activity; it's a way of developing the lifelines that may be needed in a crisis. This is a main job of FCL's retail advisors, who frequently have experience themselves as GMs and know something about running a co-op. FCL region managers and directors also tour co-ops in their districts. Similarly, commodity specialists will visit, advise, and observe. And every summer since 1987,[51] the entire FCL board goes on tour in some district of the system, and the senior management group does the same thing. But if local boards or managers don't want to be visited, they probably won't be. In an extreme case, to get a hearing and present information, FCL's one option is to ask to meet with the local board to express concerns they may have about the co-op or its manager. This process looks a little like the missions to local co-ops in the crisis years of the 1980s, and it serves a similar function.

I made a point of asking co-op general managers how they felt about the possibility of Federated representatives going over their heads to talk to their boards. One or two were noticeably troubled by the thought. Most bravely answered that it was no problem, because only a manager who was not performing would have to worry about that happening. The fact remains that intervention by FCL is the only real check on a general manager's power, if the local board is not doing its job.

~

T HE INTERPLAY OF MANAGEMENT, GOVERNANCE, and system support, and the necessary tensions among all these, is evident in the 1998–99 crisis at Calgary Co-op.

It's not always easy to tell, at the time, when a co-op is going off-course. In the mid-1990s, Calgary Co-op was written up as a model of member, community, and employee participation, with innovative approaches to member involvement, employee representation, and social auditing.[52] In retrospect, one insider suspects the problems in Calgary became serious when its biggest competitor, Safeway, was shut down by a strike in 1997. The strike, of course, buoyed Calgary Co-op's already dominant market share. The co-op posted a 10 percent increase in sales over the previous year, to $591 million; earnings swelled 21 percent, to $22.7 million; membership stood at 340,000 people.[53] The next year, with the strike over, sales dipped a couple of percent, to $580 million; but costs didn't dip as much. Earnings fell to just $13.8 million, and then to $12.5 million in 1999, which means Calgary Co-op was losing money on its local operations, and was in the black only because of $18-million-plus patronage refunds from FCL. Long-term debt rose to some $23 million; member equity was beginning to slide.[54] One board member talked of a "disturbing erosion of market share."[55]

Meanwhile, staff and management appeared to be in turmoil. Employee groups were organizing to elect or unseat directors.[56] The co-op was publicly mocked for bringing in a spiritualistic advisor and using New-Age tactics and love-ins to motivate grocery managers. Managers claimed staff morale was pretty good, while staff said in the press it was the worst in years. Grievances were coming in, on average, every three days. Discontent appeared to centre on a restructuring in which supervisors lost long-held responsibilities, and were moved through different departments instead of developing expertise within one.[57]

Apart from the managerial experiments, which reportedly found favour with some staff, it appears that after years of success, the co-op had become complacent. The spending habits of senior managers had come loose. It was "just general sloppiness," one source says, and also "kind of, favouritism to friends and contracting, you know, supplies, or expense accounts to senior management.... There were very rich fringe benefit packages and things like that in place.... Spending was pretty much out of control and it wasn't really noticed ... during the strike." Another person, from outside, says the co-op "lost a little of their focus. They were so successful that ... I don't think they remembered why they were successful." They "did some silly things as far as expansion goes," and they "paid everybody too much money.... Co-ops are not famous for overpaying people, but Calgary did." They not only allegedly paid managers excessively, but also had too many layers of them. Some people talked of empire-building. For whatever reason, the board was not on top of things. This may have been because the CEO insisted that the board meet with him, only with him, and not with other managers or staff. And the CEO, it appears in retrospect, was not on top of what other managers were doing.[58] In the face of all this, the board hired external consultants in June 1998 to conduct a management review. Ernst & Young confirmed that the management team was not performing at the level needed for the co-op to compete. The board parted company with its five-year CEO in October 1998.[59]

From FCL's point of view, this was something the system had seen before: low earnings, negative local earnings; high costs; rising debt; internal turmoil. The system's largest co-op now qualified as a "priority retail." If this had been 1982, Calgary would have been on the "B" list, sliding hard and fast towards the "A" list with no CEO at the wheel.

"I can remember Regina, Saskatoon, and then Calgary, the untouchable," one rural co-op manager told me, citing a list of city co-ops that he had watched get into trouble and be rescued. Kindly, he did not mention Winnipeg and Edmonton. "Went into damn near the same condition the Wheat Pool is in. I would have to say that [the problem in] Calgary was totally management. The other thing was that there were probably some directors who if they did know what was going on, fell asleep on the job. Having been involved in so many levels of the retail system, I've seen that happen too many times. You can't ever relax; you've got to be on the ball," he says with feeling.[60] The perspective of people who've seen similar things in other co-ops is clear. The system almost lost Calgary Co-op; it was that close.

The board had certainly lost confidence in its entire management team. Asked for help, FCL sent in a delegation in December 1998. Within a week, the co-op had laid off twenty-three head-office staff, including three members of its former Executive Management Committee and all but one of the organization's vice-presidents. While the severance packages were officially called "adequate" in the press, others found the total cost enormous. Employees were said to be "stunned" by what was happening.[61] Within weeks, the clean-up team dispensed with more head-office staff and twenty-two middle managers in neighbourhood co-op centres; reversed the management experiments; and contemplated more layoffs.[62] Federated's involvement, coinciding with the layoffs, aroused a storm of fear and suspicion.

From the system's point of view, Calgary Co-op had not been a team player in recent years. FCL senior managers were aware of problems brewing over Calgary's dealing outside the system for bargains from suppliers, while at the same time claiming funds from internal pools generated by the system's own contracts with suppliers. The co-op was double-dipping, going it alone in approaching suppliers and also wanting some of the money other retails generated by their purchases through system channels. This and other complaints from Calgary itself—that the co-op couldn't get by on the margins it had between cost and prices, that FCL had to provide lower costs for them— were intimations that the co-op, internally, was out of control. Nevertheless, directors who opposed FCL resigned when the board invited Federated in, claiming that FCL was in a "conflict of interest"— basically that it was just one of Calgary Co-op's suppliers and had its own advantage at heart. Another claimed that Calgary's cost of goods from FCL, at 80 percent, was too high, and that it should be only seventy-five to seventy-six cents on the dollar—in other words, the co-op needed and deserved a 25 percent gross margin on which to operate. The problems were all FCL's fault.[63]

Initially, three FCL directors went in to talk to the Calgary board and offered help. "I was one of the directors who went in, and that was probably one of the toughest meetings that I'd ever been in on," one of them told me. "You know, when you have a whole other board kind of looking at you and saying, What are you going to do for us? And our basic story was that we can't do any more for you than what we would do for any other retail co-operative; but your sheer size would indicate that we're going to be fair and offer you all the assistance that we can."[64] As it turns out, "all the assistance that we can" was quite a bit—perhaps in keeping with the 1980s idea of least-cost solutions. There was no way FCL or the system could afford for Calgary Co-op to go out of business.

FCL provided a transition team to guide the co-op through restructuring. FCL VP, Retail Operations, Ken Hart went in as leader of the team and became chief operating officer, living in Calgary while also covering duties back at home office. CEO Wayne Thompson called former FCL VP, Marketing, Elmer Wiebe out of retirement, and he moved with his wife to Calgary to help out the co-op. Four more FCL vice-presidents—Peter Zakreski, Art Postle, Lynn Hayes, and Terry Bell—moved in and worked as needed in Calgary while remaining based in Saskatoon. Many others from FCL Home Office pitched in as well; it was as if most of the people from Federated's eighth floor went to work for Calgary Co-op. "At one time I walked into a room," a Calgary Co-op person told me, "and there were thirty-eight FCL people in that room from head office in Federated. They gave us everything they had.... There were probably two hundred years of experience in the building from Federated."

"As the team leader who went in there," Ken Hart says, "I certainly had lots of resources from FCL to assist me in doing it, and had weekly contact with our CEO." He was a little surprised at what he found. "It was difficult at first because we weren't aware that the problems were so deep-rooted as they were, nor that they were as severe as they were. We initially thought this was going to be somewhere in the neighbourhood of a three- or four-month task, and it ended up being a year." He calls it "an intense experience." Others talk about the personal toll on Hart and his team. As Hart looks back now, he says he wouldn't change anything the transition team did; he would just have done it quicker. Hart insists on crediting the new CEO, Milford Sorensen, who came in when the transition team was done in 1999. "I'd just as soon Milford get credit for the successes of Calgary Co-op," Hart says simply,[65] "He's worked hard building on the foundation we were able to establish."

What the transition team did resembles the lessons the system and other co-ops had gone through in the 1980s. "We had to do some terrible things," Wiebe says. "We likely took half a million dollars out of the structure" through layoffs. "And the people who I interviewed one-on-one, before we got started, nine times out of ten—because they were very talented people in a lot of cases—they looked me right in the eye and they said, 'to be truthful, Elmer, you don't need me.'" Luckily, Wiebe says, "We caught it in time, or we'd have lost our largest retail." But there is a certain frustration in his comments about no one being able to do anything sooner. "You know, many times that year I [said to myself], it's hard to explain how smart people could do something like that, but it was allowed to happen because until they got into trouble, nobody could do anything."[66] What Wiebe means is that FCL can't go in, can't even really provide advice, until it's invited to do so. And when people are hostile or suspicious, FCL doesn't get invited until things are desperate.

"It was probably one of the most difficult assignments, much more difficult than '82," says Zakreski, "because [in] '82, at least you knew the people, you had worked with these people, you knew what some of their strengths and weaknesses were. When you walk into an organization like that and suddenly there's about six hundred management people and ... you don't know them all, how do you then start analyzing?" Zakreski says the process involved a complete restructuring, focussing on the basics of what the co-op was doing, "and then determining which people qualified for those positions and which didn't, and getting rid of those who didn't.... That was a very, very difficult assignment, but very rewarding seeing how they're doing now."[67]

The obvious dedication and self-sacrifice, particularly by Hart and Wiebe, who spent the most time in Calgary, earned personal gratitude from Calgary Co-op board members and staff. They must also have liked the bill. FCL did not send invoices for much of the time their executives spent there. In light of the feel-good outcome—the co-op saved, back under its own management, forging ahead with a new CEO and increasing sales and earnings in 2000, '01, '02, and '03—there might be a tendency to gloss over how difficult those months were in 1999 when FCL managers were running Calgary Co-op. It's important *not* to gloss it over, because it says a lot about the dynamics of the system.

The Federated team encountered a hostile environment where everyone, it seemed, thought they were the bad guys. The fear and suspicion were deeply ingrained, the result of years of criticism and blame by managers and staff. I talked to people who were amazed anyone in Calgary even knew what FCL was. In most places in western Canada, few people would have more than the vaguest idea. In Calgary, staff, members, even people on the street not only knew, they had an opinion; and it was negative. Federated staff had to listen to this one-on-one and in meetings; they could read it in the newspaper. "Anti-Federated sentiment" was common. "These folks who were ... putting their lives on hold to do this"—to help Calgary Co-op—"were having to hear it, which wasn't very nice for them." What's worse, these same Federated managers were the ones who had to come in and lay off staff, when the previous management had left with severance packages. "There were people here who were scared to death," one person recalls. They "were afraid that they [FCL] were going to make Calgary Co-op a farmer co-op and, you know, that Federated just wasn't sophisticated, didn't know what they were doing, and there was no way that they could understand a large retail like that."[68]

At root, the issue is one of size. Calgary Co-op directors frequently quote statistics: their co-operative has a third of the system's total volume, perhaps a third of its members; they own 12 percent of Federated; yet they have only one seat on Federated's board (out of nineteen),* one general manager on the EMC (out of seven), five voting delegates at FCL's annual meeting (out of about four hundred). The implication is that FCL serves small co-operatives, and Calgary is in a league of its own —FCL a farmers' organization from Saskatoon, Calgary Co-op the sophisticated big-city business.

The idea that an FCL manager would have the title of Calgary Co-op CEO was too much for some. As a result, Hart acted as CEO without the title, and board chair Alice Brown was appointed as a figurehead CEO. When FCL offered to do Calgary Co-op's executive search for free, as it would for other retails, and a private consulting firm quoted $100,000, the board was badly split—despite the co-op's shortage of money—and wavered before deciding narrowly to accept FCL's services, an indication of the great fear that FCL might attempt to control the

---

* Since 1 January 1989, Calgary Co-op has had an electoral district all its own (C13), ensuring that a Calgary Co-op director is always on FCL's board. (FCL Board of Directors minutes, 21–22 December 1988.)

manager selection. The search produced two candidates, one from within the CRS and one from outside—current CEO, Milford Sorensen. Privately, board members say they were relieved at the outcome: "It was convenient for the board; it was a nice coincidence that the person who was the best candidate didn't come through Federated, you know, because it would have been harder if it was the other way around."

Barry Ashton, current chair of Calgary Co-op's board, was a new director elected in February 1999, in the midst of the crisis and after the FCL transition team was in place. "I campaigned, actually, on the basis that Calgary Co-op needed to take control of its own destiny," he says. "While it may be okay on a short-term basis to appoint Federated executives to run Calgary Co-op, they would be in a conflict of interest in running the co-operative," he says. (I can't help but notice that Ashton is following in Janice MacKinnon's footsteps by getting involved on the basis of running against an existing co-op board and management.) Ashton says that getting a responsible, autonomous management team in place was the top priority for the new directors, followed closely by improving Calgary's board procedures and training, areas in which the co-op has since made great strides. Ashton remembers attending FCL's annual meeting in Saskatoon as an observer shortly after he was elected, and getting his hands on one of FCL's director manuals. He and another new director exchanged knowing looks and talked about how these were the things Calgary Co-op needed: policies, procedures, training, orientation, models for all of which were available in the wider system and could be tailored for their co-op's use.[69]

"Federated is very, very important to Calgary Co-op," says Ashton. "I don't think Calgary Co-op could stand on its own without that. Federated demonstrated their commitment to Calgary Co-op huge-time in my mind in 1998, '99, when they brought in the interim management team. They never charged us a penny for that. Of course it was in their interest to do it, I have no doubt about that," he says, "but I also watched very carefully as they did this, the skill with which they worked; and knowing something of management techniques and so on, I was very impressed with the management and the discipline that they brought to Calgary Co-op in restructuring and refocussing [it]. We've benefited enormously from our membership" in FCL.

New CEO Sorensen puts things into perspective like this: Under "the previous management régime" and maybe even earlier, "there was obviously a rift" between management and the board at Calgary Co-op, which affected relations with FCL. "It would appear to me, observing what I have over the last three years," he says, that the previous management "did everything they could to thwart the relationship between Federated and Calgary Co-op.... Here's an organization that I think became somehow intrigued with their own success and felt that they could do nothing wrong, [that] they could go out and stand on their own which, from my perspective, is absolute suicide. And so we had this militant relationship between Federated and the management of the day. Management did a good job of sharing this with our employees. Our employees had what I have to describe as a hatred for Federated, because they blamed everything on Federated. The truth be known, the problems at Calgary Co-op were not because of Federated. They were because of mismanagement," Sorensen says. But managers shifted the blame to FCL, until even employees at the shopping-centre level were blaming Federated for their co-op's ills.[70]

"When I joined the organization," Sorensen continues, "I realized that the only way we were going to be successful is if we leveraged the benefit of the Co-operative Retailing System in western Canada, and it would be folly for us to try and do anything on our own." At the same time, Calgary, he believes, has a lot it can teach the CRS. "Federated has a huge problem because they're dealing with such a myriad of stores from small rural stores—and there are many more of those than there are urban stores like ours—to a big centre like ours. Federated Co-op is faced with the dilemma where they have to try and treat everybody the same," says Sorensen. "We're an urban retail co-op, and we require more services than a rural co-op. We are dealing with much more challenging competitive circumstances. I have great empathy for what Federated is attempting to do [to] be fair to all co-operatives in the Co-operative Retailing System. As a consequence of that, there are many things that Calgary Co-op has to do itself because the services aren't there from Federated." These are the areas in which the co-op can contribute to the wider system, by showing FCL new ways of doing things.

Like every general manager I interviewed, Sorensen makes a point of asserting his independence of FCL, his willingness to criticize them, his dissatisfaction with the speed of change. "They are very successful and they've done very, very well, but I think we need to embrace technology quicker, sooner, faster, in order to build systems that will ensure that we continue to be competitive in the long run, and that's nothing new. They've heard me say this. I've been beating the drums, and as I say that, they are listening, they are doing things, they are heading in that direction. I'm impatient. I just don't think it's fast enough. The bottom line," though, is simple: "The relationship with Federated, since I've come here, has been phenomenal. They are providing excellent services for us, and they've been very, very helpful in the process."

Calgary Co-op's recent history is a dramatic illustration of the importance of management in co-operatives. It is also a demonstration that even the biggest local consumer co-op isn't big enough to make it alone, in the long run, in today's competitive environment. Individual co-ops can do quite well, for a time; but they benefit from the experience and examples of the wider system, and they may need the system to carry them in a crisis. Calgary also illustrates the fundamental dynamics of the Co-op Retailing System, the fierceness of local pride and local identity, the way in which central power is both used and checked, which is essential but not always pretty. It's yet another illustration that, in western Canada at least, people begin to co-operate when they recognize that they have to, when they are persuaded of the benefits. On that fragile beginning, a whole system can develop a co-operative culture.

◦

T HE RELATIONSHIP BETWEEN THE RETAILS AND FCL is, of course, like the relationship between individual members and their local co-operative, because FCL is a co-op, too, one whose member-owners are the local retail co-ops. Retails deciding whether or not to participate in FCL, to be part of the system, to be loyal, face the same kinds of decisions individual members do. Often this is a matter of trade-offs between short-term welfare (a quick deal available today) and long-term interest (what will happen if there's no co-op, or it's too financially weak to invest in needed services?). But generally speaking, the leaders of retail co-ops are better integrated with FCL—understand it better—than most local members are with their own co-ops. This is because of the well-developed structures on both the management side and the elected (directors') side to engage co-op leaders in the system.

The elected side of the system has its own patterns and institutions. Directors from retails serve as delegates, attending the June meetings in their districts, the fall conferences in the regions, and FCL's annual meeting in Saskatoon. Portions of all those meetings are devoted to marketing, to training, to a consideration of new programs and initiatives, to discussions of bylaw changes, and debates on resolutions. Within the districts, they elect directors from among themselves to sit on FCL's own board, and these directors take on a special responsibility for liaison with co-ops in their districts.

The region meetings are an example of how the CRS does things. At one I attended in the fall of 2002, the room was decorated with marketing placards: Co-op: Your Community Builder; product displays of gasoline and food; designs of prefabricated homes; and other folding displays. More than 160 people were in the room, very attentive to a series of presentations. One of these, by Brian Gustafson, Market Research and Member Relations manager, was titled "What Do Women Want?" It was a one-hour précis of research and ideas about marketing to women, based on the idea that, according to sociologists, we are shifting from a male-oriented society to one that is more equal, and that marketing should reflect this without being ostentatious about it. I noticed that many of the recommended techniques were already incorporated to some extent into the system's new food programs and store designs: marketing to peripheral vision; holistic marketing, including attitude and role in the community; natural lighting, angle displays, curved lines, wide aisles; convenience; and so on. Following this, the region chair, one of the co-operatives in the region, and the region manager presented their reports; time for discussion appeared later on the agenda, after an entire morning of reports.[71]

None of this might seem remarkable, but I saw it in a little different light because I was sitting at a table with eight co-operative officials and managers from China. They assured me that attending this meeting was a highlight of their visit to the region; through the interpreter, they told me that what struck them was how "democratic" it was. I was a bit bemused by that comment, since at that point we hadn't actually seen any debate and no voting had occurred. I thought perhaps they were just being polite, but after further consideration, I think I saw what they meant. The idea that democracy is about confrontation and voting is only one concept. The meeting had begun with a procedural introduction that referred to the importance of discussion, the opportunity to influence the CRS, and to learn more about FCL. An FCL director (the region chair) gave a careful account of the resolutions process, explaining that resolutions should, if possible, be discussed here, at the fall conference, before going to the annual meeting the following spring. What the Chinese visitors picked up on was the fact that participation was positively encouraged, with well-thought-out procedures. The presentations respected the delegates, giving them knowledge they needed, and making their leaders accountable.

The annual meeting is like all that, only more so, with the marketing in particular bumped up a notch. Anyone who hasn't attended an FCL annual meeting might consider doing so for the atmosphere alone: the Harmonie Brand Band (volunteers from around the system) that calls people back to order after a break; the door prizes; the myriad colourful displays; the marketing exhibit with free food from fried chicken to new varieties of ice cream—it's a bit like a mini-expo. But this isn't diversion. It's actually a statement about the purpose of the meeting, the purpose of the whole system. Old-timers talk approvingly about when the meetings stopped being "political," that is, stopped debating farm policy and what the government should do about this or that, and became focussed on marketing. At the annual meeting, resolutions are debated on a variety of matters, including how co-ops are represented, how patronage refunds are determined, new initiatives delegates would like FCL to investigate, and so on. The debates are quick, set-piece battles, rehearsed already at the preceding regional and other meetings. Most delegates have heard the positions, talked about the resolutions, and likely made up their minds before they come. Occasionally a surprise debate breaks out when someone thinks of a new angle on something, but this is not a clashing, decide-on-the spot democracy. This is a democracy of year-long dialogue and near-continual interaction. This helps ensure that the annual meeting is primarily a show of unity, with opportunity to fix problems ahead of time, along the way, or in a side corridor discussion with a senior manager.

Perhaps because voting isn't the main activity at the annual meeting, there has been no major overhaul of the democratic process within FCL. Reforms to FCL's internal democratic structure were discussed throughout the 1990s, resulting in task forces and specific proposals. FCL management made a point of staying out of these discussions; its directors were uncomfortable with some of the proposals and did not push them.[72] One issue increasingly mentioned up to 2002 was the need to limit the number of delegates, which was slowly growing due to a combination of real growth and inflation (because it is based on purchases of the member co-ops, up to five delegates per member), even as the total number of member retails declines. A revised delegate entitlement formula was approved at the 2003 annual meeting.

FCL annual meeting, Centennial Auditorium, Saskatoon.

The cycle of meetings, the regions, the delegates, and the FCL directors have something to do with communication and unity within the system; so, too, does training. As with individual members, improved services and high patronage refunds also reward co-operatives for being part of the Federated system, and integrate and link them into the wholesale. But at a deeper level, the increasing cohesiveness visible in recent years among FCL's member co-operatives is a matter of shared purpose, a recognition of a need to focus on marketing, and a recognition, as in the case of Calgary Co-op, of interdependence. Some of this goes beyond what can be achieved by any particular structure. It is a question of vision, dialogue, and experience together.

Vern Leland, president of FCL from 1978 to 1996, is well situated to comment on the changes over the years. Thinking back to when he first became directly involved in FCL, Leland recalls, "The thing that really bothered me when I became a director and eventually president of Federated was that it was a we-they situation. It was a retail vs. Federated." He goes on to explain: "And I think that a lot of the times—and I think I'm right on this—it was the retail managers who were driving that, because they were always driving for a better position with Federated. Which wasn't bad, but ... they fed that into their directors as well, and their delegates, and it was that constant we-they thing until the eighties," he says. "It really bothered me to have to deal with that. To me, it wasn't right." Leland remembers trying to counteract these attitudes by visiting retails, sitting down with the boards, "always trying to bring us together as a system." He wasn't alone in this. "I think everybody worked at that," he says. "It was not just myself but the directors, management, the retail advisors, everybody was on-board, and that was the direction we were going. And a lot of retails bought in, but there was still a very pronounced battle being fought, you know—this is our turf, we're going to go the way we want.... Some continued to go their own way and went bankrupt. It's sad, but what do you do? People won't change, won't admit the reality, won't accept advice. They all knew better, they knew better than Federated did. It was a heartbreaker in a lot of cases, but you know, I guess you can't win them all. And then you saw the others, on the other hand, who accepted this, and went out and did something about it."[73]

Al Robinson, who as senior vice-president, Corporate Affairs, worked with the board and with the elected side of the organization, agrees that "the system has never, in its history, been as cohesive as it has been in the last twenty-five years.... Nowhere near." He attributes this in part to FCL's financial results and to the flow of refunds through the system; but he believes it's also due to the experience of working through problems together. An example he gives (as do many others) is the corporate bulk-fuel program. "I think that that one [initiative] produced more value and provided more cohesion and did more for this organization than most of the other things we have done in the last twenty years," he says—a reason for a closer look at innovations of that kind, in chapter three.[74]

A critical piece in the whole structure is, of course, the FCL board. When I asked FCL directors about it, they said, mainly, that it was similar to a retail board: you review operations, set policy, work with the CEO. Some of them talked about succession planning and what they are doing to ensure qualified candidates are available to replace them; others mentioned the importance of training and board evaluation. In terms of differences from local co-op boards, they mentioned two things. One was the scale of the business, the volume of information, the size of the expenditures, which is staggering in comparison to most co-ops. The other was the size of the board, which, with nineteen members, is more than three times as large as some retail boards, twice as large as most of them. Of course, it's not just the size of the board—it's the number of districts, which is embedded in the structure of meetings, representation, and services. To change the board size implies changing the representative interface with the member co-ops. Like proposals to reduce the size of the delegate body at annual meetings— about four hundred—proposals to reduce the size of the board don't go very far. Everyone wants to be involved; and perhaps it also has something to do with that defensiveness about local autonomy, the resistance to centralization that is deeply rooted in the retails.

No one knows the FCL board better than its president, Dennis Banda. A key issue is how to integrate new directors into an organization that has a strong sense of its own history, identity, and purpose. The main thing Banda seems determined to communicate is the importance of paying attention to fundamentals. "They're coming on the board, and have to recognize that you can't, for one minute, lose your focus.... You have to come back and say at the end of the day, what does this do, or ... what does this mean [for members]?... We have to maybe do some things differently, but we also have to keep in the back of our minds [things] can slip real fast.... Look at how fast Calgary went backwards. It's almost unbelievable that you can go back so fast or things can turn bad so fast." Having a strong management team helps, because board members quickly pick up the fundamentals from them. "That doesn't say at times you're not concerned with trying to get them into line, because you don't run a dictatorship," Banda says—a reminder that the president may control the process, but not the people.[75]

"You know, when you come onto the [FCL] board it's a new experience. You've taken off; it's a big difference from being on the Spalding board or the Marcelin board. I mean you get into here, it's a big learning curve." The steepness of the learning curve is evident for new directors who join the board at the time of the annual meeting in early March, and who, within weeks—with only one initial board meeting under their belts—have to be out making speeches to represent the system at local meetings. In recent years, the board has gone through significant renewal, with the departure of directors who had served for two and more decades. Only four directors, Banda says, have more than his own ten years' experience. "So there's been a major shift," he says, "and yet I think we've still been able to bring a fairly strong board with different perspectives, and I guess part of their strength is that we've got [people] from every walk of life on the board. Well, I think it's a strength because, you know, we have everything from lawyers to business people to teachers to farmers to housewives, so there's a different perspective."

I ask Banda what makes a good director. He furrows his brow slightly and replies, "Well, I think first and foremost, they've got to be committed to their members and to the work of the co-op system. They've got to be committed to the system. Once they get here on the Federated board, they change hats in the sense that they're not representing the local retail, but now they're representing a system across western Canada and their focus has to be first on that, and then secondly back to their local membership." I ask President Banda whether it's a bit of a conflict of interest to ask a representative of a single local co-op to help make decisions on behalf of the whole. "Well, absolutely," he answers, "and what I mean by that is when you're making the decision now at the Federated board level, you're making it on behalf of three hundred co-ops, not one retail, not your own, and that's the big difference.... Your thinking has to change from making the decision at Federated that's going to benefit your local retail, to making one for all of us. Secondly, you then go back and say well, now that I've made this decision at Federated, here's how it's going to affect my retail. I have to communicate to my co-op now; my job is to tell them why Federated is doing this, how it will affect us, what it will mean for the whole system."

Ed Klassen was also president of FCL during the period covered by this book, in 1996–97. When I ask Klassen about the relationship between the Federated board and management, his comment is, "I think it was very cordial. We were encouraged to ask difficult questions, but you could get yourself in trouble if you questioned their [senior managers'] integrity, which is quite understandable … but if you had a strong case they wanted to hear it.… They were very eager to hear what you had to say, but you had to have your homework done," is how he puts it. A careful relationship, one might say. "We have a bit of a different philosophy from some of the co-ops," Klassen reflects, a philosophy that deliberately keeps board and management a little separate, to the point of not socializing too much together. "I think it's a good thing," he says, because it helps preserve objectivity, the capacity to take courageous action when needed, if directors and managers aren't "buddies."[76]

The FCL board works with management in a twelve-month planning cycle that was an exemplary model when it was developed in the 1980s, and is widely copied and adapted by retail co-ops. The cycle begins in January with a board-management planning retreat. Participants review overall progress and direction, focussing on the key departments—food and petroleum—every year, and other selected departments. With the highlights identified, they develop a business plan and pass it on to each division, which would then have a planning session of its own, and from there down to clusters and subteams within the division. The planning process is designed to lead all the way down to individual performance targets discussed between employees and managers. Thus the board meshes at the front end into a plan that cascades down to every individual employee in the company.

As with the delegates' meetings, the idea of board-management relations in FCL is not to seek confrontation, but it's important to the process that the potential for conflict exists. FCL Senior Vice-President, Corporate Affairs, Lynn Hayes puts it this way: "The directors keep the grass-roots part of the organization alive and make management realize everyday who they are working for. I'll give you the comparison—and I do this with the young people I interview—of working for a multinational versus working for the co-op system. At the multinational, everything is absolutely top down and driven from the top down, whereas here, if you tried to manage that way, you'd ultimately be a failure, because our system is so culturally created from the grass roots up. That's the nice thing about this organization: it makes people think before they act." The accountability of management to a member board is part of what makes that happen. "It's easy if you're the CEO of a large conglomerate," Hayes says, "to make a corporate decision and drive it down, because anybody who doesn't like it can get disciplined or even fired if they don't follow it. But in the CRS, the retails own FCL and would not accept that style of business." Innovation in the CRS can't happen, or not often, by central decree. Hayes uses the terms "plant" and "seed" to describe the way FCL managers spread ideas to the system.[77]

∼

THE FCL BOARD IS ALSO LIKE RETAIL BOARDS IN that its most important task is the selection of the CEO—a task it has not actually had to perform since 1983. A twenty-year-plus CEO is an institution in any company, and Wayne Thompson is no exception. Thompson earned a reputation in the 1980s by bringing the company through the crisis, as described in chapter one, but after that, he surprised people. At first, having been treasurer, he was seen as a finance person. "When he came in, he was exactly what they needed," one retail manager says, "because we were in serious financial trouble, and of course his background is financial." But, this manager continues, "although he's strong in finance, he understands the importance of marketing … he's always very eager to see that the system is on the leading edge of new trends in the market."[78] A second GM said, "Where he came from, on the other side of business, from the accounting side, had a lot of people at that point doubtful if an accountant could lead this organization. Many said it should be a marketing individual." As it turned out, while "he's not a marketer himself naturally, he understood that it needed to be a marketing organization" and assembled the team of people to make this happen.[79]

It's important to realize that shrewd GMs want both things out of FCL. They want strict economy, efficiency, savings, low costs, and high refunds that help their co-ops grow. But they also want a marketing-oriented company, one that is innovative and develops new programs, and supports the retail co-ops to do the same. If FCL has been successful and its CEO has lasted over two decades, it would be because he did both things. As we have seen, retail co-op managers are a demanding audience—and it's an audience that loves Thompson.

Thompson's office on the eighth floor at FCL Home Office is not quite Spartan. Prominent on the walls are sports memorabilia, notably Montréal Canadiens gear, including signed pictures of famous players Jean Beliveau and Guy Lafleur. He says they serve as icebreakers when employees first visit and don't know what to say to the CEO of the company; but there may also be another message in mounting pictures of the classiest and highest-scoring leaders on the most successful hockey team in history.

Most of the time, Wayne Thompson seems to use his authority like he uses his height—that is to say, he doesn't have to use it consciously at all. Everyone knows that it's there. Staff and managers do not relax when they are preparing to meet him; they want to have their ideas and arguments clear. He will give people a hearing, but he is not the kind of person with whom you want to mess up your first chance. This makes his personal, one-on-one manner all the more striking. He rises to greet people, his body language is open, his smile is wide and genuine. Only his eyes don't seem to smile quite as much as the rest of him does, hinting at a cool intelligence that runs behind them, and possibly at years of accumulated worries and strains. After a couple of decades as CEO, you get the distinct impression that Wayne Thompson doesn't need to be tough with people very often.

Among general managers in the system, Thompson's one-on-one skills are legendary. In person or over the phone, he can motivate people, he can support them, he can direct them. His support means something to his managers, precisely because it can't be taken for granted. He'll leave you in no doubt where you stand with him, and they say his word, once given, is as good as law. But other than in front of his managers, he rarely takes a podium, does not often stand in front of a camera or microphone, usually avoids the limelight. He manages a multi-billion dollar enterprise primarily through personal contact and through a closely-knit team of senior managers he has hand-picked and developed for their roles. Policies and programs are important, of course, but often the management of the system happens in a personal way. This is difficult for outsiders to see and has led to Wayne Thompson being both highly respected and also a bit of an enigma to people outside the system. He seems remarkably private for so public a figure. People say FCL is not brash, does not boast; and in this, the organization reflects Wayne Thompson's character. Beyond that, Thompson also appears to be careful about observing the invisible line between management and elected leadership in the system. The podium is primarily for the elected leaders. Thompson's realm consists of the managers at FCL and throughout the system.

Thompson's heartfelt speech at the March 2003 FCL annual meeting was an exception to his usual public reticence. Barely out of hospital, he spoke plainly and simply about his reflections on what mattered to him, above all—the system and its accomplishments. Being present in that room, you could feel the anticipation and the appreciation of his brief remarks. Delegates wanted to see him, to hear him, and were clearly moved by what he said.

To understand what makes Wayne Thompson an effective CEO for Federated Co-op, one can list the qualities people—especially retail managers—attribute to him, and the consensus is remarkable. He is an extraordinary individual, highly intelligent, sees the way to go before others see it, has an amazing command of detail, does not mince words or suffer fools gladly. But it is also worth reflecting on the fact that few CEOs, even brilliant ones, can last twenty years at the helm of a company. What mistakes has Thompson avoided? I found a convenient list of the seven habits of spectacularly *unsuccessful* executives, which according to the author are usually their strengths followed to excess:

1. They see themselves and their companies as dominating their environments, not simply responding to developments in those environments.
2. They identify so completely with the company that there is no clear boundary between their personal interests and corporate interests.
3. They seem to have all the answers, often dazzling people with the speed and decisiveness with which they deal with challenging matters.
4. They make sure that everyone is 100 per cent behind them, ruthlessly eliminating anyone who might undermine their efforts.
5. They are consummate corporate spokespersons, often devoting the largest portion of their efforts to managing and developing the corporate image.

6. They treat intimidatingly difficult obstacles as temporary impediments to be removed or overcome.
7. They never hesitate to return to the strategies and tactics that made them and their companies successful in the first place.[80]

Such a list puts some of Thompson's distinctive leadership styles into an interesting perspective. This includes his avoidance of the public limelight, the sharp boundaries he draws, his tendency to remind people how serious the problems are and how tough the solutions, and his disciplined approach to co-op marketing and finance, avoiding quick fixes.

⁓

THIS CHAPTER HAS LOOKED BRIEFLY AT MEMBER-ship, staff, management, governance issues, retail-FCL relations, and has ended by examining the institutions and the chief executive officer of the whole system. Any one of these topics merits a chapter all its own, but the purpose of a brief survey like this one can only be to make a few simple points. The key words I would use to sum it up would be *transparency* and *quality*—How does the Co-op Retailing System create trust among its members? How does it prevent or fix problems? By what means does it promote success and higher standards? The answers to these questions have to do with a delicate balance and interplay of forces, with dialogue, experience, and interaction.

The key, in my mind, is the situation of the retail general managers. They have the autonomy to be genuine entrepreneurs in their communities, and yet they are embedded in a member-based framework that, as Vice-President Hayes points out, reminds them for whom they are working. The co-op manager means something because the co-op board is there behind her or him.

If there is a problem in a retail, and the internal board-management dynamic is not fixing it, then there are two, somewhat soft and indirect, ways the system can work at it. It can be approached through the managers' side—the committees and networks and conferences and training, as well as informal dialogue—or through the elected side, with similar networking among elected directors. These dual networks are used not only to work on problems, but to promote good practice, to share ideas, to train, to gain input, to design better programs. It is almost as if organizational charts for CRS co-operatives need to include not only the board and the management, but also the wider links to FCL. The embeddedness and interaction in the wider system are factors promoting performance and sound practice. At the same time, none of this would work as well as it does if it were not based on local autonomy. The advocates of local autonomy and of standardization or centralization both have their points, and in a successful federation neither one of them will ever win.

Of course, members—whether individual consumers or co-op stores—are much more likely to be happy when results are good. Record earnings, huge investments, patronage refunds, new store designs and marketing programs, are tangible evidence of how the system is working.

All of this is like other businesses in some ways, and unlike them in others. I asked many managers about differences between co-ops and other businesses, especially those managers who had worked outside the system. The most eloquent answer came from Milford Sorensen. "From my perspective," he says,

> I think being a co-operative and having the members as owners of the co-operative, you tend to spend a little bit more time on communications, on evaluating the processes that you are implementing in the retail, and I think it's probably something that business should do more of. The co-operative model forces you to look at all eight corners of the box rather than just four. In other companies you will see people forge ahead without thinking of the consequences, and thinking too narrowly. I think you tend to think in broader terms in a co-operative because you have so many constituents out there that are looking at what you are doing.

As a result, "the management task is tougher in a co-operative" because you have a board to report to, but the results can be better. "I think that if you embrace the process and the model and work it ... you have the opportunity, if done well, to have a better-managed business than you would otherwise have," Sorensen says. "You need to really pay attention to that ownership, and I think there's a huge strength in that if it's done correctly. I think from that you get a deep sense of loyalty, a deep sense of commitment, and I sense that in Calgary Co-op. I mean, the membership is hugely loyal to the Calgary Co-op and that has and continues to overwhelm me. It's phenomenal; it's a marketer's dream, quite frankly."[81]

CHAPTER THREE

Cognition

Innovation
and Adaptation

ARKETING AND WELL-STRUCTURED ROLES AND relationships alone will not ensure the success of co-operative systems. They also have to adapt to changing conditions. They need to change, and in the right ways, with the right priorities, to succeed in the face of constantly evolving circumstances. This is even harder than it sounds, in some ways, because co-operatives are not fixed or monolithic structures. They are bundles of relationships and interdependencies, tensions and compromises, stakeholders and members and leaders. The co-op has not only to change, but to change *in a co-ordinated way* so that all of its pieces change together—so that the key relationships remain intact or are strengthened after change has occurred. This chapter is about how co-ops, FCL, and the system have learned to think in new ways and do new things in the last two decades. It puts together the story of the system's new marketing focus (chapter one) with the roles, relationships, and ways people work together in the co-op system (chapter two), in order to show how adaptations and new initiatives come about.

The system's determination to market, its attention to image and service, its use of mechanisms such as patronage refunds to reward loyalty, are innovations in a sense. They are ways of getting the basics right, doing the kinds of things co-ops were always supposed to be doing, but better. Innovations can also change co-ops and bring new structures, new ways of doing things, and, above all, new ways of thinking about things. Most of the innovations discussed in this chapter are important because they touch on the co-op fundamentals of community, autonomy, and cohesion, but they approach these essential elements in new ways.

There are two innovation processes in the system, one that begins more at the grass roots, and one that proceeds more from the centre outward. When they are successful, the two processes meet in the middle, in mutual interactions between Federated and the retails.

At the grass roots, innovation is often horizontal. Local co-ops extend themselves to meet new community needs, or to do things in different ways in response to local pressures. They may spread out existing services geographically, or they may diversify into new services. This is a process of local creativity that often depends on the critical role of the co-op general manager, as emphasized in chapter two, and sometimes on the direction and community base of the local board. Certain innovations, when they have proven themselves, spread widely in the system and are picked up and promoted by FCL.

The centre-outward process generally revolves around innovations that have to do with deepening expertise, tighter integration between levels, bringing in leading marketing ideas from outside, and building leadership in areas where the system has already established itself. Food and petroleum marketing are the main areas for this kind of innovation, often led by FCL. But FCL rarely launches fully developed innovations. Instead, the system works by feedback and dialogue, so that even when the initiative comes from FCL, what it puts forward are proposals that retails have already bought into.

~

A T THE LOCAL LEVEL, SENSITIVITY TO COMMUNITY IS a source of co-op innovations. This sensitivity involves a range of things. It may be a general attitude of openness towards the community, facilitated by the fact that the co-ops' decision makers live in the communities they serve. It might encompass particular involvements of the co-operative and its staff in community events and networks, which generate contacts and ideas. Or it could be planned and organized responses to specific community needs and opportunities. The results of all these influences are variations among the system's co-operatives.

If you know where to look in the Co-op Retailing System today, you can find unusual examples of local ingenuity. These include a senior citizens' housing complex in Winkler, Manitoba, built under retail co-op leadership, with integrated co-op store facilities. Then there is the same co-op's highway truck stop, under development between Winkler and Morden. Not much more than an hour's drive away, still in southern Manitoba, you can find a co-op funeral parlour in Portage La Prairie. A bit further south, Pembina Co-op—a retail—has a business manufacturing prefabricated homes.

Across the border, in eastcentral Saskatchewan, Midway Co-op (formerly LeRoy-Watson) helped develop a large, community-based, hog-production enterprise. Nearby, there is a grain elevator with a CO-OP® logo on it, purchased by the same co-op to help its members ship their grain. Just down the road, the small, rural co-op in Naicam has acted, in effect, as a business incubator to help rescue or launch small businesses in the town. There is a comprehensive co-op agricultural service centre shared by two co-ops—Naicam and Spalding—located on the highway between them. Drive up the highway to Melfort and you'll find a co-op that owns and operates a Grandma Lee's sandwich-and-baked-goods franchise, in place of maintaining its own cafeteria. Other co-ops are creative in the businesses and services to whom they lease space.

Further west, Calgary Co-op has numerous innovations all its own. One of the best known and longest established is the Kiddies Korral childcare centres in the stores. Parents can drop off their children under the supervision of trained staff, in a secure glassed-in environment. As they wander the store, they can observe their children on television screens. Newer are the self-service checkouts recently piloted in two Calgary Co-op stores, and the Internet-based, home-delivery food-ordering system for co-op members.

On the West Coast, there is Hornby Island, where an initiative by a staff member who is also an artist turned the co-op into the most important gallery space on the tiny island. Down the way in Victoria, Peninsula Co-op (described in chapter one) operates its own subsidiary chain of Save-On Gas stations.

The character of co-operatives as community-based enterprises is nowhere more apparent than in Canada's North. Co-op stores in the Arctic are not only critical suppliers of food and other necessities in remote locations; they also market handcrafts made by their members. They operate co-op hotels, co-op cable-television distribution networks—in fact, whatever the community needs that the co-op can supply. The northern co-ops are members of their own central organization, Arctic Co-operatives Limited, which is an affiliate member of FCL.

From childcare to funerals, art to truck stops, there aren't many things that some co-op, somewhere, hasn't tried. The range of these activities testifies to the creative, entrepreneurial character of co-ops in responding to local needs. In this chapter, we will take a closer look at some of these examples. Since there isn't space to deal with all of them, an arbitrary selection will have to suffice to give a sense of what kind of things can go on in retail co-ops.

At the same time, we must keep in perspective the fact that most of the wacky or wonderful activities are marginal to the CRS as a whole and often, financially, to the co-ops carrying them out. Most co-ops stick to their knitting—food, petroleum, marketing—and those that do other things are in a position to do so, generally speaking, because they've taken care of the basics first.

~

M OST DIFFERENCES IN THE SYSTEM ARE *COMMUNITY* differences, and not based on regional or provincial considerations. I asked many people I talked to whether they saw differences between the co-ops and leaders in the four provinces, and they generally said no. There are some perceptions that people in Saskatchewan are more familiar with the co-op model, and people in BC less so, and that this makes Saskatchewan co-ops more steady, well managed, and well supported. Others argued, though, that Saskatchewan co-op members had excessive expectations of their co-ops, and said it was easier to run co-ops in other provinces, where members would accept simple good services, prices, and facilities without always demanding more. In any case, there is a perception that operational approaches, effectiveness, and efficiency have been converging over the last couple of decades. This is what FCL President Banda, who makes a point of travelling the system, means when he says, "Yes, there are some differences ... I'm not pulling any [punches] here. It's a little different experience when you go to British Columbia." But he adds, "I wouldn't say that they're extreme or they can't be handled."[1] Another FCL manager told me, "Retailing is retailing. WAL-MART doesn't differentiate," and neither can its competitors, at least in the larger urban centres. "You weren't overly proud of some of these retails" that diverged from the system's standards, he says, but "they weren't large retails ... they never were big enough to be of any major concern, so why make an issue out of it?"[2]

That's one side of it. Marketing is marketing, and the basic concept won't be fundamentally different from one location to another. But to the extent that the communities differ, or the leadership of the local co-ops differs, even equally good marketing will lead to different things in different places.

Others describe it as a striking experience when they progress high enough in the system to have the opportunity to tour other co-operatives. "I found it interesting to see the various kinds of services, the kinds of facilities that people had, what it is that they were trying to accomplish, and some of the problems they were having. It was quite an eye-opener." Despite the similarities, "they certainly do reflect their communities."[3]

"Every co-op's got its own culture," a retail manager told me. "There are a lot of leadership differences in them."[4] To a manager's eye, they differ, first of all, in the commodities they handle. Some have "quite diversified merchandise. Some are just straight petroleum and groceries"—or indeed, perhaps only one of these, as we have seen in some cases. Then there is their competitive position. Some are just one business among several in the lines they handle; others are the dominant businesses in the places they serve. We can think of setting up a grid to classify local co-ops: diversified or specialized; large market share or small. To this we need to add a rural-urban dimension, particularly as the large urban co-ops tend to be more specialized, with the rural co-ops being more diversified and often having larger shares of their markets. And there could be a fourth dimension—single-point-of-service versus multiple—but we'll get to that later.

Most co-ops make a significant demonstration of support for the communities in which they are located. I was struck by this when driving through St. Paul, Alberta, two hours east of Edmonton, on my way to interview General Manager Bob Scott of St. Paul and District Co-op. St. Paul and District is a prosperous, diversified co-op in agro products, petroleum, hardware, and food. The co-op anchors both ends of a large mall, in which Field's department store sells clothing, a private operator runs a café, and there is everything from western wear to jewellery, a florist, hair styling, a photo shop, and more. All these businesses are tenants of the co-op mall, but the co-op's presence in the community is apparent elsewhere, too. As I drive through town on the main street (Fiftieth Avenue, as in most sizeable Alberta towns, it seems), a group at the École Racette School has a trailer sign proclaiming Thanks to Our Sponsor, St. Paul Co-op. Further along the street, banners salute volunteers. There are signs from local voluntary organizations and charities, from the credit union, and, of course, one that reads St. Paul Volunteers are out of this world. CO-OP.

St. Paul Co-op Mall.

"The owners of the co-op live right here in the community," says General Manager Scott. "It's their community and we feel, as a co-operative, that we have a responsibility to the community. That's why we try to support most nonprofit organizations; and many of the members of these nonprofit organizations are also members of the co-op. We do try to support as many of them as we can. I know that one of our competitors has a strict policy that they will not make any donations.... I'm hopeful that the members of the co-op are able to figure out that if they want us to support their organization, they're going to have to support our organization, the co-op."[5]

The co-op was not always in a position to generate employment, patronage refunds, and support for community projects. Like many co-ops, St. Paul was in trouble in the 1980s. They had built a mall in the late 1970s, Scott explains, leading to heavy debt and large interest payments. "The member equity dropped from 69 percent to 29 percent"; the co-op ceased paying patronage refunds; and at the same time, new competition moved in across all product lines. Scott, who joined the co-op as GM in 1992 after wide experience in the system as a GM and retail advisor, says the basic problem in St. Paul was a common one for agricultural areas of the Prairies: larger farm sizes, declining rural populations, consolidation of services into larger towns and cities, where there was strong competition. "We were forced to face the reality that the good old days were gone," Scott says. "It forced us to operate a lot more efficiently and close some departments that were inefficient, and forced us to make sure that our standards of service in merchandising and marketing were high. It also led to a closer working relationship with Federated." The basic retailing strength of the co-op is what enables it to make its donations to community causes.

It is not only rural co-operatives that play this role of community support. You can find the same phenomenon in the largest co-op in the system.

In Calgary Co-op there is a tendency to refer to the twenty or so different stores as "the co-ops." In one sense, this is simply shorthand for "the co-op stores," but it is also a significant way of thinking and talking, because each Calgary Co-op store really does take on a distinct neighbourhood identity, almost as if it were a separate co-operative. Calgary's neighbourhoods differ from one another, and the stores reflect the lives and patterns and needs of the members in those areas. One store is busy during the day with nonworking parents doing their shopping; another does very slow business until the afternoon, when parents from two-income families are off work and start coming in to shop. The managers, too, have a considerable degree of independence, reflected in their strategies for pursuing connections to their neighbourhoods and partnerships with community organizations. Different stores have different strategies for their donations, community sponsorships, and activities in their immediate neighbourhoods. In fact, it's written into the managers' work plans that they are to work with a certain percentage of their budget to develop local community connections, and they are evaluated on the results.

The Taradale Centre in northeast Calgary illustrates community connections. The food and petroleum operation (there is also a detached Calgary Co-op liquor store) is one of Calgary's newest and most modern stores, opened only in November 2002, a few months before I visited it. From the outside, the store design might be called homey; it's impressive but warmer and more human than some other co-op stores. There are the common touches, for Calgary Co-op stores, of two-tone brickwork, tan and red; but the homey feel is provided by a peaked roof, covered with green shakes, and with gables at regular intervals. Burgundy highlights under the green roof echo the inside colour scheme. Inside, the store features the best of contemporary system design. You enter to find baskets of fresh fruit in front of you, fresh flowers on your right, an inviting deli and table seating to your left; and behind all this an expansive fresh produce and baking area under hanging track lighting. The aisles are long and spacious, the selection large. Huge colourful murals adorn the walls. This store seems designed to make shopping a pleasurable experience—shopping as recreation that upper-middle-class consumers would enjoy. And yet, this co-op does not serve a particularly upper-middle-class neighbourhood.

Calgary Co-op's food store at Taradale.

The Taradale area is burgeoning with new construction, and in this case—in today's Calgary—this means families of every description, including immigrant and non–English-speaking people. A large Sikh community is a presence here, but a multicultural mixture is the real character of the neighbourhood. There are places in the world where this kind of mixture is perceived as a social problem, but here, co-op and community leaders are quick to characterize the people of this neighbourhood as upbeat and positive. The neighbourhood school and the neighbourhood co-op store have a kind of partnership, collaborating for quality of life and high standards of interaction among the people in the community. While visiting the co-op, I hear from both community leaders, who are also co-op members, and from Terry Singer, the store manager, about the ways in which the school and the co-op work together. The co-op donates to the school; it provides food and volunteers from among its staff for school fundraising activities; its Fuel for School initiative donates food for school breakfasts and nutritional education programs for children who need this; it invites in classes for educational visits and puts up their art in the co-op. The co-op organized volunteers and donated refreshments, supplies, or services to help the school build a frost fence, and later a playground. These were more than just co-op events; they were community-building events.

Like other newer Calgary Co-op stores, the Taradale Centre includes a meeting room and a kitchen for community use. Classes and demonstrations are held here on how to cook nutritiously and economically, or on how to do Chinese cooking. Experts are brought in to do presentations on first aid or fire safety. Local co-op members can book the room to give seminars on financial management or any other area of their expertise. These presentations are well attended, with often twenty to thirty people, who are required to register in advance by paying a $10 registration fee, which can be redeemed for a $10 gift certificate if they do attend. This store is too new, as of when I visit, to have built up a frequent cycle of events, but other stores reportedly host three community events per week, and members are constantly inquiring about and trying to sign up for the next one.

Calgary board chair Barry Ashton comments, "Corporate social responsibility has become a … fashionable term in business parlance today, and co-operatives in my mind have always been corporately, socially responsible … but we weren't very good about telling anybody what we were doing," he says, "and we weren't very good about recognizing social responsibility in its broadest sense. You know, it's not just grants and donations to worthwhile causes, or giving up a little bit of food to the food bank." Ashton mentions environmental responsibilities, community investment, and, particularly, the personal contributions of thirty-five hundred Calgary Co-op employees—one of the largest workforces in the city, Ashton estimates, and heavily engaged. "We have no idea of what the total impact of the volunteer effort of our employees is, but it is massive. I can't talk to too many employees in Calgary Co-op who aren't involved in some way." Along with local ownership and quality service, community involvement is one of the ways in which Ashton sees the co-op distinguishing itself from competitors.[6]

Two of Ashton's comments deserve special emphasis: that many co-ops have not sought much credit for what they do in sponsoring community causes; and that these activities need to be integrated into a wider strategy of community involvement and co-operative identity. These are important points, because donating money to good causes is not an innovation and does not distinguish co-ops from competitors. Other businesses make donations as well. The difference in co-ops is the degree of such activity, and the fact that it is integrated into a wider, community-oriented strategy.

Another co-op president admitted to me that in his community, "some of the larger corporate stores have a tendency to raise money for charity," too, but he drew the distinction that "they set up a collection unit of some sort in the store, and they'll say, donations accepted." The customers put "their nickels and dimes and their dollars and their five dollars into this collection, and at the end of the day the amount is totalled" to say store A donated X dollars to the charity. But "it didn't come from store A. It came from the customers, you see."[7] The co-op may do some of that, too, such as matching customer donations, but in addition, co-ops operate community granting programs directly out of the stores' profits.

Another Alberta co-op helps illustrate some effective ways in which co-ops can use community involvement to market themselves—what experts refer to as "marketing our co-operative advantage" (or MOCA).[8]

Medicine Hat's co-op mall looks like one of the best kept and most prosperous of its type in the system. It is located on a main traffic and commercial artery, Thirteenth Avenue, with a gas bar at the front of the parking lot and the mall at the back. Ad banners line the light standards in the parking lot with familiar system slogans: Co-op Equity and Cash Back, Personalized Service, Quality CO-OP® Label Products, and Your Community Builder. From food and pharmacy on the left, the mall stretches through a credit union and other tenants over to the co-op cafeteria on the right—which has a good fifteen to twenty cars in front of it at 8:30 in the morning, half an hour before mall opening. Perhaps they are there to take advantage of the "$2.99 Breakfast Every Day— plus GST," in small type. Along the mall are signs for a hair stylist, a health centre, an optician, a hearing specialist, a dollar store, a comput- er shop, a denture clinic—a range of health, financial, and personal services, for the most part complementing the co-op's offerings rather than competing with them. The one co-op department still located along the mall is a furniture and appliance store. This is, of course, only the co-op's urban face. The ag hardware, general hardware, and crop supplies centre is located some distance away; there are satellite facili- ties in Acadia Valley and Oyen, and bulk fuel delivery and chemical application out around the countryside.

The gas bar and store have neat, clean signage and design consistent with that used across the system ... with one exception, for those who know. On the side of the gas-bar building is a large CO-OP® logo, in the familiar five-sided crest, but the outline of the crest is in green. This two-coloured version of the logo has not been officially used in the sys- tem for decades. "A touch of nostalgia," a manager admits. When queried about whether FCL representatives give him any grief over this, he nods. "Yes. But they go away."

In his office, General Manager Ted Rodych sits below posters, large and small, for a petroleum marketing campaign: Gas Up At Co-op— Cash Back; In 2002 Members Earned 5.0¢/L Co-op Equity and Cash Back. "Medicine Hat Co-op, I think, is a very valuable part of the com- munity," says Rodych, even "one of the elite companies of Medicine Hat ... a leader in this community for many years." "Just [in] the last ten years, we've paid over a million dollars each year back in cash. That in itself is a big contributor of support to the community—nobody else does that in town. And we support ... minor baseball, a local hockey team, numerous, numerous groups (the Girl Guides, Boy Scouts, service clubs in town)," he adds. But even so, the co-op's profile in the community was not as high as it wanted, so several years ago management decided to have a closer look. "We put together a focus group and one of the things that came out," he says, was that "Medicine Hat Co-op is around town, but it's not visible enough in the community. So we had to raise that, you know, and it was one of the things that maybe we got, I don't know, complacent, or just took it for granted. So you want to raise that awareness." The co-op decided on a television advertising campaign made by a local producer.[9]

Medicine Hat's March 2003 campaign might serve as a model for locally produced marketing of the co-op advantage. "What Medicine Hat business has been locally owned since 1956," asks a "teaser" spot— "and shares its profits every year?" Viewers of this and five other teasers were not immediately given the answers, but were encouraged to "Keep Watching! And find out!" A series of subsequent commercials revealed the answer: "Your Medicine Hat Co-op ..." with the stress on the word *your*. "By being a member, you are part owner." Reinforcing advertisements featuring actual members and employees give reasons for supporting the co-operative, many of which focus on the equity and cash pay-outs. Board members and senior co-op managers spent four days handing out the cheques in person, in co-op stores, during which some of the commercials were filmed. In one televised example, a member explains what she spent on food and gas per month, and that at year-end the co-op gave her a cheque for $261. "What other store pays you for shopping there?" she asks on-screen.

∽

ONE OF THE CHIEF INNOVATIONS AMONG RETAIL CO-ops in the last few decades is not often recognized as such: amalgamation. The region served by the CRS, and especially the Prairies, has seen an ongoing out-migration from agriculturally dependent rural areas into the large cities as well as towns that have a diversified economic base. This trend has affected even the largest urban co-ops, in that they experience the influx of new members from rural backgrounds. In the face of a social and demographic trend that seems as

inexorable as it is devastating for the adversely affected people and communities, co-ops have responded by adjusting one of their basic principles—local autonomy—and by changing the nature of their connection to community. In place of what might be called the old principle
of one town, one co-op, we now see the widespread development of
multibranch, regional co-operative systems. Sometimes these are centred on a city at the core of the region, as is the case for Medicine Hat,
Swift Current, Prince Albert, Yorkton, and others I visited. In other
cases, the territory and character of the co-op does not centre on any
one focal point, and this is reflected in neologisms, made-up names for
new co-ops. Examples include Eastalta, discussed in chapter one; Delta,
formed when four communities in western Saskatchewan joined their
co-ops; Heritage, encompassing Brandon and Minnedosa, Manitoba;
and Pembina, which stretches across southern Manitoba. But whether
they adopt new names or not, the co-ops created by amalgamations are
effectively new co-ops.

Not everyone amalgamates. Saskatoon Region Manager Larry
Rupert sees a trend in the development of more shared services among
co-ops in his area, some of which maintain local autonomy by sharing
services under contractual arrangements with neighbouring co-ops. "I
think it might have even had its start in this region," says Rupert, going
back to the 1980s, when an agreement was signed for Rosetown Co-op
to manage Eston Co-op. "They'd gone through a series of disappointing operational years, they'd gone through a series of managers, and the
board was kind of frustrated and exasperated; and they signed a management and accounting agreement with a neighbouring retail and it
was a bigger one. We have, now, four [more] of those management
agreements in effect in the region, and they're working well. They're ...
a model now for how retails can continue to provide the service in the
community in spite of the fact that they have difficulties in getting
competent management, and they can do it without giving up their
autonomy."[10]

"Actually," says Rupert, thinking of the difficult economy, declining population, and changing demographics of the rural area, "I think
co-operatives, for the most part, have been very much in tune to the
changes that are going on about them, and have found ways to adapt
and try and still provide services that are of value to that community,

because there are some small communities that have diminished over the years where the co-op really is the only remaining service.... It's quite a credit to the determination of the people who are there in the community, to try and hang onto the service and find a way to make it work, and I guess it's probably a credit to the co-op model that it can get through that and can survive. The strength of the central organization helps, too, because of the patronage refunds, the cash that goes back to them. But in a lot of the smaller communities, when you see reinvestment going back into retail co-op facilities, you don't see much happening in the private sector. It's usually the co-op that's reinvesting back into the business and modernizing or rebuilding. The model works."

One of the successful examples of amalgamation is also in Rupert's region. "I think that Prince Albert Co-op is a really interesting study," he says, "of a market-area approach to what they did over the years." P.A. Co-op amalgamated with smaller co-ops all around, "and through that process continu[es] to provide a valuable, important, and [sometimes the] only service" in each of the branch communities. Where other competitors have shut their doors—in effect, moving the services and business volume into the city—P.A. Co-op's branches remain open.

Amalgamations have been a big part of the recent history of Prince Albert Co-op, with eight of them altogether since the original one with Paddockwood decades ago. Today the co-op stretches across a broad rural and urban region of northcentral Saskatchewan, a hundred kilometres wide and more than that tall. It's in P.A. at multiple locations, but it also has services and facilities and branches to the west and northwest in Shellbrook and Big River, south to Domremy (that's pronounced DOOR-emi) and Wakaw, north to Paddockwood, Air Ronge, and La Ronge, and east to Smeaton and Kinistino. Within this county-sized chunk of territory, the co-op is both regional and local.

General Manager Wayne Pearson comments, "I want the phone answered at Shellbrook as the Shellbrook Co-op, not as Prince Albert Co-op. We don't have the Prince Albert Co-op name on our trucks, we have the co-op name. So it's not Prince Albert Co-op at Paddockwood; it's the Paddockwood Co-op. Everybody knows they are a branch of Prince Albert Co-op," he says, but it has a local flavour.[11] The regional network seems to provide a combination of local community identity and regional scale and strength. Each branch has a local committee of six people who work with the local branch manager. There are also local annual-meeting presentations; and three delegates elected from each outlying location join fifteen from Prince Albert itself to constitute the larger meetings of the whole co-op, where the board of directors is elected. There are no designated directors from individual branches; instead, the emphasis is on getting the best possible people from the total delegate group to serve on the board.

"It works well," Pearson says. "That's not to say we don't have difficulty at some of our branches," he adds, and observes that it can be a burden for managers to deal with many different local committees and branch managers, and to travel out for presentations and discussions in so many locations every year. But when I ask him what the co-op gets out of it, he answers without hesitation. "Well, we get the involvement," he says. "And we get the fact that they feel a sense of ownership and responsibility, and I'm talking about the committees." As a result, when the co-op from time to time had branch managers who were not aggressive enough or too aggressive, "the feedback from those branch committees has helped us to fix that kind of problem."

There are difficulties in an environment characterized by consolidation. Even with its regional strength and efficiencies, the co-op does have to close branches sometimes. The difference the wider co-op makes, though, is to keep the branches open as long as possible, and provide an easier transition for the local people to accessing services from the next, larger community. "Oh, many times they think of it as [being that] their own service is gone," Pearson admits. "So we have to convince them of the fact that, well, it's not really gone; it's just moved from here to there. How well we communicate that to [the local] committee is how well we do from there on" at the location in question, he says. "We're different, you see, in their minds." Many people will drive from their small community into Prince Albert to shop at WAL-MART, Canadian Tire, or Superstore "and think nothing of it.... But let us take something out of [their local town] and all hell breaks loose!" As a result, the co-op has to explain itself carefully, show that it makes an effort to support the branch locations, demonstrate that what it's doing isn't working (if that is the case) before introducing changes. In

Pearson's experience, members go along with it if educated and involved in this fashion. The role of the local committees is critical, because the people on the committees are leaders within their respective communities. If the committee is convinced the time has come to close their branch and relocate the service, then the community is likely to follow.

Pioneer Co-op, centred in Swift Current in southern Saskatchewan, is at least equally impressive in extent. Pioneer Co-op is much in evidence as you drive along Highway 1. Coming from the west, the first outpost you see is the gas bar and convenience store in Gull Lake, and by the time you get to Swift Current, it seems as if the co-op is everywhere. There is the big lumber piling yard beside the co-op's bulk petroleum and cardlock complex. There is a large agro centre in front of the Sask Wheat Pool elevator, supplying grain bins and the like, and nearby a co-op–owned agrichemical service. The size of these facilities reflects the fact that they supply not just the immediate Swift Current area, but also the strong and growing lumber, agro, and petroleum business of the co-op's far-flung branches in more than a dozen towns and villages. Then, further down, you can see the sign for a gas bar a little north of the highway, and—at the junction of Highways 1 and 4—is Pioneer Co-op's huge Wheatland Mall, perhaps the system's biggest and most successful co-op mall. It has, of course, a large food store; a pharmacy; a home centre and hardware store, with carpets and plumbing; a cafeteria; a family fashions area; and numerous tenant businesses.

Pioneer Co-op's agro centre, located at Ponteix, Saskatchewan.

I had a heck of a time trying to get to Swift Current to interview General Manager Stuart Dyrland. In March and April I cancelled two scheduled trips because of blizzards, and in May—trying to sneak in from the west—I was almost stranded in snow over a foot deep that reduced Canada's major east-west highway to a single ploughed lane. But I really wanted to talk to Dyrland. Not only does he head one of Saskatchewan's largest businesses—Pioneer Co-op—but he also has an almost unique history in the system. Dyrland started off as a member and volunteer in Kyle, Saskatchewan, serving on co-op boards and eventually on FCL's board. In 1991, he made the unusual jump from the elected side of the organization to become general manager. "Actually, the transition probably wasn't too bad," he says today, "considering I was on the Federated board for thirteen years, and while being on the board there, I took the opportunity to take a lot of management cours-es." He credits the training and his experience owning and operating a farm with giving him the confidence and comfort to deal with man-agers and staff.[12]

Pioneer's development as a regional enterprise has been almost nat-ural, to hear Dyrland tell it. "I think most of the amalgamations have taken place because of necessity," he says. "An awful lot of the people in this area ... were down to where they just didn't have food [in their smaller communities] and were already shopping with Pioneer Co-op. We find a lot of times when we amalgamate, there's not a lot of change as far as numbers; everybody has a number with Pioneer already.... They're already coming in to buy some clothing or some food or some-thing, groceries, and so the acceptance is quite positive. In fact, [in] a lot of cases I think they're quite relieved when Pioneer takes them over. We're not overly aggressive in closing [branches] unless it gets to where there are hardly any sales any more. Whether that luxury will be there into the future, will depend on the competition there is in the cities." Pioneer sees about an eighty-mile (133 km.) radius around Swift Current as the central trading area, plus about twenty-five miles (42 km.) sur-rounding each smaller branch. The trading area still includes other, independent co-ops, whose members often purchase both from their local co-op and from Pioneer for other products.

Amalgamations and the development of integrated, rural-urban co-op systems such as Prince Albert and Swift Current are innovations, particularly when they are combined with changes in the identity or services of the co-operative. Co-ops like these, which have extended themselves over a region and diversified into a variety of rural and agricultural products, can be referred to as "super-locals."[13] Even some much smaller rural co-ops, however, exhibit many of the same features. Indeed, in some cases, there is nothing more entrepreneurial than a small rural co-op that sets its sights in that direction. Successful innovation depends upon good leadership, and this is what all these operations have in common.

~

WHEN GORD DMYTRUK CAME TO NAICAM CO-OP in 1988, it was his second GM posting.[14] The small co-op in the town of nine hundred people operated a grocery, hardware, and garden-supplies store; a full-service garage; a lumberyard; and a branch in the nearby village of Pleasantdale. After several years of cutbacks in the 1980s—the deletion of the dry-goods department, a crackdown on credit to members—Dmytruk found a co-op with few resources. He describes the planning process he went through with his staff as a kind of brainstorming: shut the door, start with a blank page, "and work on marketing strategies.... Have an open mind and try not to think about anything that's happening out there ... [just] ask myself what else can we be doing ... that we're not doing [now], to better the community."

"When we first looked at the Naicam Co-op," Dmytruk says, "we looked at the strengths and weaknesses; and one of the weaknesses was our branch store in Pleasantdale." With a declining population, it was hard to keep the branch viable. "We sat down with staff—I think that's critical—and said, what can we do differently to help us survive in the future? We left it at that. And I came back to them the next week and said, well, what have you come up with to make us better in the years ahead?" The staff proposed a lunch counter to bring more people into town to buy groceries. The co-op invested about a thousand dollars in equipment, re-merchandised the store, and according to Dmytruk "it worked out really well. It did what it was supposed to do. It brought the community together again, brought people to the store, and was able to help the bottom line as well." Later, they added a post office. "With those two additions we kept that branch operation going for many, many years—where we could have said nothing, shut it down, and that would have been the end of it. The key to it is that we realized that we don't know everything and went to the people who were at the grass roots in that community, and listened to them."

Naicam and Spalding Co-op's jointly owned agro centre.

Having worked on a weakness, Dmytruk and his team turned to a strength, and at Naicam Co-op that means agricultural services. "In those days," Dmytruk recalls, "we really didn't have agronomists in the Co-operative Retailing System. We were able to see that there was a need for that type of service for the members, and we were one of the first co-operatives to hire an agronomist" to provide farm-related technical advice and information. "Next, we developed a new fertilizer facility." Not having much cash to work with, the co-operative built the new facility in partnership with a private fertilizer company. The partnership got the farmer members' attention, showed them something dynamic was happening in the co-op, and lasted eleven years before it was time to do something new again. At that point, the co-op approached nearby Spalding Co-op, six miles (10 km.) down the highway. "The first thing we did was try to de-isolate the two communities and break down the barriers that existed," Dmytruk says. The two co-operatives collaborated in the first corporate bulk-fuel plant built in the CRS (see later in this chapter). Based on that success, they launched a joint agricultural centre located on the highway halfway between the two co-ops and near a community-built grain terminal. The shared Co-op

Agronomy Centre offers a range of fertilizers, replacing both co-ops' older fertilizer plants; on-site agronomists; and meeting rooms for training, and for co-op and community functions.

Naicam Co-op pioneered the Agricultural Input Management (AIM) program, which combines agronomy services, crop scouting, fertilizer and chemical sales, equipment rental services, and financial services in one package that can be accessed at a single site. In partnership with a for-profit bank—Dmytruk was unable to convince the credit union system to go along with his idea—farmers purchase their supplies on credit without having to make an extra stop at the bank, and access expert advice or services at the same time. The program was so successful that it was subsequently "rolled out" by Federated and made available to interested co-ops across the CRS. The AIM program is perhaps the classic example of innovation from below, driven by local creativity in response to local needs.

Significantly, the Naicam approach was not limited to agriculture. It considered, instead, community economic development in a broader sense. For example, since the new agro centre meant that Spalding lost its fertilizer plant—and small Prairie towns are sensitive about lost jobs and services—Dmytruk began to look at what the co-op could do for Spalding. "We wanted to make sure that we put something back into Spalding," Dmytruk says, and they eventually came up with a semitrailer- and car-wash unit. After the requisite feasibility study, the facility was constructed at the Spalding Co-op, and serves anyone who needs it from the wider region. "Those are the kinds of things we did to meld and mesh the two communities and bring the two communities together," Dmytruk says.

Within Naicam itself, a local bakery had been shut down for a couple of years. "And then one day, walking by, we said, you know, maybe there's something we can do with this bakery." The credit union owned the building; the co-op could access expertise from FCL's bakery department; so the co-op approached the credit union about relaunching the bakery. With the credit union supplying the building and Naicam Co-op the labour, the bakery was soon up and running. A couple from Bosnia initially took charge, and subsequently turned it over to a new group of owners who are still operating it today. Essentially, the co-op incubated a small business. If you go to Naicam, Dmytruk urges, you should stop and see it. "We really believe that the people there today ... have the best doughnuts anywhere! Again, what we did was take a facility that just as well could have been torn down, and made something out of it with the resources that were available to us from Federated."

"That's the key," Dmytruk stresses. "We don't have to do everything on our own." And of course, while undertaking these other initiatives, the co-op also did the kinds of things all co-ops do: they redid the lumberyard, renovated the store, added a hardware department in the basement, and so on.

He has since moved up the highway to Melfort Co-op, where he is at it again. Dmytruk showed me around the store there and pointed out recent innovations in the co-op's marketing. He begins with the Wall of Fame beside the administrative offices at the back of the food market, where there are photos of grade twelve students from the local community who have had jobs in the co-op. Their faces show confident smiles; their images here on this wall bring an aura of youth to the store, and constitute a statement of faith in the future of Melfort. Next is the Grandma Lee's coffee-shop area, a new twist on the old institution of the co-op cafeteria. Dmytruk explains that they never could get the coffee-shop to work the way they wanted, so the co-op purchased a Grandma Lee's franchise. Now the area is bright, clean, and attractive, with a focus on fresh foods that complements the marketing thrust on the renovated sales floor.

Nearby is the baked goods section. Dmytruk explains that the co-op has started supplying doughnuts to a couple of local people, who sell them out of the Tempo service station on the main highway. In effect, the co-op has turned into a wholesaler supplying some local businesspeople. This approach is part of Dmytruk's business strategy, which sees the co-op succeeding in the community by helping other people get ahead, not by competing against them.

At the tills, Dmytruk points to another successful experiment. Signs announce that co-op members who purchase groceries will receive "free gas," specifically, $2 off when they present their grocery receipt at the gas station on a Tuesday or Thursday. This cross-merchandising is designed to encourage members to be strong in both areas of purchases. Not incidentally, it also promotes member loyalty to the co-op gas bar at a time when new competitors are entering the market.

Not all the co-op's innovations are visible at the grocery store. Its expansions into agricultural service have resulted in a new development on the highway west of town. A petroleum cardlock and new fertilizer bins hint at a growing role in supplying inputs to farmers.

There is a restless creativity to all this that can only be called entrepreneurial. Many co-ops in the system exhibit it, not only Naicam and Melfort, and many GMs have it, not only Dmytruk.

◦

W INKLER CO-OP IS EVERYWHERE." THAT STATEMENT by General Manager George Klassen pretty much sums up the philosophy. The co-op has multiple facilities in town: a grocery store, a gas bar, a cardlock, an appliances outlet, and more in development. This is not to mention the store and gas bar in Morden, or the new agro centre twenty miles (33 km.) to the southwest. With a $200,000 per month wage bill, it makes a big impact on the economy of a small city, even one as prosperous as Winkler; and the $50,000 annual donations budget has a significant effect on sustaining community services and volunteers.[15]

Winkler and Morden, Manitoba, are another interesting study in rival towns that are learning to work together. They are about ten kilometres apart, connected by a four-lane divided highway lined with businesses. Even the new regional hospital is on the highway between the two. Now, the communities are linked by a co-op, too. Winkler Co-op acquired a service station in Morden with some operators whose Shell contract expired; and recently, with FCL's help, they bought the Foodland supermarket. After the co-op sign went up on the gas station, they signed up a thousand new members at Morden in a year; with the food store open, they signed up another thousand in six months.

Winkler Co-op has also been a site for numerous innovative ideas. One of them, right next to the downtown Winkler food store, is a nine-storey seniors' housing complex, developed with the co-op's leadership. "We had a group of seniors who were trying to establish the senior housing," says Klassen. "When they did a survey, the survey said that the seniors wanted to be downtown, would like to be attached to a grocery store, and have those amenities. And so they came to us and asked us whether we'd be interested in doing a joint project." The feasibility study led to a major redevelopment of a downtown block, closing and relocating businesses, and removing older commercial buildings in order to make room for the new housing complex. The co-op works with a tenants' association to operate the building, and has itself put millions of dollars of investment into its own commercial space in and adjacent to the complex. The bottom floor houses commercial tenants, connected to the co-op food store by an interior hallway. From right to left, you see the co-op food store; a fashion and casual-wear store (men's, women's, youth, sports, shoes) that opens out from the food store like another department of the co-op; a photo lab; a Co-op Café; a real estate office; an insurance office; a health store; a hair stylist; a hearing centre; and a drugstore—convenient services for the seniors on the floors above. "They can actually phone to our restaurant and get a meal delivered to their apartment upstairs," says Klassen.

Winkler Co-op's downtown food store, attached to a seniors' housing complex. Photo courtesy Art Wiebe, Winkler Photo Studio.

Another innovation is the new truck stop being developed in 2003. "We have a huge amount of trucks in this area. At last count we probably have ownership of over 150 trucks locally," says Klassen. "There's been a need for a truck stop here for quite awhile, and seeing nobody was putting [one] up" the co-op began to think about doing so. After numerous studies and hearings and discussion at two annual meetings,

Winkler Co-op is going ahead with a $4-million highway truck-stop development, including a restaurant.

Youth is a third area of innovation for the co-op. A number of years ago the co-op brainstormed with its younger staff about what young people would appreciate from the co-op, and they came up with the idea of offering people up to $50 credit for gas—not demanding cash or credit cards, but trusting everyone with a small credit account. The idea went over big with the teenage main-street cruisers. More recently, in 2003, Winkler added two youth directors to its board.

All of these innovations—the partnerships with Morden, with seniors, truckers, and youth—are no accidents, but are part of a pattern of innovative thinking and perception of community needs. When I talked to General Manager Klassen, I got a sense of two distinct factors that went into these innovations. One was a distinctive way of thinking about management, performance, and service, which is instilled throughout the organization but certainly evident in Klassen. The other factor is the character of Winkler as a community, a primarily Mennonite community considered conservative by some, yet progressive in business. The connection between the two things is Klassen and other managers who grew up in the local community.

When I asked Klassen about Winkler Co-op's Mennonite membership, his comment was, "They like to be informed … they like to know what makes things tick, and they want to see people being credible. And then their morals, their church background … extends very much into the life of everyday," he says. "That's what they like to see, and that carries right through business; like if you make a promise in business, you need to keep it." Klassen shares these values himself and likes to work for a company that has a community orientation and high ethical standards. These attitudes are rooted in a strong sense of community and co-operation. "They've learned from their past, they've had many hardships," he says. It's ingrained into them to work together. This is changing somewhat with young people, he thinks, who are not so dependent on each other; but the general attitude has still shaped the co-operative.

Klassen's approach is clear. "We no longer have the mentality that we're nonprofit," he says. "That had to change. If you're nonprofit, you go broke. People want to be with winners. They want to shop where there's a winner. They want to work for a winner." This is the same attitude he expects of his staff.

Winkler Co-op was not always in such good shape. It went through difficulties in the 1980s, largely due to overextension, and was on the verge of collapse when he came. One of the ways it turned around was by growing emphasis on customer service. Klassen remembers that one thing he did was to meet personally with key staff to motivate them. Then they started weekly department meetings where department managers would be critiqued by their colleagues—the rule was that they were not allowed to interrupt or defend themselves until they had heard the other person's views. Gradually, people became less defensive, and the attitude of customer service began to spread. "When I came here," Klassen recalls, "the mentality was, if it's something that's not on the shelf or something went wrong, they would blame Federated Co-op. That was the easiest way, to blame somebody who wasn't here" to defend themselves. "We got rid of that mentality. If we had missed ordering something, we would be honest to the customer and say, sorry, we misordered, our fault; we'll try and do better next time. And I sort of sense that customers appreciated the honesty." Klassen also talks about promoting and cultivating younger staff members, younger board members, a "younger mentality" of people not set in their ways and interested in doing interesting and creative things. Listening to him talk, it becomes clearer where the co-op's success, and its innovations, have come from.

~

I HAVE TOLD DMYTRUK'S AND KLASSEN'S STORIES at length because they illustrate how sensitivity to community needs leads retail managers, staff, and boards to innovate. But there are many other intriguing examples.

Sometimes individual staff members launch new things. I was struck by this at Hornby Co-op in BC, where a staff member's after-hours volunteer work turned a blank wall into gallery space for the island's artists. Hornby Island has a large number of artists and creative people, and a shortage of space to hang exhibits, so it was a perfect way to reinforce the co-op's role as the centre of that community. It also gives customers waiting in line something interesting to look at.

Some innovations happen apparently by coincidence. Yorkton Co-op in Saskatchewan was struggling for years with what to do with a money-losing, main-floor cafeteria in its new building. They looked to lease out the prime space to generate higher earnings, and the eventual solution looks like something out of a textbook on leading-edge marketing. First, the co-op rented the space to a furniture/appliance dealer, who left after a time. At that point, they considered expanding the store into it, but the ceiling was too low. Then, a couple of years ago, a Curves women's fitness business asked to move in. One local person told me the result has been "unbelievable." It's convenient for women, the parking is excellent, and large numbers of them are coming into the store who never came in before, and are becoming members. The co-op didn't exactly set out to implement new ideas about holistic and relationship-based marketing to women, but it discovered a winning formula.

Then there's that funeral home. Portage Co-op in Manitoba got into the funeral business many years ago when a local, family-operated funeral business was looking to sell out. A transnational chain was buying up businesses, and co-op members and management were concerned that if local control was lost, residents would be exposed to higher prices. The co-op bought the business and still operates it today under the name Omega. Co-op officials estimate they probably do about two-thirds of the funerals in town. "I'll shop here to the end and Omega will bury me," one of them told me, but hastened to add that it's a sombre business and they don't like to joke about it.[16]

Some of these innovations are the result of unique circumstances and are unlikely to be copied elsewhere. Some of them are not even intended to make money, but only to provide a service to the members. But in the new thinking of many people in the CRS, "providing a service" doesn't mean what it used to. By some accounts, it used to mean a kind of blank cheque to the membership, no questions asked, use it if you want to. More and more often, services, like donations, are linked to the co-op's identity as a community-based and locally owned business, an identity the co-op uses to build up a name and reputation. Even activities where little or no money changes hands are contributing to the marketing success of the co-operatives. There is no doubt, though, that revenue-generating or cost-saving innovations are critical to the health of the Co-op Retailing System. Some, such as the AIM program for farmers, spread from retail initiatives.

FCL, and the meetings and networks it organizes among managers and directors, has a role to play in helping innovations to spread among the co-ops. As president of FCL, it's Dennis Banda's job to be sensitive to the politics of how the system works. He recalls one innovative idea he saw developed by a local retail. "First of all, they made the presentation at their annual meeting, and I heard them." (FCL directors attend all the annual meetings they can within their districts.) "And then they asked if they could do it at our June district meeting. So then we had thirteen retails hear it. Then, when we heard it again, we said in the region ... well, that might not be a bad idea to do at the fall conference. So now you have four districts that [have] heard it. And when we had it at the fall conference last year, we decided that now maybe it's time that we should put it to the annual meeting."

The key in the process that Banda describes is that it is a retail talking to other retails about its new idea. It's not Federated telling retails it's good or, heaven forbid, telling them they have to do it. By using the district, region, and annual meeting structure, the idea gets put out to hundreds of co-op representatives from across the system. "Okay," says Banda, "the consequence of that is not going to be a big leap; the consequence is that I got two or three calls, all right? Some other provinces are saying, how do we get information on this, or is Federated prepared to do something to help this along? I guess that's the next question ... certainly if it gets to the point where we're starting to get a request that they need some help in some of it, then we'll have to consider that. This is an example of how we can grow within the system. We can take something like that, that's a good idea, and because of our structure with June, fall conferences, so forth, [we can] keep it in the minds of those delegates out there and those managers not to just sit on their butts."[17]

If there is a new idea in the system, Banda says, "the chances of it surviving are greater if you can get it supported" by people at the grass roots, at the local co-ops. "We can give them the mechanics, and assistance ... But ... just like forming the co-op, it's got to start at the bottom. To start up here, it isn't going to survive, because it just doesn't work. And the key is to get them sold on the idea, get them supporting it, and then they might need some help, sure they will"—and FCL will perhaps at that point create and offer a program for it, once retails are asking for one.

~

J UST AS IT USED TO BE ALMOST UNTHINKABLE FOR two retail co-ops to share ownership or management of facilities, it also was once unthinkable for Federated Co-op to own local facilities used by or shared with local co-ops. The multiplication of FCL "corporate assets," as they are called, in towns and cities and rural areas across western Canada is one of the biggest changes in the CRS in the last fifteen years. This dramatic evolution was made possible by the trust that developed between FCL and member retails, by recognition of common needs and interests, and by dialogue. It's also impossible to understand the acceptance of FCL's new role without keeping in mind entrepreneurial managers like the ones we met earlier in this chapter— what they're trying to do in their communities, what resources and issues they have to work with locally, what they are looking for from Federated. FCL's corporate assets are accepted as legitimate because people see how they fit into local, community-based, and community-oriented local plans.

CEO Wayne Thompson of Federated was one person who never thought he'd see the day when retail co-ops would accept FCL owning local petroleum or food facilities. He remembers saying as much when asked a question at a Fairmont Conference; and he recalls the retail managers who spoke up to suggest he reconsider. "The corporate bulk-plant program," Thompson says, "really came out of the Fairmont Conference, which told us that some of the things that we had come to believe over the years had to be changed." The Fairmont managers' meeting has also provided the encouragement in recent years for FCL's new corporate stores.[18]

FCL managers, retail managers, and board members I interviewed are unanimous in their view that the 1988 corporate bulk-fuel program was the key that unlocked a new kind of co-operation within the CRS.

The problem, and the solution, sound deceptively clear in retro-spect. Individual retail co-ops had long operated big petroleum tanks where they filled their trucks for deliveries to farms and businesses. But with facilities in every town, it was hard to keep up the image, equip-ment, training, and so on. And as the petroleum tanks aged and rust-ed, governments introduced higher environmental standards that would require even more expensive clean-ups and new investments. The cost of doing the improvements—or the cost of *not* doing them—was going to weigh on many co-ops throughout the system. Individually, none of them could do much about it.

But what if *Federated,* with its bigger balance sheet, built the new bulk-fuel plants that were required? And what if it built them, not in every town where a co-op was located, but *regionally,* so that each plant served a group of neighbouring co-ops? The wholesale, moreover, could also finance the inventory in the tanks—local retails wouldn't own the product until the truck was filled. They could pay FCL a throughput charge, but they wouldn't have to finance so much up front and hence wouldn't be so exposed to price fluctuations. Economically, it all made sense. People in the system seem a little surprised that politics and sus-picion, among retails and between retails and FCL, didn't get in the way. The co-ops did have to give up a little of their independence. They had to give up on having proud new facilities within their immediate town; they would have to drive further to pick up product; and they had to give up the option of speculating on price changes on petroleum inven-tories. But these considerations were offset by large gains. The program was accepted because it made so much sense.

Lynn Hayes is now FCL's senior VP, Corporate Affairs, but at that time he was involved on an FCL committee that was trying to figure out what to do about the bulk-petroleum problem. He remembers the first bulk plant that was built—the same one Gord Dmytruk spoke about, the one that helped bring Spalding and Naicam co-ops closer together. "The first one was like pulling ... teeth," Hayes recalls. "The second one was a little easier; and the amazing thing to the committee and to everyone was that after about six or seven corporate plant projects, it almost became fashionable to be involved in the corporate bulk-plant program." In effect, the participating retail co-ops marketed FCL's pro-gram to the others. "The retails that had done it actually said, this is one of the best things that ever happened to us. We've still got our truck, we've still got our driver, we moved the environmental hazard out of town, and now we've got this state-of-the-art new bulk plant. We can load our truck in fifteen minutes instead of an hour," Hayes recalls. "Soon we couldn't keep up to the demand. It has made the Co-operative Retailing System so much money in the last fifteen years because of the efficiencies that were generated. And the other thing is that it frustrated the heck out of the competition," Hayes says with a little satisfaction. "For years they had been consolidating their bulk-petroleum facilities and losing volume to the co-ops that stayed in the rural locations. And now co-op found a way to consolidate and stay in the rural communities. Well, we ended up closing 175 bulk plants, replacing them with thirty-five, and virtually never lost a litre because we never left town. We never had to do that ugly thing that the majors had to do, which was leave town and put people out of work."[19]

The corporate bulk-plant program, says Hayes, was "one rung in the ladder of the whole concept of area development, which is shared services, shared assets, shared expertise. Retails learned that they could work out of one bulk plant, and now we've got retails that are sharing general managers; there are retails that are sharing accounting services; we've got retails that are sharing agro facilities. It was kind of a precursor to other things the retails found out that they could share." He hesitates for a moment, thinking back. "There's a saying that seems to be applicable here: If it's going to be done, it will be done in petroleum first." It's petroleum that is the cornerstone of the CRS, in Hayes's view, and it is the developments and innovations in petroleum that set the tone for the system as a whole.

The initiative never would have worked if local people had been more suspicious of Federated. You could say it was *because* of local autonomy that Federated was able to play the role it did. One director told me that "the fact that there's still a certain amount of autonomy locally … means that the directors on this co-op and all the other co-ops around here do have their own financial statement." As a result, "it becomes painfully obvious" to local directors when something isn't working, when something has to change in the way the local co-op does things. He contrasts this with centralized organizations, where "there was no local authority," where whatever happened to the local facility "didn't cost them anything." People could simply dig in their heels and resist change, demand that their facilities be kept open. "Whereas for us to try to keep every bulk plant, it would have cost us something," he says.[20] Local responsibility is educative, and brings with it the discipline of the income-expense statement and the balance sheet. It's because of this that local directors know when it makes sense to have Federated do something for them. And the local people knew that *they* were the ones actually making the decision, not FCL.

Grassland corporate bulk plant/cardlock facility services both Boyle and Plamondon Co-ops.

While we're on the subject of petroleum, it's important to note that what the retails and FCL were doing around bulk plants, not to mention gas bars and so on, was the front end of a supply chain in which Federated was investing massive resources through the 1980s and 1990s. You can't tell the story of petroleum in the CRS without the story of the development of the Co-op Refinery. Expansion and technological innovation at the refinery were critical to the system's success. So, too, was the single-minded determination with which FCL concentrated its attention and resources to sustain, protect, and promote the refinery.

~

FROM THE 1940S TO THE 1970S, FCL AND ITS PREDECESSOR organizations invested in an expanding array of manufacturing enterprises. One might have concluded from the company's trajectory that it was aiming to become a manufacturer of everything members purchased—which would be close to saying, a manufacturer of everything.[21] That trajectory has changed noticeably since the 1980s, with a rigorous approach of focussing on where the greatest benefit is to be found. There are still many CO-OP® label products, but in general the system is interested in using its buying power to negotiate advantageous prices and quantities from private suppliers, without aspiring to manufacture the products themselves.

For similar reasons, FCL is involved in what may seem like rather few joint ventures for a company its size. One of the most prominent, IPCO (Interprovincial Cooperative Limited), is really an umbrella that controls the use of the CO-OP® label across Canada, does purchasing for co-operatives, and has an agricultural chemical production facility in Winnipeg. FCL manages IPCO under a management contract. FCL similarly has sole management of the NewGrade Upgrader in Regina, but more about that shortly. Federated has been involved in other joint ventures, and has got out of them when they did not meet FCL's standards of profitability or consumer benefit. These included CO-ENER-CO, a once-promising, crude-oil exploration company jointly owned with other Canadian co-operatives, and Western Co-operative Fertilizers Limited (WCFL), a fertilizer manufacturing company also jointly owned with other co-ops. In both cases, the company might have been seen as doing all right, but was not aggressive enough, not efficient enough, or did not produce enough consumer benefit to meet FCL standards. Some CRS co-ops still use WCFL as a supplier, but they do so directly, without FCL being a member of the fertilizer venture.

So FCL has been choosy or hardheaded about joint ventures, looking for synergies, close linkages, and member benefits. It treats its own divisions and subsidiaries in much the same way. In terms of manufacturing, FCL has remained involved in the manufacture of feeds and of wood products.

FCL's feed plants at Brandon, Melfort, Moosomin, Saskatoon, Weyburn, Calgary, and Edmonton continue to receive investment and upgrading to enable them to supply livestock and poultry producers. While other areas of agricultural supply have suffered due to droughts and market conditions, feed has increased in demand due to drought conditions in recent years. Every plant has seen investment over the past few years to increase storage and production capacity; in particular, all the plants have now been outfitted with new truck scales capable of handling today's large delivery units. As many commercial livestock operations increase in size, FCL reports success working with a number of these large producers.[22]

FCL's Forest Products Division, located in Canoe, BC, consists of forestry and logging operations, as well as lumber and plywood manufacturing. Although the industry has not been stable for the last few years due to weak markets and trade barriers, Canoe has continued to expand its focus on productivity and efficiencies. As examples in recent years, capital expenditures such as a log deck modernization project, the addition of a small-log, curve-sawing process line, the installation of a six-head sander and a new automated lay-up line for plywood production, have increased productivity, improved product quality, and enabled the production of more specialized products, thereby improving Canoe's competitive position. Canoe plywood now reaches US markets (as well as CRS co-operatives), a reorientation from earlier sales into Japan.[23]

But while FCL remains in areas like feed and forest products because, over the long haul, they are profitable and meet member demand, it is clear that the Co-op Refinery is a special case. FCL has focussed attention and investment on Consumers' Co-operative Refineries Limited (CCRL) over a prolonged period. As a result, the refinery has been transformed in the last generation through a constant process of technological innovation.

Former FCL President Vern Leland says that one of the things he is most proud of is "the development of the refinery, because I sensed when I came in [that] the focus was away from that, going into lumber mills and manufacturing other commodities. Until we got our focus back on the things that were really important to the system—number one, the refinery— ... we were wandering.... Really [it] was necessity that drove it," Leland says.[24]

Up until the 1980s, innovation at the refinery seems to have retained some of the bootstrapping character of its early history—or perhaps shoestrings are a better metaphor. The refinery's constant quest for efficiencies in process and equipment was carried out with immense creativity and hard work, and with capital investments that were large for the system at that time but not large in the grand scheme of the refining industry. One could say that CCRL successfully substituted intelligence, labour, and imagination to accomplish what other refineries might have done with larger inputs of capital.

What has changed since the 1980s can be captured in two key words: *upgrader* and, in 2002–03, *expansion.*

The NewGrade Upgrader adjacent to and integrated with the Co-op Refinery in Regina—sometimes referred to as the Co-op Upgrader—is a joint venture between CCRL and the Government of Saskatchewan.* Its purpose is to upgrade Saskatchewan heavy crude oil to a so-called light, sweet crude that can be used by the refinery. The construction of the upgrader was discussed, planned, and completed on time and under budget between 1982 and 1988. It was a mammoth engineering and technical task that ranks among the most complex pieces of construction in the province's history. But completion was only the beginning of a difficult series of technical, managerial, and political problems. To understand them requires at least a brief recounting of the upgrader's long history.

"Way back, in the seventies," recalls Harold Empey, "there had been discussions with Federated about being involved with a major oil company and doing an upgrader, and that fell through the cracks for a number of reasons." Empey was senior vice-president, Corporate Affairs, for FCL and was involved with the upgrader idea from more or less the beginning to the end. It is well known in the system that Empey and current CEO Wayne Thompson were the finalists for the CEO position in 1983. As Empey describes it, once the board picked Thompson to become CEO, the two of them worked out a complementary division of responsibilities that left Empey in charge of the upgrader file. "The day after [Wayne Thompson] took over he said to me, the upgrader's your responsibility." And indeed, it remained his responsibility even after he retired as vice-president in 1991. With Thompson's approval, he stayed on the upgrader file even after he retired from everything else. Empey

---

* In what follows, it is important to understand the relationship between CCRL and FCL. CCRL is a wholly owned subsidiary of FCL. Its function is to manufacture petroleum products from crude oil. It is managed by FCL, and the board of directors of CCRL is identical to FCL's board of directors.

recalls that Allan Blakeney's NDP government (1971–82) had talked to Gulf as well as perhaps other companies. What motivated the government was the recognition that Saskatchewan had huge, known reserves of heavy oil in the ground, greater reserves than what were recoverable in Alberta with the current technology. Saskatchewan was the logical site for the first heavy-oil upgrader in Canada.[25]

Like Empey, refinery Manager Bud Dahlstrom, also now retired, was there at the beginning. "Prior to the election" of 1982, "everybody had been talking about building an upgrader," Dahlstrom remembers. "There were at least four of them that were being talked about." One of the proposals had Husky building an upgrader north of Moose Jaw, but the other oil companies did not want to let Husky be the leader. "We were on the sidelines," says Dahlstrom, when the promoters approached FCL and CCRL. Just as it made sense for the upgrader to be in Saskatchewan, it also made sense for it to be attached to a refinery, as this would drastically cut the costs—and the co-op system's refinery was the only one left in Manitoba or Saskatchewan. "And we said, yes, we know that," Dahlstrom recalls, "but we're not going to build; we're not in the upgrading business; we're not in the production business." He explains: "Heavy oil doesn't really hold that much interest as far as we're concerned, because we [FCL] don't have any of the [heavy] oil. [This thing] was being pushed of course by producers, not refiners." SaskOil, which was a crown corporation, kept the idea alive, and at the end of the day all the other oil companies were gone from the table, leaving only CCRL, which hadn't initiated or driven the proposal. Dahlstrom recalls that a "50 percent partnership was established relatively early; but there was no way that Federated, of course, was even going to ... think about the capital involved, as far as 50 percent was concerned." This was the 1980s. Co-ops were dying, departments were closing for lack of capital. But the project didn't die, "because the argument had always been that if the ... infrastructure of the refinery was going to be used, that in effect was our contribution."[26]

"We could bring to the table a reduction of about 50 percent of the cost of an upgrader," says Empey. "A stand-alone upgrader at that time would have been one and a half billion dollars, and the upgrader was built for $800 million, on time, on budget," he emphasizes. Even today, the synergy of the refinery-upgrader combination enables it to upgrade fuel at a lower cost per barrel than stand-alone upgraders like the one at Lloydminster, Saskatchewan, according to Empey.

Following the defeat of the NDP government in 1982, the new Conservative government of Premier Grant Devine was looking for ways to generate economic activity, and picked up on the previous government's idea of a heavy-oil upgrader. Cabinet Minister Colin Thatcher made the next approach to the co-ops. Empey remembers attending a meeting with Thatcher in 1982, along with then-CEO Pat Bell and refinery Manager Bud Dahlstrom and others. "It was an August meeting; I'll never forget the beautiful day. He came to the meeting late; he was dressed in golfing clothes, and he was in a hurry because he had a tee-time," says Empey. As Empey recalls it, the message was that the government wanted an upgrader in Saskatchewan, and cost was not much of an issue. The co-op representatives were left with instructions to prepare a proposal, which they brought back to a later meeting in the premier's office.

To understand what followed, it's important to bear in mind several things. First, FCL had not initiated the upgrader. The government came to them. This was the 1980s, and the co-op system was cutting painfully in many areas. FCL was not willing to invest even a dime of its own money, as Dahlstrom says. FCL's priority was to protect its existing refinery, at pretty much any cost—they would gladly have walked away from the deal if it had been necessary to do so.

A "lengthy" discussion by the FCL board on 27–28 July 1983 clearly shows the co-op system's approach to the project. The upgrader was thought to be beneficial, as reflected in a comment in the minutes that "petroleum operations have been a strength for the Co-operative Retailing System and management feels the upgrader project will add to that strength." However, much more of the discussion seems to have hinged around how CCRL's finances could be protected from any adverse effects. Directors were told that CCRL would be buffered from any negative impact of debt or losses, or even failure of the project. The importance of these considerations is underscored by the fact that another agenda item had to do with meetings with financial institutions to discuss their assistance with the co-op system's recovery program, then still ongoing. The government's interest was characterized as being royalty revenue on the crude oil used in the upgrader, as well as the earnings from the upgrader itself. "A good return is expected." Also, "everything possible has been done to reduce concerns that might arise through changes in government." On the basis of these understandings, the directors approved CCRL's participation in the project.[27]

The internal politics of the co-op system were such that FCL could have done little differently if it had wanted to. Retail co-ops would not have supported FCL signing deals that might undermine "their" refinery. I remember attending co-op meetings in the 1980s where Empey spoke about the upgrader deal. Two things stick in my mind. First, he told co-op delegates that the upgrader would make money as long as the differential between heavy crude and light, sweet crude was at least US$6 a barrel—an accurate but fateful comment, as the differential fell below that for a number of years and put great pressure on NewGrade. Second, Empey assured the delegates that the deal with the government could never affect their refinery. On the basis that it was an ironclad deal and absolutely safe for the co-op system, delegates who might otherwise have been skeptical, including those from the other provinces, accepted the partnership with Saskatchewan.

When estimated construction costs went up and crude-oil differentials went down in 1985, the FCL board executive actually passed a motion to withdraw from the upgrader project. The discussion made clear that FCL was totally prepared to walk away from the project and swallow the costs incurred so far—mainly research data. Any further negotiations would have to be on FCL's terms.[28] When the matter came up again a couple of months later, the motion was rescinded, as FCL's terms had been met.[29]

The fact that FCL could take the upgrader or leave it, whereas the government badly wanted one and needed the use of the Co-op Refinery, gave FCL a strong bargaining position. It didn't help that the government announced the deal before figuring out the details, further weakening its own hand. So FCL's stringent conditions were met. It initially invested no money of its own in NewGrade, though it did undertake about $100 million of renovations to its refinery so that it could mate with the new upgrader. Neither would CCRL take responsibility for any losses NewGrade might run—that was the government's obligation. By all accounts, CCRL representatives were adamant on this point at every stage. Also, CCRL insisted on managing the upgrader, especially because of its integration into the Co-op Refinery. There was, moreover, a clause to the effect that if the upgrader were a failure, NewGrade would have to pay to restore the Co-op Refinery to its original functionality, and even dismantle and remove the upgrader. It was surely hard to say no when the government offered a deal that appeared to answer all the co-ops' concerns.

Vern Leland, who was president of FCL at the time, remembers that "the [Devine] government wanted a project and they came to us and, through a study, [showed that] this was the only logical way it would work, was to attach it to the refinery. So our position was, fine, if we can make it work, but we're not giving anything up in the refinery… [let's] make that perfectly clear. The earnings of the refinery, the management of the refinery, were so vital and key to the organization. [There] was just absolutely no question on our part.… It was just protection of our system, that was all we were after."[30]

As is well known, the Devine government unravelled. Tax cuts and spending were out of control, and the province ran deficits every single year, escalating to nearly a billion dollars before the NDP took power again in 1991. According to reliable accounts, the province was closer to financial collapse in the early 1990s than FCL had ever been. Provincial leaders were seriously worried that New York creditors would push the province into bankruptcy, forcing the federal government to step in and administer Saskatchewan. The debt was crushing, the highest per-capita in the entire country; the deficit was huge. The government faced billions of dollars in shaky investments and loan guarantees on projects approved by the previous administration, what Saskatchewan's Finance Minister Janice MacKinnon called "some of the most outrageous economic development decisions of any government in Canada." In a desperate effort to save the public finances, the government felt more than justified—it felt mandated—to reopen contracts and change deals. The NewGrade Upgrader was part of this agenda, leading directly to a "public brawl" between the provincial government and the co-ops.[31]

It may be that the government misunderstood the internal dynamics of the co-op system. The only way FCL could justify the interests of all of its member-owners was to defend staunchly the existing deal, which was exactly what those members had been promised when they agreed to the upgrader. The co-op system as a whole rallied around their refinery. Resolutions at all six fall region conferences in 1992 urged FCL to "stay the course" in its relations with the Saskatchewan government. The bottom line for the CRS co-ops was that "the Co-op Refinery, its operations and assets, must not be placed at risk"; that "system dollars must not be used for the upgrader project"; that there must be no risk of direct financial loss; and that CCRL must continue to manage the upgrader.[32]

Government representatives said that FCL, which they regarded as a Saskatchewan corporation, was more recalcitrant than some of the hard-nosed multinationals they had dealt with in rewriting other deals. FCL felt that "the Romanow administration was absolutely terrible to deal with in terms of reason, rationale, [and] straightforwardness"— that's Empey—and that they listened to oil-industry consultants and civil servants who were unsympathetic to the co-ops. At the height of the dispute, the government introduced legislation to rewrite the deal, which would also permit the nationalization of the refinery. Government and NDP representatives pressured co-op meetings and co-op leaders to make FCL do what was right for Saskatchewan. Co-ops pressured the government and the NDP to respect the autonomy of co-ops.

Vern Leland says the upgrader controversy was "a horrible thing to go through," one of the most difficult experiences during his FCL presidency. "It got so mean that I'd come home and NDP members had been on the phone to [Leland's wife] Sylvia, chastising her. Now that's how dirty some of that politics [went] ... it was just terrible. I don't know who drove it or how it was driven, but from our standpoint it was rotten, really rotten." The governing party did succeed in mobilizing some co-op members to put pressure on FCL. "What I noticed out there was [that] a whole lot of members were more NDP than they were co-op," Leland says, but this was more than balanced by pressure from the co-ops to protect the refinery, especially by co-ops outside Saskatchewan, a factor the government did not seem to take into account.

Out-of-province co-op directors who talked to me about the upgrader controversy convey a sense that they were mystified and appalled by what was going on in Saskatchewan—that, and deeply concerned, because it was *their* equity, too, not just Saskatchewan equity that was at stake. A Manitoba director said to me, "You know, for all the NDP is supposed to be supporting co-ops verbally, they don't *do* much, at least from my experience." He got more satisfaction out of his province's (then) Conservative government. "I don't think the people living in Alberta could understand it any more than we could."[33] Another Manitoba co-operator called the episode "a trauma for the whole movement" and explicitly compared the threat of expropriation to what past European dictatorships had done to their co-ops.[34]

Basically, if FCL held the bargaining power before the deal was signed, the government had more control after the upgrader was built. The co-ops could not afford to have their refinery disrupted (or expropriated), whereas the government had little to lose and possessed the power to rewrite contracts. "Finally," Leland says, "somebody came to their senses and realized that we've got to sit down and try to come up with something that's mutually beneficial."

Judge Willard Estey, appointed to lead an inquiry into the upgrader deal, facilitated a solution. Delivered in April 1993, the Estey Report confirmed that from the beginning, "FCL did not solicit anyone to establish the Upgrader. Neither did FCL wish to dedicate its Refinery to such a project if it entailed risk in FCL to either capital loss or diminution or cessation of earnings.... Neither did FCL undertake to make any capital contribution to the project." The judge's review also made clear, however, that the upgrader could never be profitable unless its debt load was reduced, and he did propose that FCL participate, to a degree, in reducing the debt by purchasing equipment from NewGrade and by contributing to a debt-retirement fund.[35] The eventual agreement seems to have conformed fairly closely to Estey's recommendations.

In the final deal, CCRL agreed to write off $5 million in operations fees, purchase assets from NewGrade worth $50 million, contribute a $5-million grant and a $20-million loan to NewGrade, and take responsibility for potential loans of up to $40 million of cash-flow deficiencies at the upgrader. In addition, CCRL agreed to a new pricing formula for crude oil. CCRL was thus putting in or foregoing $10 million in cash, offering loans of up to $60 million, and purchasing assets worth $50 million, for a total of more than $120 million in cash, loans, and guarantees injected into the upgrader.[36] The Saskatchewan government backed away from taking closer control of NewGrade, and from its threats to the refinery, and both it and the Government of Canada put new money into the project.

As it turns out, the reduced debt load, falling interest rates, and rising differentials on crude oil have made the upgrader a profitable undertaking today. But while it may one day be free of debts, it is harder to reduce the long-lasting burden of mistrust and ill will the controversy created. "I think that in time, the government involvement in the upgrader should be reduced to zero," Empey says, because as it stands, no substantial change or expansion can happen without new negotiations, "and I think the co-operative system is not ready to go through that mess again." In conclusion, he comments, "The memories are long," and ruefully adds, "Our experience with the upgrader … led us to understand very quickly that going to bed with the government took all the fun out of going to bed."

What did the upgrader bring to the co-ops? There were extra earnings for the refinery, some new efficiencies, and enhancements such as the ability to produce higher quality diesel fuel. The refinery was able to run full-out more of the time, bringing greater stability. When demand for more fully refined petroleum products was weak, the refinery/upgrader could sell synthetic crude. All of this is hard to quantify, and the co-ops might have achieved equivalent benefits by other means. The one thing the upgrader certainly did is diversify the refinery's feedstock, giving it some security against the possibility that light, sweet crude might one day become more expensive. While co-op representatives bristle at government claims that they reaped windfall benefits and got to modernize their refinery at public expense, it is true that there were some benefits and there was modernization, and not all of it at NewGrade's expense. Perhaps the best way to put it is that the refinery was challenged to take its operations to a new level of complexity and sophistication. After the start-up problems—and there were problems—there was a larger refinery, the first integrated upgrader-refinery complex in the country, and a position of technical leadership that has spin-offs in terms of dynamism and confidence. Dahlstrom also observes that "the upgrader changed the nature of the refinery" to a less tightly knit workplace, a larger and more complicated organization. "It was a step change"—like stepping up to a whole new level—"as far as people were concerned."

While all the politics were going on, CCRL staff were struggling with immense technical complexities. Bud Van Iderstine, FCL's current vice-president, Refining, started at the Co-op Refinery in July 1989, just when the upgrader was going through its start-up pains. The complex had suffered a fire in the hydrogen plant in March, and then a big heater explosion and fire in the ARDS reaction unit in June. "When I started, I spent those first weeks and months down there in the upgrader control room," recalls Van Iderstine, "and trust me ... for the first two years that I was here, I literally spent 70 percent of my time either in the control room or right out in the field. I was rarely in the office area around here for two years," he says. "What I saw was a lot of talented, very well-experienced refining people who were frustrated because they were having difficulties with some aspects of the new technology. They had a tremendous spirit of teamwork and a very positive drive and tenacity to not let the frustrations (and there were some) get to them. They just kept going because it was their refinery and they were not going to let this upgrader get the best of them." Van Iderstine remembers that the start-up was a very up-and-down kind of thing. The managerial staff had regular morning meetings to review progress and pick two or three key items to work on every day. "It was a whole lot of small steps to climb the mountain," is how Van Iderstine puts it. "It took another couple of years from there, so I would say it was in about 1991–92 when we really stabilized the plant. We then started to get good crude processing rates and we kept the upgrader components all running well. Everyone felt good about that."[37] As throughput increased and crude-oil price differentials improved, the NewGrade Upgrader began to repay loans. In 2000, its debt dipped below $100 million, on track to be eliminated within a few more years.

~

M EANWHILE, THE REFINERY MOVED ON TO OTHER things, essentially a long stream of improvements that did not end with the upgrader. The system undertook the largest expansion in the refinery's history, which was completed in 2003. The upgrader, in retrospect, may look like just one step—perhaps a side-step—along the way.

CCRL's 2003 expansion is both huge and complex. Van Iderstine points out that in the early 1990s, the Co-op Refinery was averaging 42,000 to 43,000 barrels per calendar day. This increased over a decade to

55,000 to 58,000 barrels. When there was no shutdown, the plant was able to run as high as 65,000 barrels per day, but did not maintain this production because of the need to suspend activities periodically for maintenance turnarounds. Gradually the length of the turnarounds has been shortened so that each is now down to twenty-three to twenty-five days. The expansion adds 30,000 barrels per day of capacity, but it will also be combined with a new maintenance cycle that will further reduce the turnarounds. Van Iderstine expects to exceed 90,000 barrels per day. "And I don't have any number I'm going to stop at," he adds.

CCRL's 2003 Refinery Expansion Project.

The expansion is not only about higher capacity, however. It simultaneously enables the refinery to take in a wider range of types of crude oil, and to put out products that meet higher environmental standards.

The expansion allows the refinery to process heavier crude, increasing its options for feedstock and reducing its dependence on the upgrader's production. In the short term, it is likely that much of the upgrader's output will be lightly processed and sold on the market, rather than fully processed through the beefed-up refinery. In the long term, if the co-ops' petroleum volumes keep expanding at current rates, they may need both what the refinery expansion does for them, and the upgrader's capacity, to supply members' needs.

In addition, new fuel standards coming into effect in 2005–06 require lower sulphur contents in gasoline and diesel fuels. Meeting these new standards alone would have required a very large investment; the 2003 expansion does the same thing and also adds something like 50 percent to output. Four hundred million dollars is a large investment in the Prairie economy, and some might wonder at how high it is. By comparison, CHS Inc., an American agricultural co-op that owns two refineries totalling 140,000 barrels per day, is also spending $400 million to meet 2006 environmental standards—and those are US dollars. Their improvements will bring no increase in output, and they, too, may have cost overruns before they are done, such as those that raised FCL's figure. A CHS co-op member is quoted as saying, "It's amazing how much it costs to keep manufacturing fuel with environmental costs going up, but we have to keep the environment clean."[38]

If all this hasn't been enough, Van Iderstine sees a constant stream of challenges in the future. His reaction: "I think passion is a large part of what we're all about ... whatever we're working on, whether it's the expansion project or the safety program, whether it's the turnaround, whether it's the desulphurization project," he says.

It's one thing for the refinery staff and managers to feel passion about their work, but for $400 million, the whole co-op system has to feel passionate about what is happening at the refinery. Since the co-op system claims about one million individual members, the current expansion of the refinery, by itself, is like every adult and child whose purchases go through the CRS each putting in $400. That's a lot of commitment. Choosing to modernize the refinery comes at the expense of other choices, and for the co-ops to be so united in supporting this choice is striking. Like most other aspects of the system's success, the commitment to the refinery is the product of experience and dialogue, shaping a culture in which certain shared interests, like the refinery, are emphasized.

When it comes to how FCL promotes innovation, one significant piece is the company's approach to accumulating, concentrating, and investing capital. I asked CEO Wayne Thompson about this and he answered as follows. "Part of what we've been able to do over the years is recognize the fact that if we're not going to be controlled by outsiders and influenced by them and have additional costs, then we need to generate the funds within our own system. Through our planning process we make sure that we can, if possible, put away the funds so we can pay for things ourselves. At the same time that we did that, we increased the cash portion of our patronage refunds to the member co-ops. At one time it was at 33 percent or so, and everyone was hoping we might be able to get it up to 50 percent—that went on for years and years in resolutions. Well, for a number of years now, we've been in the 80 percent range, and at the same time putting away cash for future expansion. When something like the refinery expansion comes along that we *are* able to pay out of our own cash, I think that makes the system understand why it was important we were putting that money away. If we were in the position now that we would have had to borrow the money, and we'd had these cost overruns and had to go back and borrow more and more money, you can be assured that the lenders would have wanted more and more security. So I think it's been a really good lesson for us," Thompson says.[39]

Thompson also points out that retails are increasingly doing the same thing. They have up to $100 million in cash on deposit with FCL at any one time. "So a lot of retails have a lot of extra cash. They are also building a lot of their new facilities and doing a lot of their major renovations and so on without borrowing any money…. They're starting to see the benefits of it themselves."

You could sum it up this way. Co-ops have to make earnings. With those earnings, they have to pay patronage refunds, if they can, because that will encourage member support and lead to more earnings and more refunds in future. As they earn money, they have to set aside funds for reinvestment and development. And they have to avoid borrowing. It's this disciplined, long-term approach that works for FCL— covering all the bases, no quick fixes, no spending sprees. And yet over time, FCL and CCRL saved enough to finance a massive investment to improve an important productive asset to meet higher standards and growing volumes.

~

F CL'S MARKETING STRATEGY HAS BEEN TO CONCENTRATE on pursuing excellence in petroleum and food. On the petroleum side, the development of gas bars/convenience stores, bulk plants, and investment in the refinery has increased volume, captured efficiencies, and linked the co-op system more tightly together along the petroleum product chain. On the food and general merchandise side, equivalent developments include new store designs, corporate-owned stores, the consolidation of warehouses and application of new technology within them, and selling to and through independents in order to access greater volume and expertise for the co-op system. Since this chapter focusses on innovations, let's start with the corporate stores. These are, in one sense, the food equivalents of the petroleum bulk-plant consolidation program, in that they involve direct FCL ownership and investment in localities. But they are retail, not bulk, operations, and do not involve the same kind of partnerships with retail co-ops.

Ste. Anne Co-op's bulk plant.

The new Marketplace store in Brandon, Manitoba, described in chapter one, is one example of the new corporate stores. FCL has retail facilities in selected locations, usually in partnership with a member co-op. In these cases, FCL owns the store and leases it to the local co-op to operate. This is hugely significant in a system where local autonomy is as fiercely defended as it often is in the CRS, and yet there has been surprisingly little fuss. I asked CEO Thompson whether there was any opposition, and he just says, "I think they've seen the benefit of it," and proceeded to tell me how it all came about.

> The very first one we did, that's where I'll start, was the Prairie Co-op at Melville [Saskatchewan]. At that time they had a food store that was terribly old and it was run-down, everything was wrong with it. They had a gas bar that was old. They were virtually bankrupt. So

the chance of Melville surviving was not good. They knew what they had do, but they didn't have the money to do it. So we put together the idea of the Corporate Program. That turned Melville around, their sales took off, their earnings took off, they got lots of cash. Those successes led to moving forward and doing [the same] at another retail that had similar problems.[40]

It was in the fall of 1987 that the FCL board authorized the purchase of land, demolition of an old building, and construction of a new nine-thousand-square-foot food store in Melville, to be leased to Prairie Co-op. At the same time, the board approved a more general policy for how such stores could be created. The policy placed strong emphasis on feasibility studies and on common agreement by the retail board and management as well as FCL board and management, and approval of the FCL region office.[41]

Corporately owned food store leased to Prairie Co-op at Melville.

Now, Thompson continues, "a number of retails that could in fact go out and borrow the money themselves ... *don't* do it because they see the benefits of not having to disturb the patronage refund process to the retail members and so on." If FCL owns the store, the retail can keep paying cash out to its members. "We always say to them, if you have the money, it's cheaper to do it yourself," Thompson says. "A number of retails can do that, but there are some that can't. So those are the stores we lease to retails."[42]

Where FCL owns a store, it's a long-term proposition. Federated makes its terms, conditions, and expectations perfectly clear: the lease will earn revenue to compensate FCL—and FCL's owners, the other co-ops—for building that store. It's a take-it-or-leave-it proposition for local co-operatives. There's no having FCL build the store now and then asking to buy it from them later. The clear-cut terms, the same for all co-ops, with the choice in the hands of the local retail, is probably one reason the idea has been accepted.

And then there are the cases where FCL owns *and* operates the store, with no local co-op involved. "The first one we had [like that] was Manning, Alberta," Thompson says. "Manning was a co-op at one time but left the system way back in the late seventies or early eighties and went to other suppliers. This store was horrible to say the least; they had lost money, were in receivership, and finally declared bankruptcy. We looked at this community and said, if we buy this store, maybe we can do something with it. So we bought it, made major renovations, and the results have been good. We also introduced a loyalty program where [customers] would get some cash back. We got the [customers] back because we now had a decent facility and a good merchandise standard," Thompson says. There are several such stores now in a variety of locations; in my own travels, I visited two others. Some are purchased—generally, it seems, run-down stores of the Manning type—while FCL has built others from scratch, using the opportunity to introduce its Marketplace designs to new areas. Most are food stores, while some are petroleum operations. By 2001, there were eleven FCL-owned-and-operated retail enterprises, located from Salmon Arm, BC, to Brooks, Alberta, to North Kildonan and Selkirk, Manitoba. Operating as associate members of FCL, the eleven subsidiaries are now amalgamated into a single retailing subsidiary.[43]

These are co-op–system–owned stores, but they are not retail co-ops: the customers don't invest, don't own, don't vote. They can, however, receive loyalty rewards similar to patronage refunds. In theory, a group of local customers might offer to buy a corporate store from FCL and make it into a co-op, but the capital cost of doing this is likely prohibitive, especially when they already have the store without doing anything for it other than shop there.

To have the wholesale engaged in retailing, even in a few scattered locations, is more radical than it might seem on the surface. Under other circumstances, retail co-ops might get twitchy when they see their wholesale doing this, and start wondering whether the wholesale is getting diverted from its task of supporting and serving the autonomous retails; whether it should be minding its own business; whether it might one day compete with its owners. They might be concerned that potential co-op members will be confused when they see almost identical stores in different towns, one a local co-op and one not. At the very least, one can imagine retail managers looking carefully at what the wholesale is doing in its corporate stores to see whether there are things there that might later be tried on the wider system. I know that questions have been raised, but in my interviews I picked up little reservation or doubt. This speaks to the high degree of trust that FCL has earned among the retails, to careful consultation and explanation within the regions, and to a perception by FCL members that they will benefit from the corporate stores—through larger system volumes, better deals from suppliers, better use of warehouse and distribution capacity, and more unified marketing presence across western communities. It's another surprising development, one that would have been unimaginable two decades ago.

A director in one of the regions where the new corporate-owned stores have been debated told me that the system basically sees it as a hierarchy of options, where local ownership is privileged. The best is for local co-ops to build their own stores. Second-best is for FCL to build them and lease them to the local. Third-best, and the option to resort to when the first two don't work, are the corporate-owned-and-operated stores. But the reality is that the system needs volume, purchasing power, and efficiency, and if those dictate that a store is needed somewhere, the system has to do it, one way or the other. Sometimes, innovation and flexibility mean adjusting even the most closely held principles. The same director told me there was a pleasant sidelight to the whole experience of FCL going out to purchase local stores. "The individuals involved probably could have sold to any one of the majors, but they preferred to deal with the co-operative because, for one, what they saw was very fair treatment of their employees; and … two, we're a community-based organization that was going to continue service to the community. That certainly became our advantage in those purchases," this director reports.[44]

It seems there are strengths and advantages to being a system that is ultimately based on local community ownership.

∽

INKING UP WITH INDEPENDENT, NON–CO-OP SMALL businesses is another innovation that might seem like a striking departure from past co-op practice. The idea of selling products to independent retailers actually began on the petroleum side of FCL's business when, in the latter half of the 1970s, it began supplying Tempo gas stations in order to ensure an outlet for more of the refinery's product. The benefit to the co-ops in doing this was that the larger volume lowered the average costs for the co-ops on what they handled, increasing their margins and their earnings.[45] In the mid-1980s, FCL considered purchasing the hardware and building-materials business of Sterling Distributors; according to some sources, the deal fell through because of the unhelpful attitude of the company's creditors.[46] Although FCL did not purchase the Sterling business and assets, it did start selling to independent hardware outlets, many of which were former Sterling customers. The idea expanded into the food side in the 1990s.

Following confidential negotiations that lasted much of the previous year, FCL announced at its annual meeting in 1992 that it had purchased The Grocery People Ltd. (TGP), an Edmonton-based wholesale company. The FCL board first discussed the acquisition of TGP in 1991 and granted approval for management to pursue it further. They used a code name for the project—Spitfire—to conceal the actual identity of the company in question. It is clear that directors asked many probing questions before the acquisition proceeded.[47] Teams from FCL held confidential briefings with key retail managers and boards in the system, to gain their input and ensure there was a consensus on the bold and somewhat surprising purchase. The response was basically unanimous that FCL should proceed.[48]

FCL has not bought many companies, and it does not have many manufacturing or wholesaling subsidiaries. The Grocery People was a special case because of how it fit the system's needs and meshed with what FCL needed to serve its member retails. The company was not bought to benefit FCL, but to benefit retails, a point brought home to me by retail directors and managers in various regions who spoke strongly and supportively about the move. Because of the speed with which The Grocery People was integrated into FCL's organizations, retails quickly enjoyed the benefits of warehouse consolidation (reduced costs) and improved fresh-produce operations.

FCL managers had assumed that it would take two full years to assimilate TGP into the Co-op Retailing System, and that other new initiatives would have to be put on hold until this was completed. But with concerted effort, the transition period was completed ahead of schedule, in less than a year.[49] This was made possible by the good fit between the competencies, leadership, and perhaps, above all, the cultures of FCL and TGP.

The Grocery People was in fact also a co-operative, though not a consumer-based co-op like the CRS retails or FCL. It was a type of co-operative not well known in Canada—a co-operative of independent retailers, of storekeepers and shop-owners. Local retailers, generally businesspeople who ran small-to-medium-sized food stores in western towns and neighbourhoods, joined together in 1960 to form what was originally known as Alberta Grocers. Owners of retail stores invested, they owned the company, they voted, they sat on the board of directors, and they hired themselves a CEO to run their wholesale for them—a co-operative of small-business owners, in other words. They developed a general-purpose wholesale that handled both regular groceries and perishable produce. It was well organized and provided excellent service. But retailing is a tough business. Big, integrated, well-financed competitors were moving in, and the retail store-owners were hard-pressed to finance both their local stores as well as the development of their wholesale. TGP thrived longer than most small regional wholesale companies, but by the early 1990s it was looking for a way out—one that would protect the needs of retail entrepreneurs for access to wholesale services, while removing the need for them to finance the company themselves.

Enter FCL. It took the shrewd eye of FCL senior managers, led by all accounts by CEO Thompson himself, to realize that the independent retailers' needs and the co-op system's needs were complementary. As always, Federated was looking to drive costs out of its distribution system. In particular regions and product lines, that meant it had to get higher volume, or else close more warehouses. Some retails were concerned about this. At the same time, both FCL and retails were not satisfied with the service they were getting out of their existing produce suppliers, and were concerned that their suppliers might be taken over by a competing business group. The co-ops didn't have enough money to buy out a big supplier themselves, and lacked the specialized expertise in the produce area to do the job in-house. It was a conundrum, until TGP came along.[50]

TGP warehouse, located in Edmonton.

Jim Crawford has been CEO of The Grocery People since 1989, and saw the company through its amalgamation with FCL. In 1992, says Crawford, "there were three suitors to buy TGP: the Pattison Overwaitea Food Group [best known in BC], the Loblaws Westfair company [the group behind Superstore], and FCL." As a small wholesale serving independent retail store-owners, The Grocery People were hard-pressed to continue in the competitive environment, particularly with small store-owners retiring, often closing their stores, and pulling their equity out of their wholesale. FCL was accepted as a partner, says Crawford, "as much for the culture of the company as anything else. The other companies didn't need our name and didn't need our people, didn't need our programs. In the FCL environment, they were looking for a produce supplier and they needed that expertise … it was a very good fit." There were "a lot of synergies within the companies," he says, "and the cultures were so similar because of our grocers basically being a co-op of independent retailers and Federated supplying the CRS. A lot of the culture, the thought processes, were very similar."[51]

Retired Marketing VP Elmer Wiebe recalls that while Thompson saw the opportunity, he picked Wiebe to approach the independent retailers. They weren't big operators and might not have reacted well to a direct, dollars-and-cents approach. Wiebe says it was more like "a relationship—it's almost like courting your girlfriend or wife, you know … a stage-setting thing. So he chose to send me." Wiebe's father had been a small retailer, in service stations and convenience stores. "So when we got in there and we started talking about The Grocery People and [met] their board … I could almost pretend I was one of them because I knew exactly where they were coming from. They got to like me," Wiebe says. "I wasn't the one who put the deal together, but I opened the doors." Being able to talk to a marketer like Wiebe or a merchandiser like Norman Krivoshen reassured the grocery independents through the unavoidably bumpy parts of merging a small independent's way of doing business into a big system like FCL.[52]

I asked Crawford about the similarities between co-ops and small independent retail grocers. "Well, when there's an independent retailer, an independent co-op association, they both have the same challenges and it's the same business, all the same concerns have to be addressed," he says. "The success of either one basically boils down to the management, quality, and style…. And we both do business in rural western Canada, and you have to be part of those communities to be successful. Being a co-op is one approach and being a family-owned business is another approach, and in a lot of places I think we just complement one another. Not everybody in town's going to like the Super A, and not everybody in town's going to like the co-op," he says—and true enough, in some communities, the TGP accounts and FCL members do compete with one another. TGP accounts operate under the SUPER A FOODS™, BIGWAY FOODS™, and TAGS™ banners.

Out of the similar backgrounds in western communities and small retailing came the similarities in the cultures of the two wholesale organizations. "You're always looking out for the interest of your members," Crawford sums up. "You're not a corporation that is separated from the people who own you, [so] you look at your spending habits, etc., in a different culture than a Loblaws would in relation to their retailer." Basically, "the others are corporate driven. They are corporate store organizations," he says. "The independents that they deal with, they've really demonstrated they have no real concern about the longevity and profitability of those stores. Whereas in the FCL/TGP world, the profitability of the retails, they count on it—because without them the wholesales don't exist."

It sounds like a match made in heaven, but small business and co-operatives are often perceived to be antagonistic to one another—to have little respect for each other's practices. This probably always was more ideology than reality. You just have to consider how many co-ops got into business by friendly buyouts of local shopkeepers, who often stayed on to manage the co-op for a few years before retiring.[53] Or consider managers like Gord Dmytruk, whose community economic development strategy, discussed earlier in this chapter, revolves around not competing with private businesses, and even helping launch them. But it is true that a certain perception of difference was there. In the case of TGP, it has grown into mutual respect.

Crawford admits that at one time, "aggressive and co-op were rarely found in the same sentence," but he credits Wayne Thompson with turning that around. Today, he says, people in the industry see FCL as "very high profile, very professional … in terms of the new stores, not only construction but innovation … they're very highly regarded." Crawford is enthusiastic about the relationship. "The eleven years we've been part of it, it's been a very pleasant surprise to see how they improved the standards of their operations, not only the physical buildings, etc., but I think there's a spirit that goes with that and that comes from success.… You'd be hard-pressed to find [any organization in Canada] that's been more successful, in the last ten years especially.… Everything that basically Wayne promised has happened," says Crawford. "The company kept its name. It kept its identity. It kept its programs. It kept its symbols. And it grew." Being part of FCL has meant that TGP has grown across western Canada, opening produce operations in Calgary, Saskatoon, and Winnipeg to supply the CRS. The company also continues to supply independent retail grocers across the West, as well as operating cash-and-carry wholesale businesses in various locations, and supplying food services, hospitals, restaurants, and hotels out of Edmonton and Kamloops.

FCL Consumer Products VP Norman Krivoshen—the co-ops' head grocer—says that "it's been a wonderful relationship" with TGP, particularly because of the produce business. He recalls that "when we bought The Grocery People back in 1992, their produce volume was approximately $20 million. Today, our produce volume at the wholesale level is something in the order of about $130 million. And they brought us that expertise, which we badly needed." The co-ops were able to integrate more of a supply chain under their own control. From TGP's point of view, business grew rapidly, and the company was kept intact. "When we integrated the two companies, we did it very, very quickly and we did not have very many people who crossed from one company to the other. We tried to keep The Grocery People whole so that their customers or independents did not see any change in that company," Krivoshen says. He adds that there were four areas in which the combined volumes of TGP and FCL's own departments could bring significant savings: procurement, information services, accounting, and logistics. "So very quickly, we integrated those four disciplines. We also said that TGP ... had a very, very good relationship with the independents, so we wanted to maintain that relationship and leave that part of the business with TGP. So, consequently, even though all the purchasing is done for both The Grocery People and Federated here in Saskatoon, all of the marketing for TGP still remains in Edmonton, and the marketing for FCL is here in Saskatoon. And we do not see ever bringing those two disciplines together, simply because in a number of communities, we compete against each other."[54]

I visited communities where a co-op store and a TGP affiliate were in direct competition, the only two stores in town in their product lines. General managers I asked about this basically shrugged. How did they feel about their wholesaler, FCL, supplying their competitor? Well, the competitors were a local couple, I was told; it was important for the community that they stay in business. Every local business was needed. Without them, local people wouldn't have a choice, and choice is a good thing.[55] The attitude of most GMs seems to be that they are focussed on raising their own standards to a higher level, not putting anyone else out of business. In fact, they tend to welcome competition.

The retails' acceptance of FCL's ownership of The Grocery People is fascinating, because it's not automatic or inevitable. Retails could be hostile to FCL dealing with profit-seeking competitors. But the system just doesn't think that way. The system's openness is not something to be taken for granted. It's the result of dialogue, of careful consultation and preparation of major decisions, of attention to relationships. FCL didn't just go out and buy a company. They made the case, first, why retails would benefit from it. Everything was above board. Retail co-ops are never unanimous, but when all the facts are on the table, they usually make clear choices.

~

FCL LEADERS TALK ABOUT PLANTING SEEDS IN THE system in order to bring about change. The new store designs are a good example—the Marketplace food stores, the gas bars and convenience stores, the new touchless car washes. These major changes in facilities, merchandising, marketing, and staff training are changing the face of the co-op system. So where did this round of innovations begin? In the co-op system, it's sometimes hard to tell where things started, because they arise out of dialogue and interaction; and sometimes they start locally and spread as other retails come on board. The new designs, though, are perhaps easier to pin down. The people I talked to traced them back to business planning within FCL. Federated managers looked at the system, identified a need for development, and thought about how to get the retails to share in a system vision. The important thing is that they did *not* go ahead and commission a design and then go out to the retails to pitch it to them. By now, in this book, we've seen enough of the CRS to know that retails are quite capable of getting their backs up and resisting that kind of thing. You have to involve them. Show them. And let them decide.

For a number of years, FCL senior managers from the company's home office have led study tours of retail managers to the United States to look at different retailing and marketing concepts. This is a research activity, but it's research shared with the system that, literally, brings the retail managers along. The managers discuss the ideas with each other and with FCL leaders. The EMC and other manager committees formed to look at particular commodities or programs have their say. Reactions are tested and the designs are adjusted. Ideas are floated at the Fairmont meetings before a wider audience, and perhaps fine-tuned some more. Federated staff rarely present a new idea "cold"—it almost always has some degree of verification and support from retails beforehand. As new designs develop and are discussed and tested, FCL's region offices work with retails, making suggestions, offering assistance. That's one reason FCL offers small grants to retails to assist with developing new facilities; it's a small inducement to pay attention to the system's policies and concepts. "Once there were a couple of them up and running," an FCL manager told me, "everyone else could go have a look at it, see how it works," and make comments to FCL on what they think is working and what needs to be adjusted—"and we do that. We value the feedback that comes from retails, so it works together as teamwork."[56] The successful concepts snowball as more retails adopt them.

CEO Thompson says that "the key to it"—to improving the system's marketing—"was getting our retails to buy into the [idea] that they should be and want to be the best in town." In this context, Thompson tells the story of how the study tours started. Vice-President Krivoshen was doing a major presentation on food marketing at a Fairmont Conference in the 1990s.

> Looking at how he was going to do his presentation, we wanted to involve some general managers in the presentation and during some of the breakout sessions. But we weren't sure how to go about having a reinforcement to some of the things that Norm had wanted to bring up from all of the information that he had gotten from food stores in the US, and even over in England. So we decided that we would take the people he was going to use in his presentation on a retail food-store tour to the United States. We took that group of individuals to Los Angeles, San Antonio, and Houston. When they came back, they and Norm were very much on the same wavelength as to what was happening in the United States and needed to happen in our system; they gave a lot of credibility to Norm's presentation.
>
> We found out that trip was so successful that we decided to take another group. We took the next group down, and even though we'd been saying these things, we found out that when people actually see it and feel it, and they concentrate for a number of days, and they are together and they talk about it—then all of a sudden they really understand and they really buy in.

And that just continued. So right to this day we're still taking groups of retail general managers on these store tours, and of course we've taken all of our Federated food people on these tours, and that has really created an atmosphere [for] good image and merchandising standards. And that's carried over not only in food, but it's also helped us in other departments, and in the facilities we're building, including our c-store program—all of our centres have improved as a result.[57]

The American tours take the co-op managers to see some national chains, but generally focus on regional companies that operate thirty to forty stores in large metropolitan areas such as those Thompson mentioned. These regionals have often developed interesting marketing angles that enable them to compete against the much larger national chains. Although the CRS is considerably more than thirty to forty stores, it faces competitors that are far larger, including some of the same ones as the successful regional stores in the US. That co-ops can learn from the innovative practices in cities further south is illustrated concretely by the new Marketplace store designs, which incorporate ideas from the study tours.

Many of the retail managers I interviewed had been on these tours, and what they said bears out Thompson's account. They learned from it, and they also saw the opportunity as something for the system as a whole to respond to in a unified way, not just as individual co-ops. "I was on the second batch that went," one GM told me. "I mean, it's like taking the country boys to the city … talk about opening our eyes up! And what he [Thompson] did there was—the strategy was—he got us excited about it first," so that the managers were interested and *demanding* that FCL come up with something along the lines of what they had seen. "There'd be a conventional retail right alongside a box store," he remembers, "and they're both making a living. And [the lesson is] not to be afraid of the box store, but whatever you do, find your niche and do it well." He adds, "It wasn't just all retail foods, it was c-stores and … fast-food tie-in for the retail stores, liquor stores … it was a whirlwind tour that was very educational for us. There was nothing like it. A picture tells a thousand words," he says. "They took the bigger retails, took those guys first, and of course when we came back [we] talked to the other managers in our regions as a group ... and expressed the things that we saw and anticipated the direction the retail, or the wholesale was going.... We were very happy to be involved when it happened. But that in itself, to get everybody excited about something before it happened, got them onside. Imagine if he had taken the ... region managers and the retail advisors and all the commodity managers, taken them all first and got them excited, and then he turned around and he tried to convince us, [at the] regional level or [on] a one-on-one basis. It wouldn't have flown. So, hats off to Mr. Thompson."[58]

Another, younger retail manager told me, "We toured the food stores in Los Angeles and Seattle with Wayne Thompson and Ken Hart and Norm Krivoshen, and it was an amazing experience to be ... on a casual basis with these people and learn from the experience of what they see when they go into the stores." He confirms the value of the trips. "I think we learned a lot.... Things that I've seen in the US on the store tours ... you see them in every retail [co-op] today. Everything from the slogan posters hanging from the ceiling to our delis, how they merchandise, what product offerings we have in our bakery ... what kind of lights we have on our tills ... [and] the types of value-added products ... in our produce department and how they're merchandised."[59]

∼

I N BUSINESS, OR GOVERNMENT, OR ANYTHING ELSE these days, there's the cost of not innovating, and then there's the cost of innovating badly. Both can be disastrous, and in fact, companies that jump from one problem directly to the other are not unheard of. Successful systems like the CRS manage to avoid both pitfalls.

In this chapter, we've looked at a variety of kinds of innovation in the system, ranging from the very small to the very large. Some were innovations by individual retails, or individual staff or managers, acting on their own; some were innovations by Federated within its own divisions and subsidiaries. But perhaps the most interesting examples, and the most important to the system, are the shared innovations.

Co-operatives have advantages and disadvantages. They can't throw around the capital, the R & D expertise, or the advertising dollars that their competitors can, to make something happen or to push a novelty through to consumers. They also can't give orders to the whole system at once. The co-ops' strength lies in their relationships, the relationships of the local retails to their immediate communities, and the relationships among the retails and between them and FCL. In terms of innovation, what's relevant about these relationships is two characteristics: *sensitivity* and *autonomy*. Retails can cultivate a sensitivity to community needs; Federated can cultivate a sensitivity to retail needs. Out of this sensitivity comes a recognition of opportunities and the beginnings of new ideas. We have seen, in this chapter, how local and system-wide innovations have arisen out of creative thinking within an environment of just this kind of receptivity and openness. The process may need to be driven by the kind of marketing determination described in chapter one, just to shake up the thinking; but it's the sensitivity to retailing opportunities among the members that gives co-ops an edge.

And then there's *autonomy*. Co-ops ultimately rest on the power of persuasion. Members are free to walk away from what the co-op offers. Co-ops are free to walk away from what FCL offers. This could be a cause of frustration and inefficiency, but seems, instead, to be an inducement to the parties involved to respect each other, and to listen. FCL programs work *because* FCL leaders know that they must respect retail autonomy, so they gather retail input and test and improve their programs. The chances of innovating badly are greatly reduced *because* of the discipline imposed by local ownership and local autonomy. Perhaps the members, too, listen a little more carefully and don't get their backs up, because they know that they have the final say.

In recent years, it's all worked remarkably well, but what about the future?

~

I T IS NO GOOD TRYING TO PREDICT SPECIFIC INNOVATIONS. Who, in the mid- to late-1980s, would have predicted any of the major initiatives of the last ten to fifteen years? Bulk petroleum consolidation? The Grocery People? Corporate stores? A $400-million expansion, paid for in cash? Perhaps someone would have predicted retail theatre (the thunderstorms, mooing cows, and so on), but it would have sounded like a spoof. Innovations are *unpredictable*. That's one of the lessons of this chapter. That's why you can't "plan" to have them, or when to have them, or what they will be.

But the *process* of innovation—that we can say something about.

In a system like the CRS, innovation won't happen without continuous dialogue. That's been one of the accomplishments of the last two decades—interchange between retails and Federated personnel, so that good ideas, from whichever side they may come, get planted and spread according to their usefulness. In the examples we've seen, many innovations, or their spread, have been due to an interchange among managers in FCL and in retails. Indeed, one of the questions this all raises is whether the role of managers has become so important as to make elected directors, in normal circumstances, less critical to the future of the system than they used to be, simply because managers make so much difference to the ways co-ops change over time. Of course, the directors will always be needed to select and work with management—that's how managers are put in place—but management may have become more important than ever, precisely because it is more collaborative (with other managers) and entrepreneurial.

The kind of communication needed in a federated system like the CRS is based on clear recognition of both separate and mutual interests. Both retails and Federated need to have a clear idea of what they, themselves, are about, and why the other is important to their interests. That kind of clarity has improved over the last twenty years. Federated recognized the importance of retailing to its future, and learned to work in a careful and respectful manner with retails. And retails have discovered ways that Federated is important to them, as illustrated in many ways by quotations from retail managers and directors used in this book. Usually, the relationship works—but there are always differences.

At root, collaboration in the CRS is a question of organizational *cultures,* of mental models that people have in their heads of the organizations they work for, or of their identities. Federated has defined an identity for itself. It is a marketing organization; it supports retails; it does not try to be all things to all people, but chooses carefully what it does; it is part of a retailing system focussed primarily on the key commodities of petroleum and food, as well as some others; it is frugal, driving costs out of the system, but willing to look at big investments or acquisitions when they perfectly match the strategic vision. It stresses earnings, and refunds, and financing from within. Knowing what the organization's culture is, agreeing on it, and having it understood by retails are all important, and create some of the stability in the wholesale-retail relationship.

Retails have mental images of themselves, too. While they vary, their identities or self-conceptions are local; they are autonomous; they are sensitive to the needs of their communities, large urban or farming or forest/resort, or whatever they may be; they are looking for better ways to serve their members. Many of them, taking a cue from CEO Wayne Thompson, aspire to be the best in town. It's not in spite of but *because* of who they are and what they do that they realize—most of them—that they need Federated and the strength of the wider system. The identities the retails define for themselves match with what Federated is and what it does—not that they are the same, but more important, that they are complementary and mutually beneficial.

Marketing. Roles and relationships in a system based on membership and local autonomy. Innovation and adaptation over time. These three themes come together in the largely successful ways in which CRS co-ops, today, are living the dreams of those who started them.

Cohesion and Impact

I F PEOPLE ARE TRULY CONCERNED ABOUT THE NEGATIVE *aspects of globalization—loss of local control, the power of transnational corporations—then they should be attracted* to local alternatives, local ownership, and community-based institutions. That thought was on my mind as I conducted the interviews for this book, with managers, leaders, staff, and members in local retail co-operatives across western Canada. There are some co-op members who are clearly motivated by what some refer to as ideology or philosophy, who see co-operatives as a kind of crusade for community and for local control. These people's attitudes to corporate globalization are not in doubt. But my impression is that, for the great majority, involvement with a local co-operative represents a diffuse bundle of characteristics, some of them quite practical or prosaic in nature. This should not be surprising. "Co-ops arise from need," say the leaders in the co-operative movement, a deceptively simple statement that covers some very complicated ideas. One thing "need" denotes is that co-operatives generally provide immediate, practical, and often material services. In a fundamental way, a retail co-op is and must be *about* retailing. It is not, on the surface, about being a co-op, isn't about democracy or participation. These things are a means to an end—the end being trust, efficiency, and effectiveness in meeting member needs.[1]

But there is a remarkable subtext to co-operative enterprises. It became clear to me as I listened to people talk, people who had been employees of a co-op for just three weeks and others who had been members and leaders for more than fifty years, that there is a co-op difference, beneath the surface. I talked to staff members who had only a vague idea of what a co-op was and of how to compare their own organization to others. And yet, they knew and could communicate that it was a good place to work, a place where individuals could develop themselves and go far—to the limits of their ambition and potential. A successful local co-op is these things because it is stable and diversified. It is stable and diversified because its head office, so to speak, is in the local community; it is not likely to be bought out by a competitor; it has a range and diversity of tasks to be done, and decisions that must be made locally. It can be flexible, innovative, and entrepreneurial, because it does not receive its orders from a distant, corporate head office. It is all of these things *because it is locally owned and voluntarily controlled by local people*—in other words, because of its ownership structure as a co-operative.

The character of being a co-operative shapes the experience and the identities of staff and members, even when there isn't really the language to put the co-operative difference into words.

Do people *know* what different kinds of institutions mean to the health and vibrancy of their communities? I suspect many do, to a certain extent. At root, this is a question of social cohesion. In some way, co-op members know they have a connection to their co-op and to their communities, and their co-op and their community have connections to each other, in a triangle of interactions and affective bonds that solidifies their concept of who and where they are. But this cohesive sense does not trump all other influences in their lives. Members daily make trade-offs, choose to patronize their co-operative and a competitor, and, in effect, do a social-economic calculus in their heads. *Will I patronize the co-op if it costs a few cents more? A few dollars? Tens of dollars? How do I weigh the future value of a possible patronage refund versus the present value of the sale offered by the competitor? Do I like shopping in a well-designed, well-maintained local store, or would I prefer the bare-bones warehouse style of the urban big-box outlet?* There is a perception, and a fear, that price is the only thing that matters to people. If this is true, then perhaps WAL-MART will take over, and we have our answer to how concerned people really are about corporate globalization. But whatever people say, we have considerable evidence that behaviour does not follow price alone. Local pride, local identity, competitive prices but not necessarily the lowest ones, have a chance. It's also pretty clear that it would be useful to have a better handle on how members actually think and make these trade-offs in their daily choices.

Co-ops do need to adapt to a changing environment, to new competition, and to globalization. But while they must always be changing, there are certain patterns or constants in what they do. This book has examined the patterns of continuity and change under the headings of *linkage, transparency,* and *cognition.*[2]

Chapter one was about the ways in which the system has become rededicated to marketing and relinked to serving members' needs, from top to bottom. Both retails and FCL had to change their priorities during the crisis of the 1980s. Virtually no retail and no FCL division were unaffected. As a result of the way in which that crisis was surmounted and the marketing emphasis that followed, the whole system became more united and more cohesive. FCL's financial strategy of avoiding debt, financing from within, and paying patronage refunds as a marketing tool all came out of this era and continue to the present day. The effect of the financing and marketing strategies is to accentuate the economic interdependence between FCL and its member co-ops, and between local co-ops and their members.

Chapter two, in many ways, was about trust—where it comes from and what difference it makes in co-ops. In looking at roles and relationships in the system, the chapter highlighted the ways in which the system's people and structures promote quality, and the ways in which they respond to and fix problems. These are transparency issues that have to do with governance, management, and how people perceive interests and results. Members, staff, managers, directors, and Federated board and management all have unique roles to play in the CRS. It is important to realize that problems do arise among co-ops, and a system the size of the CRS is not without them. The key is how they are dealt with and whether the system's mechanisms work in a crisis; and also whether the system has mechanisms, such as training, or checks and balances, to prevent crises in the first place. On balance, this appears to be the case—another reason for the success of the CRS.

Chapter three put the first two chapters together—the marketing thrust of the system, and the roles and relationships within it—to explain how the system has adapted through successful innovations. While looking at all types of innovations, including some mainly by retails acting alone and some mainly by Federated, the chapter concentrated on the way in which interaction and dialogue improve innovations and help them spread, voluntarily and by persuasion or imitation, through the system. The chapter concluded by stressing that sensitivity to community, and local autonomy, are key to the success of the innovation process. FCL leaders clearly exercise influence and authority, as shown in several of the examples, but they earn that authority by respecting retails.

All of this sounds quite positive, and it certainly should, given the Co-operative Retailing System's impressive financial results. Along the way, however, I have tried to pay attention to failures, problems, and tensions—how they surfaced and how they were handled. The bottom line is that the system did learn from its experiences, and that tensions, properly handled—such as the tension between local autonomy and central or standardized programs—are in fact reasons for the system's success.

That thought brings in one more word: *cohesion.*

The success of the CRS reflects several kinds of cohesion. There is, first of all, the cohesion within local, geographic communities, among the members of the co-op, or between the members and the co-op. This is especially evident in smaller or more isolated communities, but the same thing occurs in large cities, where the co-op may act in similar fashion as the focal point for a neighbourhood. In such cases, managers, staff, and members report that the co-op is seen as the centre of the community. It's the only full-service outlet, or it's the place people go to put up notices on the community bulletin board, or it has the cafeteria where seniors drink coffee together or local voluntary associations assemble for meetings or marches.

Cohesion in the co-op system is not only local. There is, second, the cohesion among the co-operatives—the cohesion of the whole system, across the communities, the multiple provinces and territories within which it operates. To some extent, there is a true bridging going on; members who patronize and support co-operatives are identifying with a brand, an image, a set of values that is consistent in some ways from one end of the system to the other. Co-operative loyalty, however, is a highly local matter. It seems probable that most members regard their co-op as an institution of their community, and are unaware of or give little thought to the equivalent co-ops elsewhere. Sometimes people are surprised to learn that co-ops even exist outside of the territory that they know well. But if members don't necessarily know a lot about the wider CRS, it appears that the leaders of the co-ops do. Leadership development is perhaps the co-ops' main contribution to bridging among communities. It is the managerial and elected leaders of the co-ops who create the cohesion of the CRS as a whole. It is appropriate that co-ops invest in training and developing those leaders, and it may well be that they can't ever do too much in this regard.

A lesson from the history of the CRS is that co-ops do not simply promote cohesion because it is a good thing to do. That isn't how commercial co-operatives work. Rather, they are challenged to meet competition, to innovate, to reduce costs, and to increase quality and service. The means they draw on to do these things often involve social cohesion, and certainly contribute to it. Perhaps the best case in point is that managers at all levels in the CRS describe the ways in which they must strive to persuade staff and members and create buy-in, rather than being able to give orders as they might do in a more hierarchical organization. The wholesale has to persuade retail managers to adopt its programs; to ensure this happens, it involves them in various ways in discussing, designing, and modifying the programs. Through this process, the wholesale also establishes its credibility—it creates trust. As a result of the trust and collaboration between levels of the organization, innovations are better designed and adopted more quickly.

This brings us to a third dimension to cohesion in the co-op system—cohesion among staff and among managers. Formally, CRS co-ops are organizations of member consumers; in the organizational chart, employees appear as they would in any other firm. But the reality may be somewhat different. Both managers and staff have a kind of "membership" in the co-op system—in investment and a voice in it, particularly because of the long careers many people have spent in the system. The CRS benefits from the stability and experience of employees who receive training and development along the way for their changing roles. This is not so much a policy or principle of the co-operatives as a necessity resulting from two things. The first is their distinctive structure, which makes it difficult to bring in outside managers past a certain level. And the second is their community-based ownership, which roots them in communities of various sizes in a stable way, with few transfers, mergers, or acquisitions such as often shake up the workforces of profit-maximizing companies. The community orientation of the co-ops also creates an environment in which it is normal and expected that staff, again especially managers, will play certain kinds of roles in their communities, as leaders, as advisors, and as community figures. It is not a universal or hard-and-fast truth, but it seems that being an employee of the co-op system may mean working in a relatively stable workplace, with good opportunities for training and advancement, and within a context of both customer service and community orientation. This, too, looks like cohesion, of a type that increases efficiency for the firm, satisfaction for the employees, and benefits to the community.

The impact of the Co-op Retailing System is immense. Taken as a whole, it provides hundreds of millions of dollars of benefits to up to a million western Canadian people every year; and beyond that, it recirculates wealth in communities it comes from, to invest in local facilities, to provide good jobs and opportunities for advancement, training, and leadership development. These benefits come about because of the cohesion within communities between members and their co-ops, and because of the cohesion within the system—the way in which a delicately balanced federated structure combines the benefits of local control and centralized programs and efficiencies. The Co-op Retailing System is cohesive, ultimately, because people talk to each other and recognize common interests. The question for the future will always be how that balance evolves and is renewed—what co-op people talk to each other about, and what common interests they recognize and identify.

Co-ops will continue to change not only because of changing competition, but because people and communities—the members—are changing, too. Co-ops have responded to some of the changes in western Canadian demographics. They have begun to deal with age and gender, for example, mapping out marketing and membership strategies that suit the realities of the communities in which they operate. In my own travels, I did notice relatively little reflection of one of the major demographic changes in western Canada—the growing proportion of people of Aboriginal ancestry, as well as visible new immigrant groups in the large urban centres. The Aboriginal influence on retailing will be large, because (if all goes as we have to hope) the impact of the rising numbers of Aboriginal people will be multiplied by their rising purchasing power; and First Nations and Métis people will be spread geographically through many communities where co-ops are active. This is not to mention Arctic Co-ops in the North, which already organizes large numbers of Inuit, Dene, and other members and leaders. I did come across southern co-ops that had visible Aboriginal members in the stores, and several that had business relationships with First Nations bands, reselling petroleum, for example, or helping First Nations set up on-reserve gas stations of their own. In future, will there be separate Aboriginal co-ops, or equivalents? Will the co-op system be more deeply involved in business relationships with Aboriginal governments? Will co-ops have marketing, merchandising, and member-relations programs geared to Aboriginal members?

I think, in any case, co-ops will need to know more about their members and their differences. Many times, when I spoke to managers and directors about members, the "member" seemed to be a somewhat colourless abstraction. Of course, co-operators value equality and are loathe to even think about differences among their members, but there is also a danger in marketing only to a lowest common denominator. You may be missing important marketing opportunities, opportunities to meet needs, in cases where it is economical for marketing to be targeted to specific groups. Doing this need not disadvantage any other groups. It seems likely, looking at the big-picture demographics, that what the system has done so far in considering women's interests and distinct ethnic needs in marketing and merchandising will turn out only to be the beginning of larger things. And then there is the somewhat connected question of board and staff recruitment and diversity. Those who can develop and access the skills of particular groups will have a wider pool of ability and competencies to choose from; and more diverse leadership, combined with training and development, can be expected to lead to general improvement in decision making. It makes me wonder which co-ops will stand out as leaders in this regard the next time a writer tours the Co-op Retailing System.

~

S INCE ONE OF THE TECHNIQUES I HAVE USED IN THIS book is, wherever possible, to give centre stage to the people I interviewed, to let them tell their own stories, it seems only appropriate to give them the last word. One question I asked most interviewees concerned their hopes and fears for the system's future. What follows is a selection of comments drawn from what they said.

One thing that may surprise outsiders is that long-serving people in the CRS are not flushed with pride and satisfaction at the system's current accomplishments. There is an undertone of slight anxiety that was put best by a general manager who said, "One fellow told me one time, 'When you're the most successful, you're also the most vulnerable.' So we can't let our success get to us. We need to continue to find ways of being more efficient."[3] People in the system who've been around awhile are concerned that the lessons they learned the hard way be passed on to their successors. It may seem incredible to think that a system generating high earnings, with high levels of member equity, could suddenly slip into debt and decline; but that worry is there. Perhaps what people have seen in individual retails—how quickly they can go wrong— gives them pause for concern.

Others commented that the co-ops would have to work hard to remind themselves of the lessons they had learned in the past. One interviewee hopes "that we will continue to make sure we know exactly what's happening in the industries [we are in] and be right on the leading edge of the marketing, and the facilities.... I think my fear is that a lot of people will forget what it was like in the early eighties."[4]

"I'm hoping," another says, "I'm hoping that there are enough ... people around" who understand the lessons "to remind them" in the future, to remind managers and leaders, of what it was like. "I guess it's not ... good enough reminding them, but [you have] to make sure that they listen." Although this interviewee was from a retail, the hope is that the wholesale—FCL—will serve as a kind of repository of memory for the system. "I know that we have a number of people in the wholesale who know what can happen, and when the red flag comes up, I know those people will say something."[5]

Another, related set of concerns had to do with turnover in man-agement at all levels of the system, and the recruiting and HR challenges this poses for the future.

"Well, I have concerns ... about that whole retirement aspect," one person told me. "I think things have been going really well ... Sometimes it's been a tough-handed approach, but it has worked and we've been successful. I guess I get a little concerned when I see a total changing of the guard, [and wonder] are they going to continue the same, are we going to operate the same as we have been? Or are there going to be major changes that might have major repercussions for us? That would be a concern of mine."[6]

Clearly, with so many long-serving senior executives, FCL is going to go through a major transition, but similar things are happening in the retails. Maybe one-fifth of the general managers of larger retails, one person estimated for me, "are less than three years into their job. It's obvious we're losing a lot of that long-term history, and certainly losing some of the managers who went through those early eighties, and what difficult times they were.... We always keep repeating, we don't want to go back into those [kind of times] again." This intervie-wee sees retelling the system's stories and mentoring of new managers as the way to pass on the learning, though "it's hard to tell the story, versus living through it."[7]

Another person thought it was natural "for older managers to sit there and have a fear about whether the younger generation is going to pick up the reins" properly. "That's like [how] you never do it as good as ... your dad wants you to," he says. But "I believe they all will. It may not be of the same passion, but it will be as strong a passion amongst themselves as what we have" now. "You've got to understand that a lot of the younger people who are coming up through the rank and file are, I would say ... much better educated" than the old managers. They "have a better understanding of politically correct and are probably not going to ... stub their toes as hard as we did when we went out there."[8]

Youth is of course a common topic for co-op people, but it becomes more acute when linked to the issue of human resources, the skills and people the system will need in future. "You know," one person said, "we keep talking about [getting] them to youth camp, and then we sort of

lose them. They talk to them in university about employment, but
there's a real gap between the fifteen-year-old who went to youth camp
and the twenty-three-year-old who's now in university. Probably one of
our biggest challenges [we're working on is] getting employees for the
system. Some of the highly professionalized roles we seem to be falling
short on, pharmacists for instance. We cannot get pharmacists in the
system."[9] So (this person asks) can we get more young people to go into
those programs? Do we need to offer bigger bonuses to get them? Or
do we need to make a connection with them before they graduate, get
them involved early in part-time placements in the system?

Others worry that young people, especially in the cities, don't have
the old understanding of why a co-op is important to a community.
"It's getting more distant," I was told. "It's not the fault of the co-op;
it's the reality of the way society is changing," especially in the cities.
"That competitor, whether it's a WAL-MART or [anyone else], they can
shut down and go tomorrow, so what? But the co-op is there forever,
[or] until members decide to fold it up or it goes bankrupt.... The average member out there" may not understand that any more, "or *think*
that way any more."[10]

Numerous people mentioned WAL-MART as the symbol of transnational and global competition. The system's attitude to such huge competitors is still a mix of lingering anxiety and growing confidence.

"It's getting more difficult, real difficult, to distinguish yourself,
simply because those people move into town. They have certain systems
and policies: they don't accept cheques; they don't allow local charge
accounts; they don't participate in community activities. Many people
don't see this. Some people do, and I guess we have to work on the people who do to get more people to think that way, who will support us
to the degree that we need to stay viable."[11]

"Well, I guess there are always fears for the system as it relates to the
big corporate box stores and their large buying powers," one person
said, "setting up these power centres where they ... draw a lot of the
consumer dollars from a lot of the smaller communities where the co-
ops have flourished. Certainly at this stage we have been able to meet
these challenges for the most part."[12]

"WAL-MART—if you ever want to go head-to-head with them,

you're not going to win. We're going to have to do the things that are successful for us. We have a niche in the market-place that WAL-MART hasn't got."[13]

"The big players aren't going away," another said, "the Superstores and the WAL-MARTs…. They're going to be there, and we have to find our niche in the market and make sure that we can serve the needs and be successful at it. And so the stronger Federated is, the stronger we're going to be. You know, I guess that's kind of a big picture, but we've got some interesting, tough times ahead of us … very interesting times ahead of us."[14]

Because of these sorts of concerns, many retail people are reassured by the size and success of FCL, and look for FCL to continue what it has been doing, or even to do more. "That's what they are in there [for], employed to do. I have to commend the wholesale on the development of the corporate bulk tanks. No question, I have to commend the wholesale on assisting to finance retail bulk-petroleum and gas-bar facilities. They helped us get into business in that area. It has also helped the wholesale in being able to develop the refinery to a maximum capacity, and now expanding. I think we need the wholesale. The wholesale took the initiative on purchasing The Grocery People to get us into the produce business, and selling to other private stores in food and related products. I'm pleased to see that Federated took that initiative."[15] People like this interviewee look for more of the same in future —more leadership, more partnership, more innovations.

Another hoped for "a more people-friendly management system that would allow more risk taking in the organization, foster creativity and ideas and give the staff ample opportunity to grow and develop and learn…. I just don't sense that the people really have that opportunity. And then from the wider level, the overall approach, I'd really like to see co-operatives stress the differences and … encourage more member participation."[16]

In terms of hopes for new areas of future development, several comments had to do with technology on one hand and community on the other.

"I think the future of the Co-op Retailing System is, we have to continue to grow" by aggressive employment of new technologies. "We have to seek out and seize our opportunities that come about, and we have to look to this electronic age. I say, as a system—and I look to our wholesale here, along with the retails—we are not on the Internet in the way in which I think we should be." Members, in this person's view, should be able to look up system catalogues on the Internet and order items to be delivered through their local co-op; they should also find the information on their local co-op's locations and services. There should be systems so that members can phone up, find a co-op that has what they want in stock, and pick it up at a convenient gas bar or other co-op facility—a seamless, co-ordinated, totally transparent system.[17] Not everyone has the same vision of how technology will be employed, but several saw it as a key to the future.

But another said, "The first example that comes to mind is [the co-op's role as] community-builder. We're a community-builder"—one of the system's four current Membership Benefits marketing slogans—"but I think Federated's position for years ... is that that's the retails' responsibility, giving money to community. Well, I agree. We give lots. It's an important part of our business plan. I think Federated should support some charities or whatever on a western Canada basis," this person urges. "We can do things locally and advertise locally and get our name in the local paper—it doesn't get us on the news—that's not the kind of things that you can get some province-wide or national advertising, or recognition [for]." As for member relations, "They let us struggle along with that; some of us really struggle. I'm terrible at publishing, stuff like that. Not a big thing. Member Relations—years and years ago—used to waste tons of money. But now there's almost nothing left. It's been pared down to nothing. It could work in the background, really help us to do a better job of it locally."[18]

The debate in the system, of course, is going to be which new programs or initiatives are compatible with the basic marketing focus, and which are not? In what ways does the recent recipe for success have to be tinkered with for the future? One can imagine a lot of conversations that will take place in the CRS in coming years to sort all these different things out, and decide what new ideas are compatible with FCL and retail priorities—how their organizational cultures and identities will change. It does seem clear that, after a long period of relative stability, the CRS is on the brink of some kind or degree of change.

Dreams live on only when they are changed and dreamed anew by different people.

"Hopes for the future?" one interviewee mused. "I guess I would definitely like to see it continue. I think it's going to be more difficult as we see more multinational and large [corporations] come into the ... cities." The big-box stores are "very large, heavily equity-financed companies that are coming in.... The main concern, of course, is bottom line." Outlying centres will be hard hit: "It's going to change ... the communities are going to change. Unless people are willing to pay the freight, I guess, they're not going to have local services in the future." But "I guess my hope is that there will be or continue to be co-operatives as reasonable businesses, and that services will continue [something like] what they are today. I think we do an excellent job of providing services, and it would be nice if the friendliness can stay within the co-operatives, and the openness between the members and management." This person's final hope is that "it doesn't get too centralized and too far away from people's needs. Whether we'll stay around forever ... that's a good question.

"Forever's a long time ... I guess the original [idea] was that if you can survive for fifty years, you're doing well," he reflects. "I guess we're starting to push the one-hundred-years [mark]" with some local retails. "We're not quite there," but close. "I hope that the system stays strong as a total, and builds and gets stronger. I don't think you want to become the only segment in the economy. I think you want to become one of the strongest ones, which I think we are, but I don't think you want to, and we never will, become the only supplier of products to people."

"Other than [that], I guess we should be thanking all of the people who started co-operatives years ago to give us the competitive edge we've got today."[19]

JUST A LITTLE DREAM

Dreams are what brought us out here
Dreams of putting our own bread on the table
That's what kept us working
To get to the point where we were barely able
Then to watch the sun dry up the things we hold dear
And the only thing that the dust left us
Year after year

Just a little dream
Who can blame a person for dreaming
Wishing on a star
What are stars for anyway
Walk beneath the stars
Hold your love close to you
Set your dreams upon a strong heart
And they'll come true

by Connie Kaldor, from the compact disk
WOOD RIVER: Home is where the heart is...
© 1992 Coyote Entertainment Group Inc.
Canada—Festival Distribution, CD—CEGCD 1010
Reprinted with permission.

APPENDIX

Composite Personalities

C HAPTER TWO MAKES USE OF ELEVEN "COMPOSITE personalities" to whom various quotations are attributed. Each name is introduced in quotation marks to indicate that the name is not a real one. All the people who are introduced, at first mention, without quotation marks around their names, are real individuals who have agreed to be quoted in this way.

Each composite person represents three to five different interviewees, grouped together by similarities I found relevant to what they said. Generally, what they have in common is their gender; position (for example, staff, general manager, board member); approximate age or length of experience in the co-op system; career path (for example, how much they have moved around among different co-ops); outlook (for example, perspective on their own jobs, management style); and/or type of co-op (for example, rural or urban). They may have geographic or ethnic characteristics attributed to them, but these are generally fictional—purely literary devices—as I found no meaningful patterns among my interviewees in these regards.

When a remark is attributed to a composite, this means *one* of the people represented by the composite actually said the exact words quoted. In other words, none of the quotations is made up; all are actual material from interview transcripts, approved by the individuals who said them. The only thing that is made up is the name of the composite person. So when the text says that (for example) Jean Derone said X, this should be read as shorthand for, many of the people I interviewed who had the characteristics attributed to Jean Derone generally agreed, and one of them put it in exactly these words: X. This means that different quotations attributed to "Jean Derone" may actually come from different individuals.

There are two reasons for doing this. The first is literary. Without the composite individuals, the text would be cluttered with dozens of repetitive references such as one director said this, several rural general managers said that. The fictional names make it easier for readers to visualize people saying these things. The second reason concerns confidentiality. By mixing together remarks from several people, it is basically impossible for even the most careful and well-informed reader to figure out who said what. This is important since many interviewees, especially staff and board members but also some managers, agreed only to be interviewed and for their remarks to be used under conditions of anonymity.

Other people, especially FCL managers, are quoted by their real names because it is part of their role within FCL to speak on behalf of the organization, or their part of it. They have authorized each of these quotations. There are still some individuals quoted anonymously at various points, largely because the characteristics of the people in question do not fit well into a composite, or because the use of the composite in a specific situation might have been confusing for some reason.

The names were chosen from figures in co-op history out of the general European ethnic background of most people I interviewed, with spellings changed or modernized. The composite characters, and the derivations of their names, are as follows:

(1) "Alicia Acland," in her twenties, has been a co-op employee for eight years in a Saskatchewan city. She sees the co-op as a good job, is proud of the work she does, and is beginning to see there could be more possibilities for her in the system. (Alice Acland was a nineteenth-century British co-operator, whose women's columns in the *Co-op News* helped start the Women's Co-operative Guild.)

(2) "Emily Freund" is in her late thirties, with twelve years experience working for the retail co-op in her home town in Manitoba. She did other work and had a family before joining the co-op. As she has gained experience, she has become a supervisor (a senior staff member, still in-scope of the union) in her department. She's considering the possibility that she could be department manager one day. (Emmy Freundlich was an early twentieth-century Austrian-German co-operator who was active in the International Women's Co-operative Guild.)

(3) "Nora Hurley" began working in her home-town co-op in Alberta soon after she left high school in 1982. She worked part time in the administrative office as a secretary, gradually developed her skills with data processing and accounting, and now serves as office manager. (Nora Herlihy was an Irish teacher who grew up in County Cork, became involved in co-ops in Dublin, and in the 1950s helped launch the Irish credit-union movement.)

(4) "Mark Thrane" worked in the private food trade before he joined the co-operative system. He was an employee at a specialty food store before he moved to a new community in western Canada in 1995 and found employment at a grocery store of a multibranch co-op. Since then he has worked in deli and produce, and in 2001 became assistant store manager. (In 1851 Marcus Thrane was one of the earliest co-operative organizers in Norway. Because of his working-class background, he was arrested and imprisoned for his efforts and later emigrated to the USA.)

(5) "Bill Haas" is one of the system's relatively younger general managers. A bit over forty years of age, he started work for the co-op with a part-time job when he was a high-school student. He stayed at the co-op after graduation, worked in lumber and hardware, became a department manager, did his GM training, and had his first posting at a small rural co-op in the late eighties. He managed three, successively larger retails before arriving at his current assignment in 1996. (Wilhelm Haas was a German co-operative leader from the state of Hessen. Prior to the First World War, he headed the largest co-op federation in the world, the Imperial Federation of German Agricultural Co-operatives.)

(6) **"Jim Mitchell"** worked part time at the co-op when he was in high school in Saskatchewan, and subsequently got a job in the co-op food store in his home town. He worked his way up the ladder: senior clerk on the food floor, then produce manager. He did GM training, gaining experience in larger and more diversified co-ops, and became a general manager in 1980. He also worked for FCL for a year as a retail advisor, until he became a GM at his current co-op in 1984. (J.T.W. Mitchell, of England, was chairman of the Co-operative Wholesale Society in the latter part of the nineteenth century.)

(7) **"Jean Derone"** grew up in a rural community, where she started working for the co-op while she was in high school. She moved through several departments of her co-op in the 1980s, also acquiring training in marketing and in management from FCL and from postsecondary institutions. She became a general manager in a rural co-operative in 1999. (Jeanne Deroin was an ex-seamstress turned teacher, who in 1849–50 set up a unified federation for all of the co-ops of different trades in Paris. Like Thrane, she was arrested and imprisoned for her efforts.)

(8) **"Abe Greenwood"** has farmed in northcentral Alberta since 1957. He became a member of his local co-op as soon as he started farming. He was asked to run for the board in 1968, was elected, and has served on the board ever since—thirty-six years. He has been president of the board for twenty-one years. (Abraham Greenwood was an adult educator who became a leader in the Rochdale Society of Equitable Pioneers, England, in 1850.)

(9) **"Bill Maclure"** has been president of his urban co-op for the past eleven years. He first became involved with the co-op, as a member, soon after he moved to the city in 1970. Through involvement in various issues and co-op committees, he ran for the board of directors and was elected in 1982. Since his retirement as a schoolteacher, he has been able to devote himself to his role as president. (William Maclure was a geologist and educator who invested more than $80,000 in Robert Owen's project to create a co-operative community in New Harmony, Indiana, in 1825–27.)

(10) **"Frank Stefchuk"** was brought up to be loyal to the co-op in his rural community in Saskatchewan. When a position came open on the local board in 1976, he ran and was elected. He has been on the board continually ever since, through all the difficulties of the 1980s, except for one three-year term he sat out. He has participated actively in FCL district, region, and annual meetings. (Dr. Frank Stefczyk was a founder of the Polish co-operative movement, founding credit unions beginning in 1899, which were known as the Kasy Stefczyka.)

(11) **"Trish Potter"** joined the local co-op in her city, where she operates a small accounting business, in 1985. She served on member committees, then was elected to the board of directors in 1991, and has served ever since. (Beatrice Potter was a late nineteenth- and early twentieth-century British co-operative publicist. Potter was her maiden name; she was also known under her married name, Webb.)

ENDNOTES

Preface

1. Interview by the author with Lorne Robson at his farm near Deleau, Manitoba, on 19 June 2003; name and quotation used with his permission. Manitoba Co-op Wholesale was one of FCL's predecessors through amalgamation.
2. Brett Fairbairn, *Building a Dream: The Co-operative Retailing System in Western Canada, 1928–1988* (Saskatoon: Western Producer Prairie Books, 1989).

Introduction

1. Confidential interview transcript 14. Hereinafter cited as Transcript plus number.
2. FCL *Annual Report*, 2002, p. 6.
3. Supplement: Federated Co-operatives Limited, *Western Grocer* 89, no. 2 (March/April 2003), p. 10.
4. Interview by the author with Dennis Banda at FCL Home Office on 17 March 2003 (and the same for the following paragraph). As described in the preface, the research interviews conducted for this book were confidential and anonymous. Where individuals are quoted by name from the transcripts, this is with their express permission for the quotations used.
5. Murray Lyons, "FCL Sales, Earnings Set Another Record," Saskatoon *StarPhoenix*, 20 December 2003, p. C1.
6. Agway operated Texas City Refining as a joint venture with Southern States Co-operative and made profits during the oil shortages of the early 1970s. It was sold in 1988 at a loss of $110 million. (Bruce Anderson and Brian Henehan, "What Went Wrong at Agway," p. 2.) Farmland recently sold its interest in Country Energy, a joint venture launched in 1998 with CHS Cooperatives, and is said to be looking at selling its petroleum refinery in Coffeyville, Kansas. CHS will be left with the only two larger refineries in co-op hands, one in Montana and one in Kansas; there is a smaller refinery in Indiana operated by Countrymark. See United States Department of Agriculture, Rural Business-Cooperative Service, *Agricultural Cooperatives in the 21st Century* (Cooperative Information Report 60, November 2002), p. 15.

Chapter One

1. Transcript 16.
2. FCL *Annual Report*, 2002. "Active" members are usually considered those purchasing during the year in question; there are considerably more than this many membership accounts in existence. But also, because there is typically only one

membership per family, the number of people represented by the CRS will be a multiple of the number of memberships. In 1994, FCL President Vern Leland estimated that the CRS represented something like 30 percent of the western Canadian population. (Leland's address to the 65th Annual Meeting, 1994).

3. Interview by author with Gerry Onyskevitch at Moose Jaw Co-op on 10 April 2003; name and quotation used with his permission.

4. On the 1930s, see Brett Fairbairn, *Building a Dream: The Co-operative Retailing System in Western Canada, 1928–1988* (Saskatoon: Western Producer Prairie Books, 1989), esp. pp. 56ff.

5. FCL annual meeting minutes, afternoon of 3 March 2003. All documents cited in this book are from FCL corporate files unless otherwise noted.

6. Minutes from 53rd Annual Meeting, Calgary, 9–12 March 1982 (re: 1981 *Annual Report*).

7. See W.H. Thompson, treasurer, to Gerry Doucet, general manager, Pioneer Co-op, 7 September 1982.

8. "Presentation to the Co-operative Managers' Association by T.P. Bell, Fairmont, B.C. (1982)."

9. Transcript 51.

10. Transcript 84. The competition to the CRS in food includes the Westfair/Loblaws wholesale group (retail outlets Superstore and ExtraFoods), the Macdonalds Consolidated (retail Safeway) group, IGA (expanding in western Canada with backing from eastern food giant Sobeys), and the growing grocery trade by WAL-MART. BC in particular has other regional competitors such as Overwaitea Foods.

11. Transcript 53.

12. Interview by author with Elmer Wiebe at his home in Saskatoon on 12 March 2003; name and quotation used with his permission.

13. Interview by author with Wayne Thompson at FCL Home Office on 14 April 2003; name and quotation used with his permission.

14. Transcript 24.

15. Transcript 16. Written documents say "over 50 percent of retail shares in FCL were assigned to various lenders." (Elmer Wiebe, "The Recession of the 1980s," 24 October 1988.)

16. Transcript 29.

17. Transcript 87.

18. Transcript 84.

19. Transcript 46. Attributed to composite because the two quotes, Drumheller and Red River, would surely give away who was involved in both places.

20. Interview by the author with Mel Adams at FCL Home Office, 18 March 2003; name and quotation used with his permission.

21. Interview by the author with Ed Klassen at his home in Carman, Manitoba, on 17 June 2003; name and information used with his permission.

22. Wiebe interview.

23. Transcript 13 (and the same for the following).

24. *Edmonton Journal*, as follows: Duncan Thorne, "City's Co-op Stores Struggle to Survive Million-Dollar Losses; Closure Fears Making it Tough to Hire New Management," 11 April 1990, p. D11; Duncan Thorne, "Suspended Co-op Board Seeks Probe of Receiver-Manager," 16 January 1991, p. D6; Duncan Thorne,

"Co-op Members Vote for Probe; Receiver-Manager's Spinoff Plans Opposed," 24 January 1991, p. D11.

25. Kurt W. Wetzel and Daniel G. Gallagher, "A Conceptual Analysis of Labour Relations in Cooperatives," *Economic and Industrial Democracy* 8 (1987), pp. 517–40. Looking only at Saskatchewan, the authors observed that co-ops had only 6 percent of the province's unionized workforce but 40 percent of the person-days lost due to strikes. They attributed this to increased professionalization of management and polarized relations with workers, and to the role of second-tier co-ops like FCL. See the discussion in Fairbairn, *Building a Dream*, pp. 190–91.

26. Transcript 29.

27. Wiebe interview.

28. Denny Thomas, Harold Chapman, and Jack Trevena, "Democracy + Member Relations + Operations—A Trinity for 'Growth from Within,'" 1982 presentation, apparently to Co-operative Union of Canada, in FCL files. See also n.a. [almost certainly Thomas, Chapman, or Trevena], "Growth from Within: A Paper for 1981 Regional Conferences," also in FCL files.

29. "Corporate Priorities for 1983" (FCL Restraint Program); similar corporate-priorities documents for 1984, 1989, 1990, 1992, 1997.

30. "FCL's Restraint Program," memorandum dictated by T.P. Bell, March 1983.

31. Interview by the author with Peter Zakreski at FCL Home Office on 10 February 2003 (and the same for the following); name and quotation used with his permission.

32. "FCL's Restraint Program"; FCL *Annual Report*, 1982; Wiebe, "The Recession of the 1980s." The quotations are from Wiebe.

33. Zakreski interview.

34. Transcript 29.

35. Transcript 44.

36. Transcript 66.

37. Transcript 13.

38. Thompson interview (and the same for the following quotations).

39. "Retail Restraint Program," undated.

40. "Retail Restraint Program."

41. "Board Resolution to be Adopted by Those Retails With Net or Local Losses in 1981 But Not Receiving Assistance in 1982," (from "Retail Restraint Program").

42. "Board Resolution to be Adopted by Those Retails Receiving Special Assistance in 1982," (from "Retail Restraint Program").

43. "Report to the Board of Directors on 36 Priority Retails or Retails With Net Losses After FCL Refund in 1981," dictated by WGM on 22 September 1982. Actually, the report mentions thirty-seven retails by name, including also Kelowna (dealt with separately) and at one point refers to the number of thirty-eight retails (possibly a typo).

44. "Report ... on 36 Priority Retails."

45. Interview by the author with Ken Hart at FCL Home Office on 25 April 2003; name and quotation used with his permission.

46. Keith McCullough, President, on behalf of the Board of Directors, North of 53 Co-operative Ltd., to T.P. Bell, 30 August 1982.

47. Bell to McCullough, 9 Sept. 1982.
48. Bell to Gerry Doucet, Pioneer Co-op, 3 September 1982; same words, to McCullough, 9 September 1982.
49. Transcript 87 (and the same for the following).
50. Transcript 44.
51. Transcript 24.
52. Interview by the author with Nick Nichol at the University of Saskatchewan on 14 April 2003 (and the same for the following); name and quotation used with his permission.
53. Wayne Thompson, FCL, to W. Nygren, B.C. Central Credit Union; B. Downey, Credit Union Federation of Alberta; D. Hillmer, Credit Union Central of Saskatchewan; H. Walters, The Co-operators; L. Williams, Co-operative Superannuation Society; D. Gillett, Co-operative Trust Company of Canada; G. Lane, Credit Union Central of Manitoba; and L. Reid, Canadian Co-operative Credit Society, 16 February 1983.
54. "Report on Meeting with Lenders—March 30 & 31, 1983, in Saskatoon," memo dictated by T.P. Bell on 4 April 1983.
55. Interview by the author with Ron McClenaghan at Yorkton Co-op on 26 June 2003 (and the same for the following); name and quotation used with his permission.
56. Interview by the author with Cliff Irving at Vanderhoof Co-op on 22 May 2003 (and the same for the following); name and quotation used with his permission.
57. Interview by the author with Warren Gill in Vermilion, Alberta, on 13 May 2003 (and the same for the following); name and quotation used with his permission.
58. Interview by the author with Allan Merritt at Portage Co-op on 17 June 2003 (and the same for the following); name and quotation used with his permission.
59. "Join Portage Co-op and Discover the Benefits," leaflet, Portage Co-op, 2003.
60. Interview by the author with Pat Fafard at Peninsula Co-op on 27 May 2003 (and the same for the following); name and quotation used with his permission.
61. On direct-charge co-ops in the CRS, see Fairbairn, *Building a Dream,* pp. 242ff.
62. Interview by the author with John Pituley in Rock Glen, Saskatchewan, on 10 April 2003 (and the same for the following); name and quotation used with his permission
63. Transcript 72.
64. Transcript 76 (and the same for the following).
65. "Marketing Division Report to EMC, December 13, 1983. 1984 Marketing Thrust" (task force documents)—emphasis in original.
66. "Marketing Division Report," emphasis in original.
67. Interview by the author with Lynn Hayes at FCL Home Office on 19 February 2003; name and quotation used with his permission.
68. Transcript 97.
69. Transcript 51.
70. Interview by the author with Al Robinson at the University of Saskatchewan on 7 February 2003; name and quotation used with his permission.
71. Personnel and Industrial Relations Division Report to Board of Directors, 29 September 1983.
72. Zakreski interview (and the same for the following).

73. Transcript 56.
74. Thompson interview (and the same for the following).
75. "Minutes of the Planning Meeting of January 19–21, 1988, Held in the Travelodge Motor Inn in Saskatoon, Sask." (FCL board minutes). The minutes reviewed progress on marketing year by year since 1983.
76. "Board Management Planning Session Held at the Travelodge Hotel, January 7, 8 & 9, 1985."
77. "Minutes of the Planning Meeting of January 19–21, 1988."
78. Interview by author with Al Roden at his home in Saskatoon on 4 July 2003; name and quotation used with his permission.
79. Roden interview.
80. Interview by author with Norman Krivoshen at FCL Home Office on 13 June 2003; name and quotation used with his permission.
81. Hart interview (and the same for the following).
82. "CEO Wayne Thompson addresses the 64th annual meeting," (extracts from speech, FCL files).
83. K.B. Gustafson, "Serving our Members in a Changing Environment," *President's Newsletter,* September 1995.
84. Krivoshen interview.
85. Dale Worobe, "Co-op Food Stores Outshine the Competition," *Western Grocer* 89, no. 2 (March/April 2003), pp. 13–20; here, p. 14.
86. Krivoshen interview.
87. Rupert interview.
88. Krivoshen interview (and the same for the following).
89. Krivoshen interview. See also Calgary Co-op CEO Milford Sorensen's comments on the same program, below.
90. FCL annual meeting minutes, afternoon of 3 March 2003.
91. There are bigger consumer co-operatives in Canada, but they are not locally based. For example, Mountain Equipment Co-op is a retailer with nation-wide membership and stores in cities from Halifax to Victoria.
92. Interview by author with Barry Ashton at Calgary Co-op administrative offices on 2 May 2003; name and quotation used with his permission.
93. Interview by author with Alice Brown at Calgary Co-op administrative offices on 28 February 2003; name and quotation used with her permission.
94. Interview by author with Milford Sorensen at Calgary Co-op administrative offices on 28 February 2003; name and quotation used with his permission (and the same for the following). On Gordon Barker and the earlier development of Calgary Co-op, see Fairbairn, *Building a Dream,* chap. 18.
95. Interview by author with Barry McPhail at the Richmond Street store in Brandon on 18 June 2003; name and quotation used with his permission.
96. Wiebe interview.
97. Thompson interview.
98. Interview by author with Bud Van Iderstine at CCRL on 16 July 2003 (and the same for the following); name and quotation used with his permission.
99. Roden interview.
100. Interview by author with Terry Bell at FCL Home Office on 20 June 2003 (and the same for the following); name and quotation used with his permission.

101. Will Zaichkowski, "Delivering the Goods on Procurement," Western Grocer 89, no. 2 (March/April 2003), pp. 29–32.
102. Sorensen interview (and the same for the following).
103. Interview by author with Art Postle at FCL Home Office on 23 June 2003 (and the same for the following); name and quotation used with his permission.
104. USDA, *Agricultural Cooperatives in the 21st Century*, pp. 13–14. The co-operatives under discussion are federated supply *and marketing* co-ops, specialized in agriculture, and therefore somewhat unlike FCL. The "dinosaurs" comment referred to independently owned, local co-op elevators.

Chapter Two

1. Broadcast of 15 May 2003; outline and partial transcript available at http://www.cbc.ca/thecurrent/2003/200305/20030515.html as accessed 13 June 2003.
2. See Lou Hammond Ketilson, "The Marketing Competitiveness of Canadian Consumer Co-operatives," *Yearbook of Co-operative Enterprise* (Oxford: Plunkett Foundation, 1988), pp. 133–45; and by the same author, "Management in Co-operatives: Examining the Marketing Competitiveness of Consumer Co-operatives," in Murray Fulton (ed.), *Co-operative Organizations and Canadian Society: Popular Institutions and the Dilemmas of Change* (Toronto: University of Toronto Press, 1990), pp. 250–64.
3. Interview by author with Hilary Brown and Muriel Rogers in the "ringside" café outside Hornby Co-op on 26 May 2003 (and the same for the following); names and quotations used with their permission.
4. Transcript 7 (and the same for the following). Composite interview: see the appendix. Hereinafter cited as (composite: see appendix).
5. FCL *Annual Report*, 2002, p. 21.
6. Transcript 36 (composite: see appendix).
7. Interview by author with Larry Rupert at FCL Home Office on 7 February 2003; name and quotation used with his permission.
8. Transcript 7 (and the same for the following); (composite: see appendix).
9. Transcript 21 (composite: see appendix).
10. Transcript 59 (composite: see appendix).
11. Transcript 59 (composite: see appendix).
12. Transcript 68 (composite: see appendix).
13. Transcript 7 (composite: see appendix).
14. Transcript 21 (composite: see appendix).
15. Transcript 5 (composite: see appendix).
16. Transcript 2 (and the same for the following); (composite: see appendix).
17. Transcript 89 (and the same for the following); (composite: see appendix).
18. Transcript 34 (and the same for the following); (composite: see appendix).
19. Transcript 60 (and the same for the following); (composite: see appendix).
20. Transcript 29.
21. Transcript 99.
22. Interview by the author with Wayne Thompson at FCL Home Office on 14 April 2003; name and quotation used with his permission.
23. Transcript 91.
24. Transcript 99.

25. Transcript 46 (and the same for the following); (composite: see appendix).
26. Transcript 68 (composite: see appendix).
27. Transcript 5 (and the same for the following); (composite: see appendix).
28. Transcript 68 (composite: see appendix).
29. Interview by the author with Peter Zakreski at FCL Home Office, 10 February 2003; name and quotation used with his permission.
30. Transcript 5 (composite: see appendix).
31. A study reported in 2003 says that 75 percent of male executives (still) have stay-at-home wives (which would make transfers easier as far as jobs are concerned), while few female executives have house-husbands. See Virgina Galt, "Is there a home-front advantage?" *The Globe and Mail*, 16 May 2003, p. C1, reporting on the study *Leaders in a Global Economy: A Study of Executive Women and Men*, by Families and Work Institute, Boston College, and Catalyst (a research group).
32. Transcript 46 (composite: see appendix).
33. Transcript 68 (composite: see appendix).
34. Transcript 61.
35. "The Executive Management Committee" terms of reference, c. 1999–2003.
36. Interview with Norman Krivoshen at FCL Home Office on 13 June 2003; name and quotation used with his permission.
37. Transcript 72.
38. Interview by the author with Bill Baumgartner at his home in Regina on 8 April 2003 (and the same for the following); name and quotation used with his permission.
39. Transcript 32.
40. Transcript 42.
41. Transcript 14.
42. Transcript 46 (and the same for the following); (composite: see appendix).
43. Transcript 68 (composite: see appendix).
44. Transcript 36 (and the same for the following); (composite: see appendix).
45. Transcript 36 (composite: see appendix).
46. Transcript 94.
47. Transcript 44.
48. Transcript 21 (composite: see appendix).
49. Transcript 7 (composite: see appendix).
50. Janice MacKinnon, *Minding the Public Purse: The Fiscal Crisis, Political Trade-Offs, and Canada's Future* (Montréal: McGill-Queen's University Press, 2003), pp. 72 and 259.
51. Policy approved (initially for three years) at FCL Board of Directors, 15–18 December 1986.
52. Lou Hammond Ketilson, "Calgary Co-operative Association," in The International Joint Project on Co-operative Democracy, *Making Membership Meaningful: Participatory Democracy in Co-operatives* (Saskatoon: Centre for the Study of Co-operatives, 1995), pp. 180–200.
53. Anne Crawford, "Calgary Co-op Celebrates Record Profit," *Calgary Herald*, 17 February 1998, p. F1.
54. Charles Frank, "Heavy Questioning Expected at Co-op Meeting: Eventful Year to be Reviewed Monday Night," *Calgary Herald*, 20 February 1999, p. D1;

Calgary Co-operative Association *Annual Report,* 2000, p. 10.

55. Anne Crawford, "Co-op Fires 22 Middle Managers," *Calgary Herald,* 14 January 1999, p. F1.

56. Monte Stewart, "Labor Concerns Play Key Role in Co-op Meeting," *Calgary Herald,* 18 February 1999, p. B2.

57. Jeff Adams, "Critics Take Aim at 'New Age' Co-op Tactic: Using 'Love-Ins' to Motivate Grocery Chain Managers Greeted with Skepticism in Conservative Industry," *Calgary Herald,* 19 May 1998.

58. Transcripts 29 and 85.

59. Anne Crawford, "Co-op Chief Steps Down: Alice Brown Replaces Gene Syvenky on Interim Basis," *Calgary Herald,* 21 October 1998, p. F1.

60. Transcript 42.

61. Anne Crawford, "Co-op Fires Head Office Staff," *Calgary Herald,* 10 December 1998; transcript 85.

62. Crawford, "Co-op Fires 22 Middle Managers."

63. Anne Crawford, "Rick Smith Resigns From Co-op Board," and "Members Fear Demise of Calgary Co-op," *Calgary Herald,* 8 May 1999 and 1 June 1999, p. E3 and p. D4 respectively.

64. Transcript 63.

65. Interview by the author with Ken Hart at FCL Home Office on 25 April 2003; name and quotation used with his permission.

66. Interview by the author with Elmer Wiebe at his home in Saskatoon on 12 March 2003; name and quotation used with his permission.

67. Zakreski interview.

68. Transcripts 12 and 85 (and the same for the following paragraphs).

69. Interview by the author with Barry Ashton at Calgary Co-op administrative offices on 2 May 2003 (and the same for the following); name and quotation used with his permission.

70. Interview by the author with Milford Sorensen at Calgary Co-op administrative offices on 28 February 2003 (and the same for the following); name and quotation used with his permission.

71. Author's notes from FCL Saskatoon Region Fall Conference, 3–4 November 2002, Travelodge Hotel, Saskatoon.

72. "Minutes of Board-Management Planning Meeting, January 22–24, 1991, Travelodge, Saskatoon."

73. Interview by the author with Vern Leland at his farm near Weldon, SK, on 23 April 2003; name and quotation used with his permission.

74. Interview by the author with Al Robinson at the University of Saskatchewan on 7 February 2003; name and quotation used with his permission.

75. Interview by the author with Dennis Banda at FCL Home Office on 17 March 2003; name and quotation used with his permission.

76. Interview by the author with Ed Klassen at his home in Carman, MB, on 17 June 2003; name and quotation used with his permission.

77. Interview by the author with Lynn Hayes at FCL Home Office on 19 February 2003; name and quotation used with his permission.

78. Transcript 50.

79. Transcript 1.

80. "Philosopher of failure studies fallen stars," *The Globe and Mail,* "Report on Business," 17 June 2003, p. B1. (Reporting on business teacher Sydney Finkelstein's *Why Smart Executives Fail, and What You can Learn from Their Mistakes*).
81. Sorensen interview.

Chapter Three
1. Interview by the author with Dennis Banda at FCL Home Office on 17 March 2003; name and quotation used with his permission.
2. Transcript 61.
3. Transcript 52.
4. Transcript 76 (and the same for the following).
5. Interview by the author with Bob Scott at St. Paul Co-op on 13 May 2003 (and the same for the following); name and quotation used with his permission.
6. Interview by the author with Barry Ashton at Calgary Co-op administrative offices on 2 May 2003; name and quotation used with his permission.
7. Transcript 49.
8. See Roger Spear, "The Co-operative Advantage," *Annals of Public and Cooperative Economics* 71:4 (2000), pp. 507–23.
9. Interview by the author with Ted Rodych in his office at Medicine Hat Co-op on 5 May 2003; name and quotation used with his permission. Rodych screened the TV commercials for me in his office; what follows is taken from the notes I made at that time.
10. Interview by the author with Larry Rupert at FCL Home Office on 7 February 2003 (and the same for the following); name and quotation used with his permission.
11. Interview by the author with Wayne Pearson at Prince Albert Co-op on 20 February 2003 (and the same for the following); name and quotation used with his permission.
12. Interview by the author with Stu Dyrland at Pioneer Co-op in Swift Current on 5 May 2003 (and the same for the following); name and quotation used with his permission.
13. The term super-local comes from the United States, where some rural supply co-ops have leased or otherwise consolidated the facilities of neighbouring co-ops, and have typically developed an added set of integrated agricultural services (e.g., soil testing, custom seeding, custom spraying, custom harvesting, and grain handling). Murray Fulton and Julie Gibbings, *Response and Adaptation: Canadian Agricultural Co-operatives in the 21st Century* (Saskatoon: Centre for the Study of Co-operatives, 2000), n. 1, p. 49.
14. The following is based on the author's interview with Gord Dmytruk at Melfort Co-op on 20 February 2003 (name and quotations used with his permission), and on Lou Hammond Ketilson and Brett Fairbairn, "Member-Oriented Business and Community Cohesion in Naicam Co-operative Association: A Case Study," prepared for the Canadian Adaptation and Rural Development, Phase II [CARD II] Leadership Development Program, Canadian Co-operative Association, 2003.
15. Interview by the author with George Klassen at Winkler Co-op on 16 June 2003 (and the same for the following); name and quotations used with his permission.

16. Transcript 86. In Canada there are also separate funeral co-operatives; these are more common in eastern parts of the country, but I was told there is a membership-based funeral co-op in Steinbach, Manitoba. To the best of my knowledge, Portage is the only general consumer co-op that operates a funeral service.
17. Banda interview (and the same for the following).
18. Interview by the author with Wayne Thompson at FCL Home Office on 14 April 2003; name and quotation used with his permission.
19. Interview by the author with Lynn Hayes at FCL Home Office on 19 February 2003 (and the same for the following); name and quotations used with his permission.
20. Transcript 79.
21. See Brett Fairbairn, *Building a Dream: The Co-operative Retailing System in Western Canada, 1928–1988* (Saskatoon: Western Producer Prairie Books, 1989), esp. pp. 214ff.
22. FCL *Annual Report*, 2002, pp. 18 and 28.
23. Ibid., pp. 18 and 32.
24. Interview by the author with Vern Leland at his farm near Weldon, SK, on 23 April 2003; name and quotation used with his permission.
25. Interview by the author with Harold Empey at the University of Saskatchewan on 14 July 2003 (and the same for following quotations lower down); name and quotations used with his permission. Although space does not permit a full treatment of the upgrader dispute and the many hours of interviews I did on the subject, the following also reflects comments from half a dozen other FCL and retail leaders besides Empey. My apologies to those I don't have space to quote.
26. Interview by the author with Bud Dahlstrom at his home in Regina on 9 April 2003 (and the same for following quotations and references lower down); name and quotations used with his permission.
27. Minutes of FCL board of directors meeting held 27–28 July 1983 at the Saskatchewan Wheat Pool Building, Regina, Saskatchewan; also minutes of board meeting, CCRL, 27 July 1983.
28. FCL board of directors executive committee minutes, 17 June 1985.
29. CCRL board of directors minutes, 1 August 1985 (note, again, that the CCRL board is identical to the FCL board).
30. Leland interview (and the same for quotations lower down).
31. See Janice MacKinnon, *Minding the Public Purse: The Fiscal Crisis, Political Trade-Offs, and Canada's Future* (Montréal: McGill-Queen's University Press, 2003), esp. pp. 29ff. The term "public brawl": p. 85.
32. *The Co-operative Connection*, 5, no. 7 (Dec. 1992).
33. Transcript 94.
34. Transcript 44. The FCL *President's Newsletter*, July 1993, similarly referred to the government's legislation as "dictatorial."
35. Minutes of board information meeting, 15 April 1993.
36. "Upgrader Agreement Reached," *President's Newsletter*, August 1993.
37. Interview by the author with Bud Van Iderstine at CCRL on 16 July 2003 (and the same for following quotations lower down); name and quotations used with his permission.
38. Kansas farmer David LeRoy, quoted in Lani Jordan, "A Heritage of Refining

Success: Two Refineries Mark 60 Years of Serving Customers, Plan for Major Environmental Upgrades," *Cooperative Partners* (published by CHS, Inc., in conjunction with Land o' Lakes, Inc.), September 2003, p. 29.
39. Thompson interview (and the same for the following).
40. Thompson interview.
41. FCL board of directors minutes, 30 Sept. – 1 October 1987.
42. Thompson interview.
43. FCL board minutes, October 2001. The corporate retails are organized into FCL Holdings Limited, an Alberta corporation, as well as in FCL Enterprises Co-operative, a federally incorporated co-op. Instead of all eleven being associate members of FCL, since 2001 the associate member is FCL Enterprises Co-operative.
44. Transcript 63.
45. Fairbairn, *Building a Dream*, p. 215.
46. EMC minutes, 3 April 1985.
47. "Minutes of Board-Management Planning Meeting, January 22–24, 1991— Travelodge, Saskatoon" and "Minutes of Board Management Planning Meeting, January 21–23 1992, Travelodge Motor Hotel, Saskatoon."
48. Transcript 56.
49. CEO's remarks to FCL board, "Minutes of Board Management Planning Meeting, January 19–21, 1993, Sheraton Cavalier Hotel, Saskatoon."
50. Transcripts 61 and 24.
51. Interview by the author with Jim Crawford at The Grocery People in Edmonton on 24 June 2003 (and the same for the following); name and quotations used with his permission.
52. Interview by the author with Elmer Wiebe at his home in Saskatoon on 12 March 2003; name and quotation used with his permission.
53. Formally organized as the "associated stores" plan of 1939; see *Building a Dream*, pp. 101–2.
54. Interview by the author with Norman Krivoshen at FCL Home Office, 13 June 2003 (and the same for the following); name and quotation used with permission.
55. Transcript 65.
56. Transcript 52.
57. Thompson interview.
58. Transcript 14.
59. Transcript 72.

Conclusion
1. This portion of the text is an abridged extract from Brett Fairbairn, "Cohesion, Adhesion, and Identities in Co-operatives," forthcoming in a collection on Co-operative Membership and Globalization to be published in 2004 by the Centre for the Study of Co-operatives, University of Saskatchewan.
2. For more information, see Brett Fairbairn, *Three Strategic Concepts for the Guidance of Co-operatives: Linkage, Transparency, and Cognition* (Saskatoon: Centre for the Study of Co-operatives, 2003).
3. Transcript 84.
4. Transcript 9.
5. Transcript 42.

6. Transcript 77.
7. Transcript 91.
8. Transcript 14.
9. Transcript 24.
10. Transcript 62.
11. Transcript 101.
12. Transcript 87.
13. Transcript 91.
14. Transcript 84.
15. Transcript 101.
16. Transcript 31.
17. Transcript 101.
18. Transcript 66.
19. Transcript 11.

INDEX